# AMERICA ONLINE'S
# INTERNET
## for Macintosh

*EASY, GRAPHICAL ACCESS—THE AOL WAY*

**SECOND EDITION**

D1240333

# AMERICA ONLINE'S
# INTERNET
## for Macintosh

### EASY, GRAPHICAL ACCESS—THE AOL WAY

**SECOND EDITION**

Tom Lichty

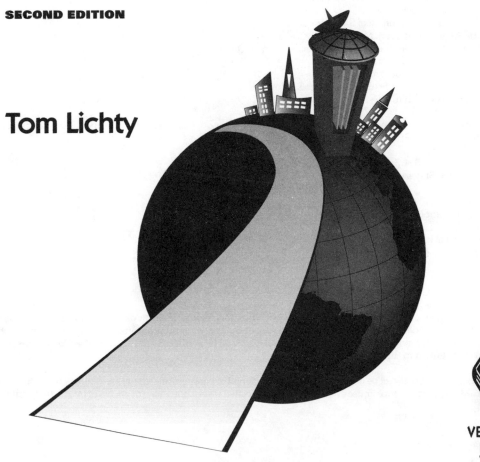

VENTANA
PRESS

**America Online's Internet for Macintosh: Easy, Graphical Access—the AOL Way, Second Edition**
Copyright ©1995 by Tom Lichty

**Library of Congress Cataloging-in-Publication Data**
Lichty, Tom.
     America Online's Internet for Macintosh : easy, graphical access—the AOL way / Tom Lichty. — 2nd ed.
        p.   cm.
     Includes bibliographical references and index.
     ISBN 1-56604-284-4
     1. America Online (Online service) 2. Macintosh (computer) I. Title.
QA76.57.A43L522 1995
004.6'7—dc20                                         95-32673
                                                                CIP

Book design: Marcia Webb
Cover design: Original concept, John Nedwidek, emdesign; Adaptation, Kelly Richmond, America Online
Vice President, Ventana Press: Walter R. Bruce III
Art Director: Marcia Webb
Design staff: Bradley King, Charles Overbeck, Dawne Sherman
Editorial Manager: Pam Richardson
Editorial staff: Angela Anderson, Beth Snowberger
Project Editors: Angela Anderson, Marion Laird
Print Department: Wendy Bernhardt, Dan Koeller, Kristen DeQuattro
Product Manager: Patty Williams
Production Manager: John Cotterman
Production staff: Patrick Berry, Scott Hosa, Lance Kozlowski
Index service: Robert J. Richardson
Proofreader: Marion Laird
Technical review: America Online, Inc.: Tim Barwick, Sunil Paul, David Peal, David B. O'Donnell, Marshall Rens,
    Kelly Richmond, Colin Steele

Second Edition 9 8 7 6 5 4 3 2 1
Printed in the United States of America


Ventana Communications Group, Inc.
P.O. Box 13964
Research Triangle Park, NC 27709-3964
919/544-9404
FAX 919/544-9472

## Trademarks

Trademarked names appear throughout this book, and on the accompanying compact disk or floppy disk (if applicable). Rather than list the names and entities that own the trademarks or insert a trademark symbol with each mention of the trademarked name, the publisher states that it is using the names only for editorial purposes and to the benefit of the trademark owner with no intention of infringing upon that trademark.

## About the Author

Tom Lichty retired from the University of Oregon faculty in June 1994 to devote full-time energies to research and writing. He is the author of six computer books, including *Design Principles for Desktop Publishers* (voted Book of the Year by the Computer Press Association in 1988), *America Online's Internet for Windows, Second Edition*, and *The Official America Online Tour Guide* (Windows and Macintosh versions), an alternate of the Book-of-the-Month Club in December, 1992, and the Quality Paperback Book Club's featured offering for February, 1993. Tom lives at the base of Oregon's Mount Hood, where he specializes in the design, desktop publishing and online communications fields of the computer industry. His Internet mailing address is majortom@aol.com.

## Acknowledgments

America Online's Internet is a *pièce de résistance*. It's a phenomenon that was ten years in the making but less than one year in commanding and receiving media, government, national—indeed, *worldwide*—attention.

It's my pleasure to describe America Online's Internet to you, but it was not a task completed in solitude. My thanks to Tim Barwick, Ken Carbone, Lyn Chitow, Ed Ferguson, Helen Gill, Bob Stoerrle, Mike Jarvis, Matt Korn, Jay Levitt, Maura O'Connell, David B. O'Donnell, Sunil Paul, David Peal, Marshall Rens and Kelly Richmond at AOL for their contributions to this project. Kudos to Charlie Armstrong, Dave Axler and the cyberjockey crew at the Internet Connection. A deep bow to Angela Anderson, Marion Laird and Pam Richardson at Ventana Press for their indomitable stamina. And special thanks to Cliff Figalo for his patience under fire and Jennifer Watson, who finds her mailbox full when she's gone for two days but who always manages to smile in spite of her mountains of work.

My thanks also to you, the America Online member. AOL is a community, and each one of us contributes to that community in one way or another. AOL's spectacular success is thus *our* achievement, and for that we can all take credit.

# CONTENTS

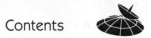

# INTRODUCTION

When I wrote the first edition of *America Online's Internet* in the winter of 1994, I began by presenting some startling Internet growth statistics. By the time the book appeared on the shelves—only four weeks after I finished writing it—those figures were out of date. Figures that were even more startling had replaced them.

A few months later, the World Wide Web made its explosive impact on the Internet—the image of the impact made by a dinosaur-extinguishing meteor comes to mind—and all previous numbers of all kinds were rendered insignificant.

I've learned my lesson: one cannot adequately identify the Internet's abiogenesis with numbers.

For the same reason, one cannot predict the Internet's future. Less than 10 percent of the U.S. population is currently online, and the United States is one of the world's most active online societies. This implies that at least 90 percent of the world's people have yet to participate on the Internet.

Figure I-1: A major Soviet strategic bomber base near Dolon, Kazakhstan. **Note:** *The illustration shown in Figure I-1 and many other recently declassified spy photos from the 1960s are available via the World Wide Web at* **http://edcwww.cr.usgs.gov** *(much more about the World Wide Web in Chapter 6).*

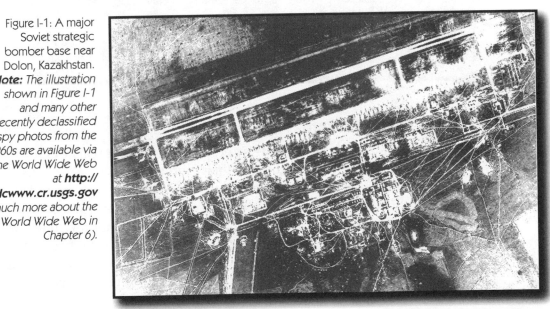

## The potential

The Internet today is like a parade that's forming but has yet to take to the streets. No one knows what's going to come of it, but something's going to happen, of that we can be sure.

We can be sure of one other thing: the Internet represents the potential for a worldwide grass-roots community. It reaches millions of people with electronic mail service and terabytes of data, most of which are free for the taking. But what is more important is that it offers truly equitable access for anyone with minimal computing power, a standard telephone line and a modem.

Ironically and contrarily, the Internet was a nearly closed fraternity until recently. Only academics, military personnel and a few stalwart adventurers were afforded access. This has changed. Somebody found the key and unlocked the door. People are flooding the Internet like the lava from Vesuvius flooded Pompeii.

**Keywords**

You're going to encounter frequent mentions of *keywords* in this book. Keywords are America Online's shortcuts. To get to an area of interest quickly, sign on and press Command+K. A small dialog box will appear, requesting a keyword. Type in the word, press your Enter key, and AOL will transport you to your destination immediately. This bypasses AOL's menu hierarchy and saves time; it's the technique for navigation that's used in this book.

## What the Internet has to offer

The Internet has no borders and it has no eyes. It reaches millions of people but knows nothing of their ethnicity, gender or age. Its only criteria for membership are a telephone line, a computer and a willingness to communicate with others. There are no uniforms, no authorities and no castes. This unparalleled equanimity offers the potential for an ideally democratic community: one where the common denominators are a desire to speak and a willingness to listen, where superficial values are simply impracticable.

There's more to the Internet, of course. You can search academic databases, transfer files or simply savor the travel of cyberspace. The Internet is a time machine, a trove of digital treasures, a cumulus of knowledge as dense as a neutron star.

### Cyberspace

The term *cyberspace* was coined by William Gibson in his novel "Neuromancer" (see the Bibliography in the back of this book). It is used in this context to denote a virtual expanse as infinite as space itself, with none of the prosaic hindrances—time, distance, geography, politics—that impede terrestrial travel as we know it. In cyberspace, all you need to do is imagine your destination, and your journey begins. For a glimpse of what cyberspace may become, read "Snow Crash" by Neal Stephenson, which is also mentioned in the Bibliography.

## What this book has to offer

This book does not describe the contents of the Internet in detail (plenty of publications do that, including the two free ones mentioned in the "Free for the taking" sidebar), but it does describe the process of accessing the Internet via America Online. Along the way you'll need a bit of explanation about what you're getting, but I'll try to keep that to a minimum. This is a user's manual, not a program guide.

### Free for the taking

America Online offers several low-cost publications that describe the Internet's contents. Two of them stand out. One is *Zen and the Art of the Internet*, a relatively short (about 75 pages) description of the network, written by Brendon Kehoe for the Computer Science department at Widener University. Sign on, press Command+K, then use the keyword: Internet. You'll see *Zen and the Art of the Internet* among the topics listed there. It's intended for online browsing and reference. It can also be downloaded: press Command+K and use the keyword: FileSearch, then search the libraries using the criteria: Zen and Internet.

An alternate is a much larger document, the *Big Dummy's Guide to the Internet*, written by Adam Gaffin and published by the Electronic Frontier Foundation. Nearly 200 pages in length, it is well written and thorough. Sign on, press Command+K, and use the keyword: EFF.

If you do download these publications, print them and shelve them alongside this book. It's not a bad way to start a first-rate Internet library.

## What America Online has to offer

With regard to the Internet, America Online is a gateway. It's hooked directly into the Net; we dial into it via telephone lines and modems for local access. That's the manifest description. But there's more to it, of course.

### It's familiar & comfortable

If you've lived in the same house for a number of years, you've come to know it intimately. You can find its light switches in the dark. You know its sounds and its smells. It's as familiar as—well—your own home.

As you may have guessed, I'm working on an analogy here. America Online, you see, is the Internet's new "home." AOL's Mac interface is familiar and comfortable. All of its commands are where you expect them to be. The days when Internet travelers were explorers of alien territory are over. The Internet's cybernauts have found a new home, and now it's as familiar as our own front door (see Figure I-2).

Figure I-2: A few of
America Online's
windows to the
Internet.

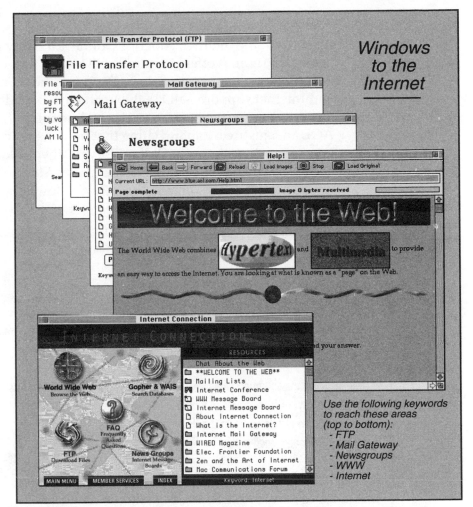

### It's toll-free access

For most U.S. households, AOL brings the Internet to the   front
door. You no longer need to depend on a friend of a friend to access
the Internet, and you no longer need to spend 20 cents a minute to
browse the Internet via a connection 200 miles away. More than
likely, America Online offers a toll-free number in your area. If it
doesn't, there's always the 800 number (investigate the keyword:
800), offering access at a fraction of the cost of long-distance calling.

### It's an online service

Apart from the Internet, America Online is a richly rewarding place in its own right. It offers hundreds of forums, tens of thousands of files for downloading, scores of online magazines, online computer and Internet support—all the things that have made it the success it is today. I've written a 550-page book describing it, and I won't do AOL an injustice by abbreviating that book here. If you want to know the whole America Online story, visit your local bookstore and ask for a copy of *The Official America Online Membership Kit and Tour Guide*, published by Ventana Press in Windows and Mac editions. Both can be purchased online as well: just press Command+K, then use the keyword: TourGuide.

---

### net.characters

Above all, the Internet is a community, and for those of us who are new residents, it's good sense to first learn a bit about the people who inhabit this place. Here are a few categories of Internet residents as defined by Adam Gaffin in the *Big Dummy's Guide to the Internet*:

*Net.gods* are the old-timers, the true titans of the Net and the keepers of its collective history. AOL has scores of them working in the Internet Connection.

*Net.geeks* are people to whom the Net is Life. If you're not fond of excitement in your life, they make good mates: intelligent, good wage-earners, and rarely demanding.

*Blatherers* just can't get to the point—they can wring three or four screens out of a thought that others might sum up in a sentence or two.

*Net.weenies* and *flamers* enjoy insulting others—those who post nasty messages in a sewing newsgroup just for the fun of it.

You can't tell *lurkers* are around, but they usually are. They're the ones who read information posted on the Net but never post or respond themselves. We all lurk at one time or another, and nearly everyone started out that way.

*Wizards* are people who know a particular Net-related topic inside and out. There are scores of them roaming the message boards at keyword: Internet, where they're called *cyberjockeys*.

*Net.saints* are always willing to help a newcomer and eager to share their knowledge. Use the keyword: Guide to learn more about AOL's saints.

## What you need

Like getting settled in a new house, moving into new electronic environs requires sacrificing the familiar for the new and improved. These are relatively small adjustments, but it's best to get them out in the open right away. You need to know where you're headed and why you're headed there. This means that you need to understand what the Internet is and what it has to offer.

## What you need to know

The Internet is an anarchy. The Internet succeeds where other anarchies have failed, primarily because of its strict—though tacit and voluntary—proprieties. These proprieties—called *Netiquette*—are the social foundation of the Net. You must know them, and they're discussed in Chapter 5.

You *don't* need to know UNIX, or what USENET newsgroups, mailing lists, FTP, the World Wide Web, Gopher and WAIS are. America Online's interface handles the UNIX for you, and this book will acquaint you with the rest. Here you'll find a complete introduction to the Internet, specifically adapted for AOL members. You will discover not only how to get there but what to expect once you arrive.

## Equipment reguired

You'll need a computer, a modem and a telephone line. The computer need not be fancy: as long as it's capable of running System 6.0.5 (or later), it'll do. The modem should be of the 9600 baud variety or faster. If you're buying a new one, buy a 28.8 kbps model if you can. The standard telephone line your phone is connected to will perform quite nicely. All of these things are described in detail in Appendix B.

## What's in this book

To begin, the "Quick Start" chapter offers immediate gratification for those who haven't yet installed the America Online software and are anxious to get on with it. It's a five-minute fix for impatience junkies.

Chapter 1: "Mastering Your Domain" draws the background upon which you will render your Internet experiential masterpiece. It explains what the Internet is, what America Online is, and how the two coordinate to provide your Internet access system. I expect many readers to skip this chapter in their eagerness to get into the action. I hope you all come back to it eventually and read what it has to say.

Chapter 2: "NetSpeak" offers a quick familiarity session before the actual body of the book begins. The Internet is rife with esoteric terminology that is, of necessity, used throughout this book. Rather than leave it to you to thumb through the glossary or discover the meanings of those terms by accident, I've prepared this orientation chapter. (There's a glossary at the back of the book as well, to serve as a more comprehensive reference.)

Chapter 2 also peeks at some of the Internet's attractions. This is my carrot on a stick: it's important that you know why you're learning AOL's Internet tools as you learn them.

Chapter 3: "Electronic Mail" discusses e-mail management. You can send mail to anyone on the Net—and anyone connected to any commercial online service. This chapter tells you how, and offers some suggestions for getting the most out of this feature.

Chapter 4: "Madame, Your List Is Served" is all about Internet mailing lists. Read this chapter and your mailbox will never be empty again.

Chapter 5: "Newshounds Anonymous" explores newsgroups and the network they run on, USENET. You may find this to be the home of the Internet's richest rewards. Be sure to read this one.

Chapter 6: "Web Walking" describes the Internet's *pièce de résistance*, the World Wide Web. AOL's software for browsing the Web is unique, and it offers some features few other browsers can match. Even if you know about the Web, you should read this chapter.

Chapter 7: "Getting the Goods (FTP)" introduces FTP, the system for downloading any of the millions of files available on the Net.

Chapter 8: "Gopher & WAIS Databases" burrows into the wealth of data that's available via the Gopher system.

Figure I-3: Looking like a sci-fi paperback cover, a NASA photograph of Saturn rising over one of its own moons, available via FTP from **naic.nasa.gov**.

Chapter 9: "FlashSessions and the Download Manger" offers operational details about AOL's offline productivity features. You can conduct much of your Internet activity offline, then sign on and let AOL do its online wizardry in a burst of information exchange. If you're interested in saving money, this chapter is a must.

The bonus section: "Roadside Attractions" offers a number of sites on the Net worth checking out—things like the Yahoo Web server, the Weather Underground and the colossal Garbo server in Finland.

Appendices include "Preferences"—where you'll find out about the AOL Internet preferences, and "Making the Connection"—a step-by-step guide to AOL software installation and sign-up. You'll also find a glossary of Internet-related terms and a bibliography of references for further reading.

## Moving on

I've tried to keep this Introduction short because I know you're anxious to begin your Internet journey. To help you get going, I have included a Quick Start section that should get you installed, connected and online in a matter of minutes. It's intended for the stalwart reader who hasn't installed the AOL software but is already familiar with online services, modems and software installation routines. If that's you, turn the page. If you've more patience (or less familiarity with the territory), or if your AOL software is already installed, skip the next chapter and begin your journey with Chapter 1: "Mastering Your Domain."

One way or another, I look forward to seeing you very soon on another page . . . .

# QUICK START

This chapter is for those who have yet to install the America Online Software and are anxious to get underway. I'm an impatient person too, so I empathize and offer this quick start on your Internet journey.

If you already have AOL's software running, or you're not in a big hurry, turn to Chapter 1 and pursue the Internet at a more leisurely pace. We'll get to know the Net and America Online in that chapter; then, if you need to, you can turn to Appendix B in the back of this book for an in-depth discussion of installation and setup.

## The computer & the modem

Almost any Mac (Mac Plus or later) capable of running System 6.0.7 (or later) is capable of running the America Online software. If you plan to make much use of the World Wide Web (discussed in Chapter 6: "Web Walking"), however, you will want a well-equipped machine. AOL's Web browser also offers a nifty local cache, and the more disk space you provide for it, the better. Ideally speaking, a frequent user of the Web should have a computer with a 68040 processor or better, 8mb of RAM or better, and at least 20mb of free disk space for the program files and the cache. If you plan to access any of the Web's multimedia features, you will find a color monitor helpful.

You should also have a 9600 baud modem or faster. Anything slower than that will frustrate you. Again, Web users will want all they can get: a 28.8 kbps modem (V .34) makes sense under these circumstances.

Unless you can tolerate Byzantine inconveniences, connect the modem to the modem port (in the back—the one with the little telephone handset icon) of your Mac. Make this connection and the connection to the phone line before you run the AOL software for the first time. Be sure to turn on the modem once all of the wires are in place.

If you've never tested your setup, and your modem shipped with some kind of system-analysis software, use it to verify the integrity of your modem and phone line before you attempt installation.

## Installing the software

You don't have to make a folder for the America Online software: after asking where you want the software installed, the Install program will make its own folder. You will need at least 3.5mb of free space on your hard disk for the program files (if you plan to install the Web browser, make that 5.5mb), and a floppy drive or a CD-ROM that's compatible with the America Online program disk. **Note:** If the disk (or CD-ROM) and your drive aren't compatible, stay calm and call AOL at 800-827-3338 for a suitable replacement.

Follow the steps below to install the software:

🔺 If you're installing from floppies, make a copy (or copies, if your membership kit contained two disks) of the America Online floppy disk(s), store the original(s) in a safe place and insert the copy into your disk drive. The America Online v2.6 window should open on your desktop when you do (if it doesn't, double-click the disk icon on the desktop). Double-click the Install icon to begin the installation icon.

🔺 The Install program's Welcome screen will appear. Click the Continue button to proceed. At the second screen, click the Continue button again to do a standard installation. Select the disk you prefer for the software installation (see Figure Q-1). The Install program will create a folder for you. If any of this isn't satisfactory, turn to Appendix B in the back of this book for further details.

Figure Q-1: The Install program assumes you want to install the software on the first hard disk it encounters in its search. Switch the disk if you wish.

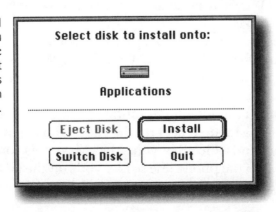

🔺 The Install program will finish the installation without your intervention now, decompressing files on the floppy and building a number of folders within its parent folder. It will keep you posted on its progress and let you know when it's finished.

## The initial online session

Before you begin this phase, decide on a screen name and a couple of alternates. This name will also become part of your Internet address. On the Internet, it's customary to use your first initial and your full last name, all lowercase: **tlichty** would be appropriate for me. Your first and middle initials plus your last name is a good alternate. AOL screen names can have a maximum of ten alphanumeric characters: no punctuation is allowed. Have a password ready too, between 4 and 8 alphanumeric characters in length.

Have your VISA, MasterCard, American Express or Discover card handy. AOL accepts selected bank debit cards also. In a pinch, AOL will accept your bank checking-account number, but there's a small fee for this. (AOL will provide specific fee information before they charge your account.)

Try to conduct your initial sign-on before 6:00 pm Eastern time. Things move along much more quickly before peak hours.

🔺 When it concludes, the Install program may leave the America Online v2.6 window open on the screen. Double-click the America Online v2.6 icon to launch the software.

🔺 When you first launch the software, you have the option of upgrading from a previous version of AOL which you may have installed on your hard disk, or simply continuing if you are a new member. If you choose to upgrade, you'll be asked to locate your older copy of AOL. The Install program will then copy all your user-specific information for each of your account names to the new installation. After installation is complete, you can safely delete the old AOL folder: it won't be needed any longer.

⚠ After a number of explanatory screens, the software will start the process of finding an access number for you. It does this with your telephone area code (which you will be asked to provide) and a toll-free number that connects to its database of access numbers (see Figure Q-2). **Note:** If none of the numbers listed is a local call for you, you will incur long-distance charges when connecting to America Online. Consider AOL's 800 number instead. There's a small surcharge for its use, but it's less expensive than most toll calls.

Figure Q-2: Select AOL's nearest access number from the list in this window. The number at the top isn't necessarily the closest number for your area: examine the entire list.

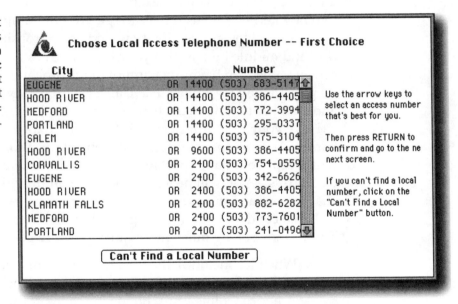

⚠ Select a primary number and an alternate from the list provided. The first one listed for your area may not be the nearest or the fastest, so look them all over. Different numbers for the primary and secondary numbers are best, but if only one is available, list it in both locations.

⚠ The software will then hang up and dial your primary access number. The remainder of the initial session will be conducted via the number you've chosen.

👈 When the software asks for your temporary registration number and password, supply those that were packaged with your disk(s) or CD-ROM.

👈 Provide your name, address, telephone number and billing information as requested.

👈 When asked, try the screen name you decided upon earlier. If it's rejected, try an alternate. AOL's initial suggestion is rarely appropriate (see Figure Q-3). Supply your password also when asked.

Figure Q-3: Use the Select Alternate Name button to provide an appropriate AOL screen name.

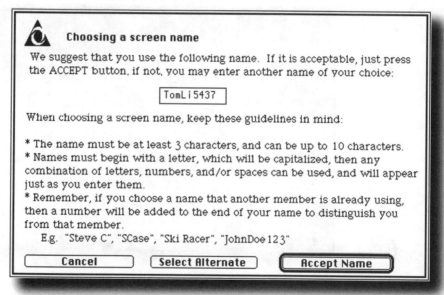

If any previous step has given you trouble, turn to Appendix B of this book and conduct the initial session again. The greater detail provided in that section may reveal the source of your trouble.

If you're *really* having trouble, call AOL's Technical Support at 800-827-3338. They're experts at solving problems related to the initial session.

## The Internet Connection

Soon after you complete the screen name/password information, you'll enter into the service proper; you'll be greeted by America Online's Welcome screen and voice. Though you're welcome to explore AOL all you wish, if you want to access the Internet immediately, press Command+K (America Online's "keyword" shortcut to designated areas within the service), and enter the keyword: Internet. In a few moments, you'll arrive at the Internet Connection (Figure Q-4), and your journey begins.

Figure Q-4: The Internet Connection is where all Internet activities occur on AOL.

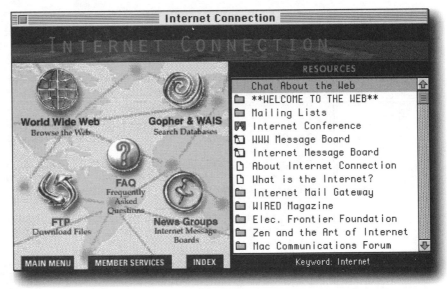

## Installing the Web browser

If you installed from a single floppy disk and you plan to access the World Wide Web, you will need to download the Web browser application, which is not included on the floppy. Don't worry: there's no charge for the browser or the time required to download it, and there are no arcane downloading protocols or settings to worry about. Just use the keyword: Web and follow the instructions you see there for downloading the browser.

## Moving on

If you know the Internet well, you'll know exactly what you want to do once you've arrived at the Internet Connection. If you're not familiar with the Internet, spend a little time exploring the buttons and listed items in the Connection's window, then sign off (the Sign Off command is on the Go To menu) and take a moment to gather your wits, offline, while the clock's not running.

Understand that the Internet is primarily a society, and like all societies it's steeped in tradition and protocol. In other words, you'd best learn how to swim before you jump in the lake. I try to help you do that in Chapter 1, "Mastering Your Domain." That's the best place to begin your journey, and it's only a page away . . . .

# Chapter 1

# MASTERING YOUR DOMAIN

The word *domain* has a specific meaning to members of the Internet community—a meaning we'll discuss later in this chapter. On the other hand, my dictionary defines the word domain as "...a field of action, thought or influence."

Yes. That's the Internet: a field of thought, action and influence. These words imply a certain responsibility—an imperative to think sensibly, to act nimbly, and to wield influence judiciously. As domains go, the Internet is not a fast-food franchise where everything is casual and familiar; the Internet is *Maxim's* in Paris: it's renowned, it's formidable and its rewards are ambrosial—*if* you take the time to learn the protocol before you start snapping your fingers.

Thus, this chapter. Here we introduce your domain and the key that unlocks its door—America Online. Here we describe the roots of the domain—the improbable marriage of the military and academia. And here we recite the liturgy—the rituals that manifest the Internet society today.

**Eschew passivity**

Cofounder of the Electronic Frontier Foundation (and founder of Lotus Development Corporation and Lotus 1-2-3) Mitch Kapor says: "In mass media, the vast majority of participants are passive recipients of information. In digital communications media, the vast majority of participants are active creators of information as well as recipients."

Decentralization! Participation! Egalitarianism! It all sounds very Jeffersonian. Indeed, Thomas Jefferson believed that the fundamental resource of his day—land— was a natural right and that its acquisition by the masses should be inalienable. Nowadays, the fundamental resource is information, and, unlike land, there's an infinite supply of it.

The Internet is our land grant. How the land is cultivated and the rewards harvested are up to us, the members. We are the pioneers, the settlers of the Information Age.

## America Online

First and foremost, realize that few of us can afford to connect our computers directly to the Internet. Direct Internet connections are costly, and they require expertise to maintain.

Until recently, the majority of Net users worked at computers or terminals connected to networks at universities or military establishments. Many of these networks were directly or indirectly connected to the Internet. In either case, the computers sitting on people's desks weren't connected to the Net; their "hosts" were.

It wasn't until the early 1990s that "commercial" accounts (accounts other than educational, governmental or military) were accepted on the Net. And it wasn't until 1993 or so that online services such as America Online established their Internet connections, opening the Internet up to any individual with a personal computer, a modem and a standard telephone line.

America Online is the mechanism you will use to connect to the Internet. You will use your telephone and a modem to dial in to AOL, and AOL will put you "on the Net."

### An online telecommunications service

America Online is an online telecommunications service, located just outside of Washington, DC, in Vienna, Virginia. There are numerous similar services—most in the form of local bulletin board systems (BBSes)—but only six are truly nationwide (see the "Six & Counting" sidebar). Though Delphi was the first of the six to offer Internet access, America Online was the first to offer access in the Mac's familiar graphical interface.

### Six & Counting

The six services I refer to are America Online, CompuServe, Delphi, GEnie, Apple's eWorld and PRODIGY. This number is subject to change. The online telecommunications industry is one of the fastest-growing industries in the world, after all, and newcomers abound. At the time this chapter is being written (June 1995), IBM, AT&T and Microsoft have all announced their intentions of entering the fray—indeed, some have already entered it. More are sure to follow.

Online services offer much more than Internet access. America Online specializes in supporting a "virtual community," where members gather to discuss interests and issues in real-time or bulletin-board fashion. AOL offers an exceptional electronic mail facility as well (described in Chapter 3), plus tens of thousands of files—graphics, fonts, programs, multimedia—for downloading from their computers directly to your hard disk. More than one reference is available for learning about America Online: see the Bibliography.

## An elegant Internet interface

AOL isn't simply an online service, however. It's not just your Internet provider, either: it's also your Internet *interface*. Most of the machines that are connected to the Net run the UNIX operating system, and prior to AOL's Windows and Macintosh interface, those of us who desired Internet access had to learn at least a smattering of UNIXspeak—a task not unlike learning to program a VCR, in both complexity and intolerance of error. This isn't your problem. AOL intervenes, with an elegant interface that's unequaled in the Internet industry.

## Packet-switching networks

But I may be ahead of myself. Before you can use AOL to access the Internet, you must access AOL itself. This is accomplished via a *packet-switching network*.

If you wanted to converse with someone via computer, you could string a wire between your two machines and carry on. But if you're a distance from one another, that wire would have to be mighty long. And if millions of people worldwide wanted to converse this way, the world would resemble a colossal ball of twine, enmeshed in the wires of personal telephony.

Instead, you decide to hire a *common carrier*—a service such as the phone company—to deliver the message for you. For a fraction of what it would cost you to string a wire yourself, common carriers do it more reliably, less expensively and much more conveniently for you.

For much the same reason, America Online hires common carriers to deliver goods to (and from) its members. These common carriers offer *nodes*—local telephone numbers—in most cities in North America. They charge AOL for using their nodes, just as Federal Express (another common carrier) would charge you to deliver a package.

Unfortunately, just as America Online's business has doubled and tripled in each of the past few years, so has business at the common carriers. The lines are becoming jammed. It is for this reason that AOL has established its own network of wires, decreasing AOL's dependence on common carriers. AOL's network, not surprisingly, is called *AOLnet*. It's the best way to connect to AOL. If you're not already using it, check to see if there's an AOLnet node near you. Use the keyword: AOLnet to investigate the potential.

Regardless of who provides them, we really haven't solved the problem of the wires. America Online handles thousands of calls simultaneously. This implies hundreds of thousands of wires, just to service AOL and its members.

Fortunately, there's a solution. AOLnet, SprintNet, Tymenet—they've all discovered techniques by which they can accommodate multiple conversations on a single wire, seemingly at the same time. Chances are, your computer is sharing a node with some corporate computer that's uploading data to a parent mainframe in New Jersey and an ATM that's polling its host for the validity of someone's personal identification number. All three computers are using the same line at the same time. This seems contrary to everything we've ever learned about telephone lines, but it works.

### Lovers' spats & cheesecake

Imagine four people conversing on an old-fashioned party line. Two of them—let's say they're cooks—are exchanging recipes for cheesecake, and two others—the lovers—are having a quarrel. Since all four must use the same line and the pairs have little interest in each other's conversations, they agree on a formality whereby each conversational segment is preceded and followed by a code word.

During a lull in the conversation, one of the lovers announces "Start spat," and the cooks agree to remain silent (and politely ignore the conversation) until the lovers announce "End spat." When the lovers pause to marshal their forces, one of the cooks announces "Start cheesecake," and continues until he announces "End cheesecake," signifying the end of that thread of conversation. Little snippets of conversation alternate like this until all dialog concludes.

Such electronic conversations occur by the thousands, all on the same telephone lines. Each conversational segment—a *packet*—is preceded and followed by codes denoting the beginning and the ending of the packet. Each packet consists of a relatively small amount of data—perhaps a kilobyte—and is sent via high-speed telephone lines in a burst taking only microseconds. Thus, thousands of conversations take place on the same line with no apparent break in transmission. The technique is referred to as *packet switching*, and it's as common as...well...lovers' spats.

The cost of time-sharing information like this is so insignificant that it's covered by your America Online membership. No matter how many hours you're online per month, AOL never charges extra for the "wires" between its nodes and Vienna. Indeed, the only long-distance charges are to those rural members who have to dial 1 before they can reach a node—and even those people can access AOL via its 800 number (investigate the keyword: 800). It's not exactly a toll-free call (there's a slight surcharge for using the 800 number), but it sure beats long distance.

## TCP/IP

This discussion of packets applies to the Internet as well. Indeed, the Internet is the Colossus of packet-switching networks.

Unlike common carriers for most online services, however, the Internet doesn't rely on point-to-point connections. Each Internet "node" is connected to thousands of others. When one node is ready to send a packet, it tosses it into the air somewhat like a basketball tip-off. The packet is broadcast on the Net, caught by the most convenient node and passed on in a similar fashion. (I'm simplifying, perhaps to an extreme—I just want you to have a general idea of the Internet's architecture.)

This process (called *Transmission-Control Protocol* and *Internet Protocol*—TCP/IP) has been compared to passing a hot potato: packets bounce from node to node until they reach their destination. It employs the Internet's least-engaged resources and tolerates the removal of a node now and then for repair or maintenance.

## The Internet

The Internet and America Online share a number of similarities. They both offer forums, mail, files to download, and chats. But the Net is much, much bigger. No one really knows how many people actually use the Internet, but it reaches over a hundred countries, and tens of millions of people use it every day. No one owns it, it has no central facility, and there's no board of directors or CEO. An advisory committee is at the helm, and they are all volunteers.

Now that I read the previous paragraph, I hasten to add that there's no "it" either. The Internet isn't a single entity. It comprises scores of independent networks—some military, some academic, some commercial—all *inter*connected. Indeed, these interconnected *net*works are the very basis of the Internet name.

### Nouns & adjectives

If you're going to live in the neighborhood, you're going to have to speak the language. Used as a noun, the Internet is referred to as "the Internet." One would never say, "Send me a message on Internet"; it would have to be, "Send me a message on the Internet."

Used as an adjective, it's "Internet mail," not "the Internet mail."

## Military preparedness

The best way to define the Internet is to examine what it was originally. Like a democracy, the Internet is best understood by observing its past. Most important, the Internet began as a military contrivance. Most Net users know this, but many have never grasped the significance of that fact. The Internet's early military credentials have more to do with what it is today than any other factor.

The Internet is a collection of an uncounted number of independent computers distributed worldwide. Most are networked (wired) together locally and connected to a hub of some sort—a *server*. These servers—and, perhaps, other independent computers—might be connected to a *domain*: a machine that's connected to the Internet and is listed in the Domain Name System (the Internet's equivalent of the phone book). Using leased high-speed telephone lines (not modems), each domain is wired to at least one—often more than one—other domain on the Net. The slowest of these telephone lines operates at 56 kbps—kilobits per second—more than five times faster than a 9600 baud modem. Many of these domains maintain a constant connection to the Net: they don't sign on and sign off as we do with AOL, they're online all the time.

A simplified map of this arrangement might look like the one pictured in Figure 1-1.

Figure 1-1: The Internet extends around the globe as a web of independent domains interconnected with round-the-clock high-speed dedicated telephone lines.

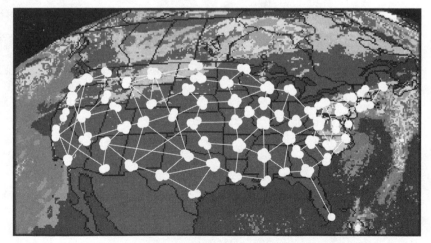

*Note: Don't interpret either Figure 1-1 or 1-2 literally. I drew the white lines, and they're not intended to represent literal Internet or AOL nodes (especially since all I've included is the U.S. mainland— a politicocentric decision if there ever was one). It would take a map the size of Wyoming to display all of these nodes (although there may be such a map somewhere).The image of the continent is from the GEOS satellite. Use the keyword: Weather, then investigate the color weather maps.*

Compare the Internet strategy with that of America Online. AOL consists of a network of host computers (in Virginia) and thousands of client computers (all of our PCs and Macs). While the Internet strategy looks like a web, the AOL strategy looks more like a star (as shown in Figure 1-2).

Figure 1-2: AOL's star-like network consists of a host and thousands of intermittently connected clients.

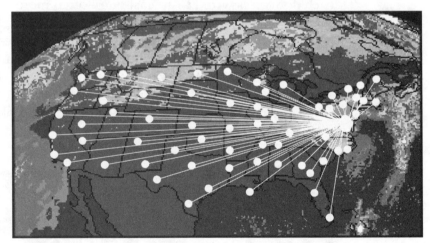

Now the military part: look again at Figure 1-2. A fictitious scenario: If Ace Excavation were to dig up a fiber-optic cable in Vienna, Virginia, most of us would be without AOL—a disheartening experience, indeed. On the other hand, if a backhoe unplugged a domain in the Internet, communications would simply be routed around it. Indeed, if a large percentage of the Net's domains were eliminated, the Net would still function.

Forever prepared, the Defense Department commissioned the Advanced Research Projects Agency (ARPA) to configure a computer network that would anticipate just such a possibility. This happened in the late 1960s; the network was called ARPANET.

## Academic anarchy

By the early 1980s, educators discovered the value of sharing research information and computing resources through interconnected computers—especially supercomputers, which are as precious as platinum. The educators weren't interested (much) in security; their interest was access. Their computers held vast amounts of data, and in a typically magnanimous spirit, they wanted to share that information objectively, without bias, to anyone within the community who wanted access. They needed a network—a worldwide network.

### Three years in search of 75 cents

Speaking of the ARPANET, meet astronomer Cliff Stoll. Since astronomers do a lot of computer modeling, Cliff is fairly adept at computers. That's a good thing, because there isn't much work for astronomers and there is a lot for computer operators, especially at Cliff's level.

Which is how Cliff Stoll came to be involved with the Internet and ARPANET (later renamed Milnet). When I asked Cliff to contribute to this book, he wrote:

"Hmmm.... Military computers on a network? A group of German programmers, adept at breaking into computers, decided to make money from their skills. For a year, they snuck into dozens of systems across the Milnet, copied data from them, and sold this information to the Soviet KGB. They were high-tech spies. With keyboards and modems, they exploited security holes in distant computers. Once on a system, they scanned for sensitive material, passwords or pathways to other computers. For a year, they went undetected. Then they bumped into me.

"In August 1986, while managing an astronomy computer in Berkeley, California, I noticed a 75 cent accounting error. Someone had used a few minutes of computer time without a valid billing address. Curious ... just nickels and dimes, but worth checking into. Zooks, but what I found! Using a printer and several PC's, I watched someone sneak through my system, onto the Milnet, and then steal information from military systems a thousand miles away.

"Instead of locking him out of my system, I let him prowl through it, quietly tracking him back to his roost. The trace took a year; but in the end, we proved that five guys were spying over the computer networks. They were convicted of espionage in 1990."

For the whole story, read Cliff's first book, *The Cuckoo's Egg*. It's the true story of tracking a spy through the maze of computer espionage, and it ought to be required reading for any Internet user.

Buy a copy of his book, read it, then send him some e-mail telling him you heard about it here. His AOL screen name is CliffStoll.

ARPANET was their answer, but there are fundamental inconsistencies in the military and the academic attitudes. The academic community elected instead to develop its own network which they called NSFNet, named for the National Science Foundation—the academics' primary source of funding. Significantly, NSFNet used the same networking strategy ARPANET used: interconnected domains randomly distributed around the globe.

Eventually, ARPANET and NSFNet established a connection, and the concept of interconnected networks became manifest.

Academe's entry into the arena distorted the military structure of networked computing somewhat: most of the academic computers were owned by colleges and universities; none were subject to any form of central control. The result could have been dysfunctional anarchy. But by definition a computer network implies some form of universal protocol: electronic standards that everyone agrees to uphold. The result is frequently described as *consensual anarchy*, whereby everyone marches to his or her own drum but all agree on a common route for the parade.

And that's how the Internet is today—an agglomeration of independent domains drawn from both ARPANET and NSFNet (and many others), each owned by organizations independent of each other, all interconnected by high-speed data lines, and none subject to any form of central control. There's no central data storage either. Data are scattered about the Net like clues in a treasure hunt—hidden in faraway places, waiting for discovery. It amazes me that the thing even manages to exist: it's one of the few working models of functional anarchy today, and it works extremely well.

---

### *WIRED* Magazine

*WIRED* is the "magazine of the digital generation"—covering interactive media, the networking community and the toys of technology. Started in early 1993, *WIRED* has quickly advanced to the vanguard of the literary aristocracy. Its design is precocious; its tone acerbic. This publication has few peers that can match its insight, candor or irreverence—and none can match them all.

Best of all, WIRED is available on America Online. Only past issues are available—you'll have to visit your newsstand for the latest edition—but its content isn't so timely that it becomes obsolete in a month or two. If this chapter interests you and you're not yet a devotee, you should read this magazine. Use the keyword: WIRED.

## Societal protocol

Enough talk about ARPANET and packet-switching networks. Above all, the Internet is people—by consensus, a group of individuals who choose to remain unowned, ungoverned and unbridled in their pursuit of a virtual community. Commercial users (that's us) already create a menace with our sheer numbers; if we further stress this delicate structure in our ignorance and enthusiasm, it will crumble. A few words of caution, then, seem appropriate before we move on.

### Be respectful

The Internet is fragile. Via FTP, for instance, we are transported directly to the operating-system level of computers anywhere in the world (FTP is discussed in Chapter 7). FTP is like your PC's C: prompt or your Mac's Finder: files can be moved, read, modified or deleted. Though not every machine on the Net offers this degree of access, some do, and they have survived that way for many years— because users are trusted. Trust is a precious thing. Honor it by reading up on the Net (see the Bibliography in this book) before you exercise your authority.

The widespread access to the Net via online services such as AOL has stressed the Net's physical and social tolerance. Though it's hardly older than two decades, the Internet is steeped in tradition, and much of that tradition is a response to its mainframe heritage. This is not the place to shake things up. If you want the Internet to survive, observe it thoroughly before you participate.

If nothing else, sign on to AOL and use the keyword: TOS. Take a few minutes to read the Terms of Service there. You will find a succinct and thoughtful declaration of online ethics that's as appropriate to the Internet as it is to AOL.

### Be kind

John Perry Barlow, cofounder of the Electronic Frontier Foundation (and lyricist for the Grateful Dead), once said, "In cyberspace, the First Amendment is a local ordinance." Each country brings its own Bill of Rights to the table. Hate, bigotry and harassment are anathema on the Net: perhaps nothing else is as threatening to its spirit. The very nature of electronic communication cloaks us in anonymity and immunity (journalist Gregg Morris dubs it "anonymosity"), provoking an immediate sense of sovereignty. It's a heady feeling. Resist it. Consider others. Be kind.

### Thou shalt not sell

One of the cornerstones of the Internet's foundation is its noncommercial emphasis. The Internet is a refreshing respite from the abundance of commercialism that floods our lives—a matter of no accident. Bearers of commercial messages on the Net are as welcome as water on a leaky ship, and they're expunged with similar determination.

There is a major exception to the discipline—that's the World Wide Web, discussed in Chapter 6—but unless you're absolutely certain about what you're doing, market your enthusiasm in a more receptive medium.

### Give back what you receive

Above all, the Internet is a community. It's content is not produced by a governing entity. You're not watching "Picket Fences" here; you're not the audience, you're a player. As in real communities, your Internet community is shaped by the interaction of those within it. Passivity under these circumstances is not appropriate.

If you read a newsgroup, post to it. If you subscribe to a mailing list, respond to what you read. If you download a graphic, upload one in return. Do all of these things with *elan* and compassion, but *do them.*

### Celebrate joie de vivre

If you share my fascination with infants' eyes, perhaps you can relate to this section. A child's eyes seem to be enthralled by the world they see: "Gee! There's so much stuff out there! Where should I begin?"

In the discovery context, the Internet is an event as close to being newborn as most of us will ever get. Its potential is unbounded. Its challenge is provocative. Its breadth is infinite.

It's a shame to neglect this kind of opportunity. Don't just subscribe to half a dozen newsgroups and fail to explore the others. Search the Net for files to transfer to your machine. Strike up an e-mail acquaintance with someone in a faraway land—someone in France, perhaps. If you don't know what *joie de vivre* means, ask your French acquaintance to define it. That's the most enchanting way to add the term to your vocabulary.

### Be persistent

The Internet is no place to be shy. There's no reward in timidity. A quick wit isn't requisite: there's lots of time to think over a reply. Ignorance begets ignorance: there are plenty of informational resources on the Net and plenty of people to ask.

## Moving on

My treatise on Netiquette has concluded. However, though you're prepared to act the part of the good citizen, you might not be prepared to converse with the natives. For that, you need a phrase book. Actually, a phrase chapter will do. It's next.

# Chapter 2

# NetSpeak

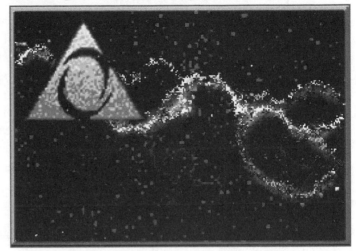

**A** friend was in the hospital not long ago, hooked up to an intravenous device. There was the obligatory bag hanging from the clothes-tree thing; there were tubes, of course, and that inevitable needle. There was also a pump: a black box with digital readouts and lots of warning lights. It reminded me of a '68 Chevy—over-sized, slightly antiquated, and warning lights for everything.

While I was visiting, the black box began beeping. A light came on: "occlusion," it read. My friend and I were in a panic: the beeping was incessant, "occlusion" sounded fatal, and we didn't know what to do.

Eventually a nurse arrived. He fiddled with a plastic tube and the beeping stopped. The light went out. My friend (and I) survived. "What was that all about?" I asked the nurse. "The tube was pinched," he said. Occlusion, in this context, meant a pinched tube. An obstruction. We could have avoided a few moments of horror if only we had known how to interpret that message.

Thus, this chapter. Here you'll learn the essential language of the Internet, so that little semantic surprises like "occlusion" won't send you running for the nearest Unabridged. I'm making no assumptions about your familiarity with the Internet; it's okay to be a net.numbskull. Einstein, you'll recall, failed mathematics. Ignorance is transitory.

In this chapter we'll also discover some of the attractions the Internet offers. Knowing how to speak its language is one thing; knowing *why* you want to speak it is another.

## About e-mail

Electronic mail, or *e-mail*, is simply mail sent from one computer to another. You can send e-mail to anyone with an Internet address (and each of the millions of people in over 100 countries has one); you can send mail to more than one addressee at a time; you can print, save, copy and paste e-mail messages; you can forward them, ignore them, delete them, file them, and—of course—read them. This you can do whenever you please, whenever it's convenient for you. E-mail is almost instantaneous and, best of all, it costs about three cents per message, even if the recipient is halfway around the world.

Figure 2-1: E-mail sent and received; it cost about a nickel and took less than 15 minutes to send and receive this mail from Johan Helsingius in Finland.

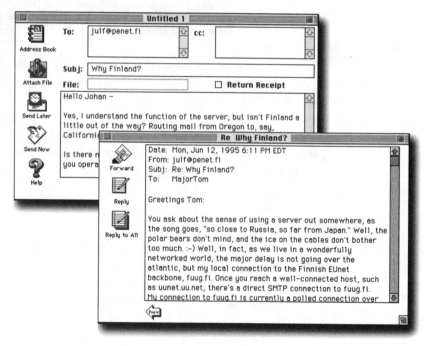

Lots of people have e-mail addresses: the writer Douglas Adams is **adamsd@cerf.net**; cartoon characters Beavis & Butt-head are **beavis@mtv.com** and **butthead@mtv.com**; Stewart Brand, founder of the *Whole Earth Catalog* and the man behind the WELL (Whole Earth 'Lectronic Link) is **sbb@well.sf.ca.us**; Bill Clinton is **president@whitehouse.gov**; Microsoft CEO Bill Gates is **billg@microsoft.com**; and the Vice President, Al Gore, is

**vice-president@whitehouse.com**. This is not a comprehensive listing. There are millions of others.

E-mail is discussed in detail in Chapter 3.

## Mailing lists

*Thwack!!* Caroming the length of the table, the solitary cue ball collides with its freshly racked brethren, scattering pool balls in every direction. The force of one is manifest in the activity of many.

*Mailing lists* are the cue balls of the e-mail playing field. Send an e-mail message to a mailing list and *thwack!!*: it provokes hundreds—sometimes thousands—of like messages careening across the I-way like a liberated rack of pool balls. E-mail messages sent to a list are automatically sent (as e-mail) to everyone who subscribes to that list. Anyone who subscribes can submit a message to a list; and for most lists, everyone is welcome to subscribe.

That, in essence, is all there is to mailing lists. Many (though not all) are automated; others are managed by humans. Frequently, a human will "moderate" a list by filtering out extraneous messages and clarifying those that are sent. Occasionally a human moderator will condense a list's activity and broadcast it as a "digest," providing mailings once every week or so.

### Some interesting lists

There are thousands of lists available on the Internet. Most of them address special interests but many discuss issues that range far and wide. With millions of people from more than 100 countries contributing, these mailing lists rarely suffer from apathy or vacuity. Here are a few examples:

- The *Fatfree* mailing list discusses extremely low-fat vegetarianism.
- The *Femail* list provides a forum for issues of particular interest to women.
- *Ballroom* focuses on all aspects of ballroom dancing.
- The *origami* list is all about the Japanese art of paper-folding.

There are thousands of others, of course. This is simply a random sample.

Mailing lists—including how to subscribe to them—are discussed in Chapter 4.

## Newsgroups

Everyone with an e-mail address can participate in a mailing list, but for those with slightly more enlightened Internet connections (which includes those of us on AOL), there are *newsgroups*. Newsgroups (or *USENET newsgroups*, as they're properly called) are similar to mailing lists, though e-mail isn't the medium. You "join" a newsgroup (rather than subscribe to it), and actively read its contents (rather than passively receive e-mail as you do from lists).

In content, newsgroups and mailing lists differ very little. Most of them are nondiscriminatory platforms for the free exchange of ideas, opinions and queries. Some, however, provide a medium for the exchange of *encoded binary data*: graphics, programs, sounds and movies. There are as many newsgroups as there are mailing lists—perhaps more. Next to e-mail, USENET newsgroups are the Internet's primary calling card.

A sampling includes ten newsgroups devoted to aviation, six for bicyclists, another ten dedicated to crafts and collecting, nine food and beverage groups; close to 50 are devoted to music, and another 40 serve the players of various games. Pets, travel, and sports—as you might expect—are among the most popular newsgroup topics. There's a newsgroup for people with foot fetishes, another for jugglers, one for autograph collectors, and three for subscribers to conspiracy theories. There are newsgroups that explore the cultures of Afghanistan, Africa, Arabia, Argentina, SE Asia, Australia and Austria—and those are just the A's. There's

**alt.cows.moo.moo.moo,**
**alt.tv.dinosaurs.barney.die.die.die** and
**alt.swedish.chef.bork.bork.bork**

(Newsgroups often have peculiar names, though these are exceptional).

As I write this chapter, America Online members have access to over 18,000 USENET newsgroups. If you have an interest and you can't find a newsgroup that discusses it, you probably haven't looked hard enough.

Newsgroups are discussed in Chapter 5.

Figure 2-2: True to form, the **talk.bizarre** newsgroup reveals this eclectic conversational thread. Most other newsgroups are more focused than this. Pictured is the AOL Macintosh software.

## The World Wide Web

The *World Wide Web* is to the Internet what the automobile is to a freeway. You might say it's just another conveyance for information, but it's quickly becoming the dominant one, and it's the one that has captured the allegiance, imagination and enthusiasm of millions of Net users worldwide.

The Web is also the Internet's primary medium for commercial activity, and commercial activity—more than any other single factor—is what's shaping the Internet today.

Figure 2-3: A typical "page" from the World Wide Web.

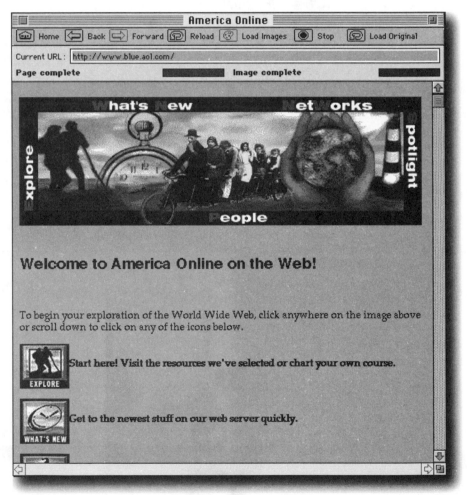

The Web offers a familiar, point-and-click interface to the Internet. Magazine-like, it also offers a medium that's resplendent with graphics and attractive layouts. The Web is an amalgam of text, graphics, sounds, video and more, yet in spite of its complexity, it's as easy to use as a toaster. The World Wide Web is discussed in Chapter 6.

## FTP

Formally, the term *FTP* is a noun—an acronym for File Transfer Protocol. Informally, it's a verb indicating the process of transferring files from one machine to another. Noun or verb, FTP is how you transfer files from the Net to your computer.

Many machines on the Net offer a public directory—a repository for files available for transfer to your machine. Many of these directories are available to anyone who logs on—thus the process is referred to as anonymous FTP—and there are thousands of them on the Net.

The beauty of FTP is that it makes no difference what kind of machine you're using or what kind of machine is holding the files; most Internet data will transfer without discrimination. No one has ever measured the quantity of data that's available via FTP for transfer. There's probably no prefix for it anyway: kilo or mega certainly won't do; giga (mega times a thousand) comes closer. We'll have to invent a new term for this kind of volume.

Figure 2-4: The boy-and-dog clip art was downloaded via FTP from **cc2sun.cs.ttu.edu**. A number of other clip-art sites are available: read the **alt.binaries.clip-art** newsgroup for their names.

What's available via FTP? Palindromes & aerodromes, programs & diagrams, the Urdu-English dictionary, photographs & holographs, toxic custard & tasteless jokes, the budget of the U.S. Government, planets & rennets, gay bars & isobars, area codes & ZIP Codes, the Russian telephone directory, Mother Jones & Mother Earth, cyberpunks & cipher funk; and, to sharpen the point, the first one million digits of pi (at **wuarchive.wustl.edu** in the */doc/misc/pi* directory, in case you're interested).

FTP is discussed in Chapter 7.

## Gopher & WAIS

On the other hand, you may feel more like browsing. You may not know exactly what you want; you just want to see what's available. For that, you might employ a *Gopher* server. Gopher servers present Internet data in a menu format: you choose items from nested menus much as you choose items from the Macintosh Finder or the Windows File Manager to find stuff on your hard disk.

The original Gopher server still grinds away at the University of Minnesota, where the school mascot is the Golden Gopher. That, they say, is why Gopher is called Gopher.

Figure 2-5: A path of Gopher menus leads to an article documenting the first "bug" in the space shuttle program. This is the AOL Windows interface.

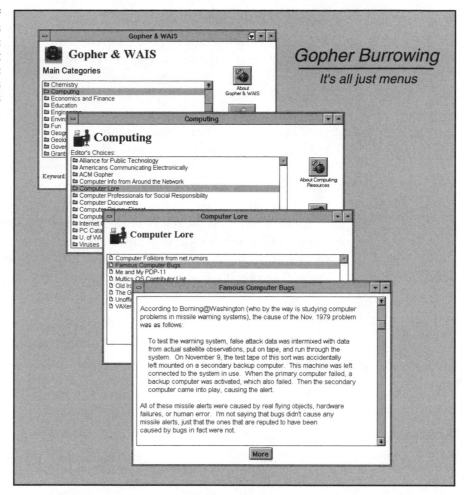

The original Gopher has been joined by scores of others, making the number of Gopher sites (or Gopher *holes*, as they're called) practically as overwhelming as FTP sites.

While we're on the subject of Gopher, we might consider *WAIS* (Wide-Area Information Server—pronounced "wayz"). Gopher is a table of contents, whereas WAIS is more of an index. A Gopher menu might disclose all files with the word *frog* in the file name; WAIS will disclose all files where the word *frog* has been included in the files' indexes.

Think of WAIS as an automated librarian: you tell the librarian what you want and it searches the Internet looking for it. Gopher and WAIS are discussed in Chapter 8.

## Moving on

Are you feeling confident now that you know the language? Don't be discouraged if the answer's no. The Internet is a vast, complex, and intimidating place (even to frequent users). The trick is to find a niche that interests you, explore it until you're comfortable there, then find another and another after that. The Internet is a bit like the Sunday buffet at a fancy restaurant: lots of tempting delights are available, but if you try to sample everything—especially at one sitting—you'll leave the table frustrated, overwhelmed, and in discomfort. This is a place that's best suited to methodical exploration. Take your time.

Before you can travel the I-way, however, you need a vehicle. Few can match America Online's Internet Connection for convenience and comfort. It's the perfect cruiser for the left lane of the Infobahn. Turn the page: it's time to roll.

# Chapter 3

# ELECTRONIC MAIL

**S**ome people remember the days when the phrase "the mail" meant only one thing: the U.S. Postal Service—and a first-class postage stamp cost 3 cents. To send something by mail, you handed it to the postman, dropped it in a mailbox or took it to the Post Office.

The impatient information age we live in today requires package delivery, overnight letters, facsimile, voice mail and e-mail. Each of these alternatives has its place. Electronic mail offers immediacy, convenience, multiple addressing, automated record-keeping and international delivery. Moreover, it's cheap—perhaps the least expensive of the bunch—and ecologically responsible. E-mail has all the makings of a darling, and it is just now entering its prime.

## What exactly is electronic mail?

Electronic mail (*e-mail* for short) is simply mail prepared on a computer and sent to someone else who has access to a computer. There are lots of private e-mail networks—computers wired together and configured to send and receive mail. Many of these networks are connected to the Internet in some way, and the Internet transfers mail from one network to another.

Most e-mail systems share common characteristics:

- ♠ Messages are composed of pure ASCII text. Fancy formatting, graphics and special characters aren't accommodated within messages.

- ♠ Messages can be sent between dissimilar computers—PCs, Macintoshes, Amigas, mainframes, even terminals.

- ♠ The addressee must be known to the mail system.

## Why use e-mail?

It's convenient, immediate and ecologically "correct." Composing a message amounts to nothing more than typing it; mailing a message amounts to a single click of the mouse; and AOL automatically keeps a copy on file for you—off-site in Virginia. For most members, there's no long-distance call, no envelopes, stamps or funny fax paper (an ecological disaster if ever there was one). Indeed, paper of any kind is rarely used when mail is sent electronically.

America Online's e-mail service is an outstanding example of this communication medium. It does all the things e-mail should do, of course, and adds to those enough features to make a mail carrier blush. You can compose mail offline, send (and receive) it when you're away from the computer, address it to multiple recipients, send carbon copies (and blind carbon copies), reply to mail received, and forward mail to others.

America Online obediently holds your mail until you're ready to read it, announces its availability every time you sign on and never sends you junk mail. AOL doesn't charge extra for e-mail, even that sent to or received from the Internet. It's not exactly a return to the 3-cent stamp, but it's close.

## Electronic fortune cookies

Before we get to the details, here's a little exercise just to show you how Internet e-mail works.

- ♠ Sign on to America Online. Leave the Welcome screen showing and choose Compose Mail from the Mail menu. An Untitled Mail window will appear (see Figure 3-1).

Figure 3-1: This window appears whenever you're about to compose some mail. AOL has already identified you as the sender; it's now waiting for you to identify the recipient.

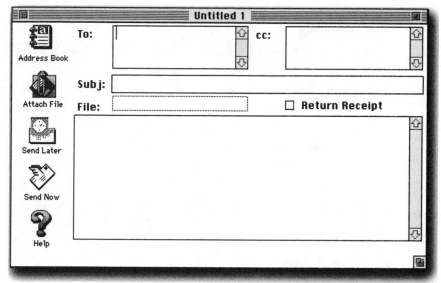

▲ The insertion point is now flashing in the To: text box, waiting for the recipient's screen name. Type in **almanac@oes.orst.edu**. OES is the name of a computer at Oregon State University where they store little daily missives just for those who request them.

▲ In the subject text box, enter the word **test**.

▲ Type **send quote** into the message text box.

▲ Click the Send button.

If you've nothing else to do online, sign off (the Sign Off command is under the Go To menu). Do something else for a couple of hours, then sign back on. By then, a reply should be awaiting you from the computer in Oregon.

### No accounting for case

America Online screen names are not case-sensitive. MajorTom works no better than majortom. On the Internet, e-mail addresses are made up of two parts, separated by an @ sign. The user name (the part to the left of the @ sign) occasionally is case-sensitive for certain Internet addresses. The domain name portion of the address (the part to the right of the @ sign) is never case-sensitive. This is really comforting: I used to be obsessed with such details, worrying that imperfectly addressed mail would end up in electronic limbo somewhere on the Net. My anxieties were needless (as most are). Even if you misspell a screen name, either America Online or a "Postmaster" will notify you that there's no match for the address you've typed. If you've misaddressed mail to another AOL member, AOL tells you the moment you click the send button. If you've misaddressed mail sent to someone on the Net, it will be returned by the remote computer with a note explaining why.

Note also that two more things have happened: (1) the mail icon on the In The Spotlight screen has changed, and a tiny mailbox will flash in the upper right corner of your screen (Figure 3-2).

Figure 3-2: You've got mail! Two visual prompts let you know every time mail is waiting for you at America Online.

 *In the upper-right corner of your screen, a tiny mailbox flashes.*

*And in the Spotlight window, a hand holds your new mail.*

▲ Click the You Have Mail button.

▲ The New Mail window appears (see Figure 3-3). (This window is a little redundant when you only have one piece of mail waiting, but soon you'll be a Popular Person and dozens of entries will appear here every time you sign on.)

Figure 3-3: The New
Mail window appears
whenever you elect to
read incoming mail.

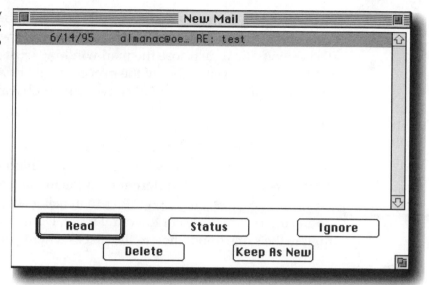

▲ Double-click the entry, which represents the message from
Oregon State University.

▲ The message window appears, with your electronic fortune
cookie therein (see Figure 3-4).

Figure 3-4: The mail is
received. The folks at
Oregon State
University post a new
quote each day: to
receive it all you have
to do is ask.

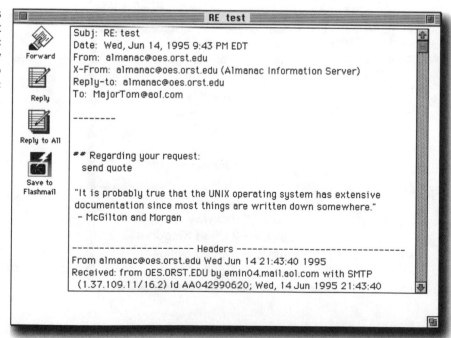

It's probably best for you to toss this mail now, before anyone sees how you've wasted network resources and your own precious time. To throw it away, just close the mail window. I just wanted you to see how simple, fast and easy the process really is. America Online's interface makes Internet e-mail convenient, global and inexpensive.

## Internet addresses

Before we go any further, we need to discuss Internet addresses. They're really not much different than the mailing addresses the U.S. Postal Service uses, although rather than being sent to you at your home, Internet mail is sent to your *domain*. Domain or domicile, they're the same thing: they're the places where you receive mail.

### International top-level domains

When my friend Kyoko writes a letter to me from Japan, the address format she uses is: name/address/city/state/usa. International Internet addresses are exactly the same: at the far right you'll find the name of the country. This is called the *top-level domain*. Figure 3-5 identifies the abbreviations for some common international top-level domains.

Figure 3-5: The Country abbreviation is the top-level domain of international Internet addresses.

| Abbreviation | Country |
|---|---|
| au | Australia |
| at | Austria |
| ca | Canada |
| ch | Switzerland |
| dk | Denmark |
| fi | Finland |
| fr | France |
| de | Germany |
| it | Italy |
| jp | Japan |
| no | Norway |
| uk | United Kingdom |
| us | United States |
| za | South Africa |

A well-known example of an international top-level domain is **username@well.sf.ca.us**. This indicates a user on the Whole Earth 'Lectronic Link (the WELL) in San Francisco (**sf**), California (**ca**), USA (**us**).

The domain name portion of an e-mail address almost always consists of groups of alphanumeric characters separated by periods (I say *almost* always because there are occasional exceptions to the rule). If a friend gives you an e-mail address that doesn't follow this rule, AOL's e-mail staff can help you. Use the keyword: MailGateway, or send e-mail to the screen name: Postmaster.

### U.S. top-level domains

At the risk of sounding politicocentric again, most domains are within the United States, and the *us* top-level domain is typically omitted for activity within this country, just as it is for paper mail that's to stay within our borders. Instead, top domains for U.S. users typically identify the type of system they're using. Figure 3-6 identifies the common U.S. top-level domains.

Figure 3-6: U.S. top-level domains identify the nature of the user's affiliation.

| Abbreviation | Affiliation |
|---|---|
| com | business and commercial |
| edu | educational institutions |
| gov | government institutions |
| mil | military installations |
| net | network resources |
| org | other (typically nonprofit) |

My Internet address is **majortom@aol.com**. Anyone looking at my top-level domain can determine that I'm affiliated with a commercial organization—in this case, America Online.

### Fully qualified domain names

The name to the immediate left of the top-level domain is (ideally) the name of the site's sponsoring agent or organization. Apple Computer's Internet connection is **apple.com**; The University of Oregon is **uoregon.edu**. A fully qualified domain name (FQDN) is defined as just enough data after the @ sign to ensure your mail's delivery. Sometimes this will be the top-level domain and a one-word site name, but not always. Domain names, especially in Europe, can get quite complex.

## Network & computer names

The domain name may stop there, but there's usually more. An additional subnetwork name may appear to the left of the FQDN. Most of my academic associates work at the University of Oregon, but the U of O has at least seven satellite networks connected to **uoregon.edu**. One of those networks is located within a building called Oregon Hall, and the people there call their network "oregon." (Everyone names their computers on the Net. Without a name, there's no domain.) A person on that network adds his or her identifier to the string **oregon.uoregon.edu**, which identifies the Oregon Hall (oregon) LAN (local area network), which is connected to **uoregon.edu**.

Putting all of the pieces together, we emerge with a string of characters like **shark.mel.dit.csiro.au**. Whether it makes any sense to you—a mere human—is inconsequential. It's a legitimate domain name, and that's all the Internet cares about.

> *Note: I'm simplifying matters here. In truth, the underlying software that makes the Internet run uses what are known as IP addresses to route information. Most Internet hosts have a unique IP address (large sites, such as AOL are exceptions). It's the IP address that's used to route data. Humans, however, have trouble remembering IP addresses such as 129.133.10.10. Humans, then, use domain names, which are translated into IP addresses when the Internet's routing software encounters them.*

> **Anarchy foils all**
>
> Now that I've offered a nice organized treatise on domain names, I'm compelled to remind you that this is an anarchy we're talking about, and in an anarchy people do as they please. Internet addresses are a case in point. Domain names don't necessarily follow the conventions I've cited and not all computers have unique addresses.
>
> A domain name such as **lawmail.law.columbia.edu** may point to a computer in the United Kingdom, rather than one at Columbia University (though such flagrant deceptions are rare). Domain names such as **coombs.anu.edu.au** and **weiss.anu.edu.au** may seem to be computers on the same network (anu) but it ain't necessarily so. Finally, a computer can have more than a single name: **rascal.ics.utexas.edu** may be where your friend at the University of Texas receives her mail, but that computer may also be named **ftp.ics.utexas.edu** for the purposes of downloading files.

## Mailing addresses

Some of your Internet activity will occur between you and a domain only—there won't be a person at the other end. You might poll a domain for a mailing list, for example, or request an article, or petition for a domain name for your own network. This is all accomplished by conversing with the domain's server, rather than an individual person.

Most Internet activity, however, takes the form of e-mail sent to people, not domains. To identify an individual, the format **username@domain name** is used. Everything to the left of the @ sign in an Internet address is the user's name. Internet user names aren't subject to the ten-character limit that AOL screen names are, so they can become quite elaborate.

**The directory of Internet users**

Remember that each of the domains on the Internet is independent of the others, and each domain may have scores of connected networks. Users come and go on these systems like evening talk-show hosts. There are millions of people with Internet e-mail addresses, after all, and thousands come and go every day.

"So what?" you say. "There are more telephone users than e-mail users in this country, and they're all listed in directories." Your point is well taken, but the telephone system is composed of a number of coordinated authorities (the baby Bells), each charged with the responsibility of publishing phone books. Not so with the Internet. No one's charged with the responsibility of maintaining Internet member directories: those that exist are produced voluntarily, and these volunteers all have lives beyond their spare-time member directories.

In other words, there's no accurate, up-to-the-minute, all-inclusive Internet membership directory. There are a few online directories, but most apply to specific sites or are an almost-random collection of addresses rather than a comprehensive directory.

**Note:** There are actually a number of "White Pages" of Internet users, but they're far from comprehensive and there are at least half a dozen of them. The best way to search them is to use the Whois directory maintained at the Internet Registry. You can search it via e-mail. To find out more, send e-mail to **mailserv@ds.internic.net**. Place the word help in both the Subject: and the message fields. You'll receive return mail within a couple of hours.

There are no real standards for Internet e-mail address formats, but there are some common practices. Many people use their first initial and full last name as their Internet name. This usually results in a unique identity (at least to the domain) and it's not gender-specific (an issue which many Net users prefer to avoid). It's not generally possible to use spaces in addresses, so you'll often see underscores instead. And Internet addresses are usually not case-sensitive. None of this should make a whit of difference to you, as your AOL screen name (minus any spaces) automatically becomes your Internet user name. Your domain (sounds regal, doesn't it?) is **aol.com**.

*Tip: Keep a written record of your important Internet addresses. Don't just put them in your AOL Address Book (you might need an address when you're away from your machine, and AOL's software stores your address book on your hard disk), and don't trust them to your own memory (few people remember the alphabet soup of Internet addresses accurately). If you carry an old-fashioned (hardcopy) address book with you, that's the best place to keep your Internet addresses.*

## Internet mail

Most Internet users use the Net primarily for electronic mail. Indeed, the Internet is rapidly becoming the spinal column of the electronic community, routing messages from locations scattered all over the planet.

Actress Lily Tomlin (in the role of Ernestine the telephone operator) once described the electronic community as "BacoBits scattered across the salad bar of cyberspace." Take a moment to reflect on that as you pursue this discussion of electronic neural systems. It helps to keep perspective.

### Sending Internet mail

Internet e-mail is composed and sent conventionally. To address an Internet user, simply place the recipient's Internet address in the To: field of the Compose Mail form (see Figure 3-7).

Figure 3-7: Sending mail via the Internet requires entries in the To:, Subject: and message fields. You can't leave any of them blank.

```
┌─────────────────────── Untitled 1 ───────────────────────┐
│                                                           │
│  📕      To:  paul_williams@orego    cc:                  │
│ Address       n.uoregon.edu                               │
│  Book                                                     │
│                                                           │
│  📎      Subj: NCCE                                        │
│ Attach                                                    │
│  File    File:                      ☐ Return Receipt      │
│                                                           │
│  🕐     Hi Paul --                                        │
│ Send                                                      │
│ Later    I'm speaking at NCCE this year and was wondering │
│          if you might be there. If so, perhaps we can sip │
│  📧      a brandy together?                               │
│ Send Now                                                  │
│          Tom                                              │
│  ❓                                                       │
│ Help                                                      │
└───────────────────────────────────────────────────────────┘
```

Note the caption for Figure 3-7. Specifically, note that it says you can't leave any of the fields in AOL's Compose Mail form blank. This is important. Along your Internet travels you will frequently encounter instructions that tell you to leave certain fields blank. (The instructions for a number of mailing lists—discussed in the next chapter—will tell you to leave the Subject: field blank, for example.) You can't do that with AOL's software. You have to type something into every field. Most people type a single period (.) into throwaway fields like this and everything works fine.

Once you click the Send button (or once you run a FlashSession—FlashSessions are discussed in Chapter 9—containing outgoing Internet mail), your outgoing mail is posted directly on the Internet. There's no waiting.

### Undeliverable mail

Because Internet addresses can be complex, you might occasionally misspell an address or accidentally address mail to a nonexistent user or domain. Fortunately, this possibility has been foreseen and you will be notified in the event of a delivery problem. Most sites will also kindly return the entire contents of your mail; but in the event the remote site does not, AOL keeps a copy of your mail for at least five days. (Use the Check Mail You've Sent command, under the Mail menu, for these occasions.) In the event of problems, you can contact the Postmaster of the remote site: address the mail to Postmaster@ (follow with the domain name) and ask for assistance. Keep in mind that most Postmasters are busy folks and many are volunteers, so their assistance might not be immediately forthcoming. In some cases AOL's e-mail staff and Postmaster can help you, but you should always ask the Postmaster at the remote site first.

Figure 3-8 shows a misaddressed Internet mail message, which looks as good as any other. But a few minutes later I receive the "User unknown" message pictured in the lower window. Note the inclusion of my message's text in the postmaster's message. When I copy and paste the text into a properly addressed message, the mail will be delivered satisfactorily.

Figure 3-8:
Misdirected Internet
mail is returned to me
with a "user unknown"
message, including a
copy of my original for
copying and pasting.

## Undeliverable Internet Mail

Subj:  NCCE
Date:  94-01-03 10:13:37 EST
From:  MajorTom
To:    paul_williams@oregon.uoregon.edu

Hi Paul --

I'm speaking at NCC
might be there. If so

Tom

*Though the message
at left looks acceptable,
the user name is in-
correct. The mail is
undeliverable.*

Subj:  Returned mail: User unknown
Date:  94-01-03 12:06:45 EST
From:  MAILER-DAEMON@mail06.mail.aol.com
X-From: MAILER-DAEMON@mail06.mail.aol.com (Mail
Delivery Subsystem)
To:    MajorTom

----- Transcript of session follows -----

While connected to donald.uoregon.edu [128.223.32.6]
(tcp):
>>> RCPT To:<paul_williams@oregon.uoregon.edu>
<<< 553 unknown or illegal user:
paul_williams@OREGON.UOREGON.EDU
550 paul_williams@oregon.uoregon.edu... User unknown

----- Unsent message follows -----

Hi Paul --

I'm speaking at NCCE this year and was wondering if you
might be there. If so, perhaps we can sip a brandy
together?

Tom

*A few hours later,
the mail is returned
from the Internet
postmaster. Note that
the body of the
undelivered message
is included in the
postmaster's message.*

*Noting the "user
unknown" message,
I recheck Paul's
address, find the error,
and re-send the mail
to the proper address.*

---

### Subordinate deities

Look at the sender's address in Figure 3-8. Isn't that a vicious-sounding word: *daemon*? My dictionary defines the word as a "subordinate deity." In this context, however, a daemon (pronounced day'-mon) is an innocuous little program—one that's usually transparent to the user—which is anything but a deity, subordinate or otherwise. The Mac has its daemons too (though we don't call them that); perhaps the most familiar example is the Print Monitor—the background program that spools the print output from your applications.

### Sending mail to other commercial services

To reach a few of the more common Internet-connected commercial services, use the address formats shown in Figure 3-9.

There's plenty of information about sending (and receiving) e-mail from other online services at keyword: MailGateway. If you are unsure about a particular Internet e-mail address, the AOL Mail Gateway staff or the Postmaster can help.

Figure 3-9: Use these address formats to reach users on other commercial services.

| Service name | Example |
|---|---|
| AppleLink | name@applelink.apple.com |
| AT&T Mail | name@attmail.com |
| CompuServe | 12345.678@compuserve.com |
| Delphi | name@delphi.com |
| GEnie | name@genie.geis.com |
| MCI Mail | name@mcimail.com |
| NBC Nightly News | nightly@nbc.com |
| Prodigy | name@prodigy.com |
| The White House | president@whitehouse.gov, or vice-president@whitehouse.gov |

**Internet mail trivia**

Actually, this isn't trivia at all. I was trying to attract your attention. If you're an Internet mail user, this is Really Important Stuff:

- The maximum message length for outgoing Internet mail is 28k, or about 11 pages of text. If you must send a message longer than that, use a word processor to divide your mail into pieces, then send the pieces.

- Don't use any special characters (like copyright symbols or the "smart quotes" offered by some word processors) in Internet mail. If a character can't be produced with the standard typewriter keys, it probably won't survive the journey to its destination.

- Don't use the Attach File button for attaching files to outgoing Internet mail. If you must use e-mail to send or receive attached files, read the section about uuencoding that appears later in this chapter.

- Some of the services listed in Figure 3-9 charge their members for Internet mail, both incoming and outgoing. Keep that in mind when sending mail to these people: they may not appreciate the gesture.

- AOL doesn't charge you anything extra for Internet mail, sent or received. If you're counting your blessings, add that to the list.

- If you're going to use Internet mail frequently, go to your local bookstore and buy a copy of *A Directory of Electronic Mail !%@:: Addressing & Networks* (see the Bibliography in this book). You'll be a better citizen of the Internet community if you do.

## Receiving Internet mail

Internet mail is received like any other AOL mail: it's announced when you sign on and you can read it by clicking the You Have Mail button in the Spotlight window. The only way you'll know it's Internet mail is by looking at the sender's address, which will appear in Internet address form. You'll also see the Internet "header" at the end of the message. Reading Internet headers is a little like reading the Bible in its original Hebrew: enlightening, perhaps, but not requisite to effective use of the medium.

A few things to keep in mind regarding received Internet mail:

 If you want to give your Internet address to someone else (it's very impressive printed on your business cards), remove any spaces, change everything to lowercase, and follow it with **@aol.com**. My Internet address, then, is **majortom@aol.com**. Steve Case's Internet address is **stevecase@aol.com**. (The period at the end of each of these addresses is normal punctuation and not part of the address proper.)

America Online's maximum incoming e-mail message length is about a megabyte. On the other hand, AOL's maximum text-file length is 32k. If an incoming Internet mail message is longer than 32k (and less than a megabyte), AOL will cut it up and deliver it to you as separate pieces of mail. Use a word processor to reassemble the pieces.

AOL offers plenty of help with Internet e-mail at keyword: MailGateway.

## The Mail menu

Nearly all day-to-day mail activities—Internet or AOL—are performed using the Mail menu (see Figure 3-10).

Figure 3-10: The Mail menu handles most of your daily e-mail activities.

**Mail**

**Post Office**
**Compose Mail**            ⌘M
Read New Mail               ⌘R
**Check Mail You've Read**
**Check Mail You've Sent**

**Edit Address Book**
Address Memo

**FlashSessions...**
  **Activate FlashSession Now**
  Read Incoming Mail
  Read Outgoing Mail

**Mail Gateway**
**Fax/Paper Mail**

## Composing your mail

The first option on the Mail menu is the Post Office, where you can access many of the same options found on your Mail menu, as well as some others. The second option on the Mail menu is Compose Mail, which you choose whenever you want to send mail to someone. This option is available whether you're online or off; you can compose mail offline and send it later—a feature I'll discuss in a few pages.

When the Compose Mail command is issued, America Online responds with a blank piece of Untitled mail (review Figure 3-1). Note the position of the insertion point in Figure 3-1. It's located within the To: field of the window. America Online, in other words, is waiting for you to provide the recipient's screen name. Type it in. (If you don't remember the screen name, use your Address Book, which I'll describe later in this chapter.)

You can type multiple addresses, separated by a comma and a space, in the To: field if you wish. Note that the field is actually a scroll box. If you want to send mail to Steve Case and Tom Lichty, type **Steve Case, MajorTom** in this box. You can type as many addresses as you want, up to 4,400 characters.

Press the Tab key and the cursor jumps to the CC: (carbon copy) field. Here you can place the addresses of those people who are to receive "carbon copies" of your mail. Carbon copies (actually, they're called *courtesy copies* now—carbon paper is a thing of the past) are really no different than originals. Whether a member receives an original or a copy is more a matter of protocol than anything else. Capacity limitations for this field are the same as they are for the To: field.

**Blind carbon copies**

As is the case with the traditional CC: (or cc:) at the bottom of a business letter, the addressee is made aware of any others who will receive a copy of the letter—a traditional courtesy.

On the other hand, you might want to send a copy of a message to someone without letting the addressee(s) know you have done so. This is known as a "blind" carbon copy, and at AOL it works whether you're mailing to another AOL member, an Internet address, or a combination of both. To address a blind carbon copy, place the address that's to receive the blind carbon copy in the To: or the CC: field, *enclosing it in parentheses.* The parentheses are the trick. No one but the recipient of the blind carbon copy will know what you've done (the ethics of this feature are yours to ponder).

Press the Tab key to move the insertion point to the Subject: field, and enter a descriptive word or two. The Subject: field can contain no more than 61 characters. **Note:** The Subject: field must be filled in—AOL won't take the message without it.

Press the Tab key again. The insertion point moves to the message text area. Type your message there (see Figure 3-11).

Figure 3-11: The completed message is ready to send. Click the Send button (if you're online) or the Send Later button (if you're not online).

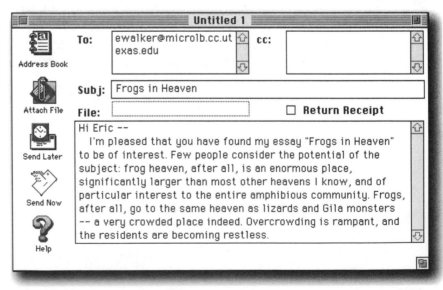

It's subtle, but note that the Send button in Figure 3-11 is dimmed; this message is being prepared offline (see the following section on preparing offline mail).

### Preparing mail offline

Consider preparing mail when you're offline and the meter isn't running. You can linger over it that way, perfecting every word. When you complete a message, click the Send Later button. The next time you sign on, AOL will note that you have mail waiting to be sent. To send it, choose Read Outgoing Mail from the Mail menu, then click the Send All button (see Figure 3-12).

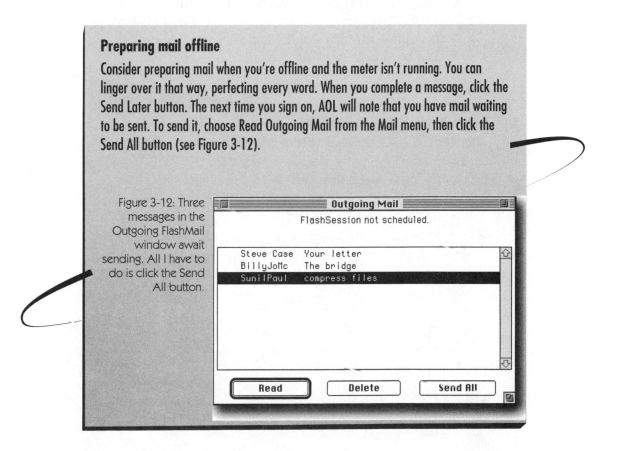

Figure 3-12: Three messages in the Outgoing FlashMail window await sending. All I have to do is click the Send All button.

### Alternative mail sources

Occasionally, you might want to send a text file on the Net. Perhaps it's a file you have created with the New command (File menu) or a text file you captured online. Regardless of the source, you can send a text file as mail (rather than as a file) by copying and pasting it into a Compose Mail window.

This feature is especially useful for those who prefer to use a word processor to compose messages. Word processors feature spelling checkers and productivity tools that AOL's Compose Mail utility doesn't offer. If you prefer to use your word processor, prepare your message there, then select the entire message and choose Copy from the word processing program's Edit menu. Switch to your AOL software, choose Compose Mail from the Mail menu, click within the message field of the Compose Mail form, then choose Paste from AOL's Edit menu. After that, all you have to do is supply the name of the recipient in the To: field and a subject in the Subject: field, sign on and send your mail on its way.

---

### A pain in the neck

Because there's no eye contact or voice intonation in e-mail messages, sometimes it's necessary to punctuate your conversation with textual symbols—"smileys," (or "emoticons") as they're called. Smileys clarify the sender's intention when it might otherwise be misinterpreted. The phrase, "Just as I thought, Billy Joe: there are no forks in your family tree," could be interpreted as slander. Follow it with a smiley, however, and most members will understand your attempt at depraved humor: "Just as I thought, Billy Joe: there are no forks in your family tree. ;-)"

The semicolon-dash-close parenthesis combination at the end of the sentence above is a wink. Turn your head (or this page) 90 degrees counterclockwise and you'll see a little "smiley face" with its right eye winking. It's a pain in the neck, but it's better than making enemies. Go ahead, smile at someone today. :-)

Below are some of the more common emoticons. Some people use them more than others, but most everybody does occasionally.

| | |
|---|---|
| :-) | Smile |
| ;-) | Wink |
| :-D | Laughing out loud (also abbreviated "LOL"). |
| :-( | Frown |
| :-/ | Chagrin |
| {} | Hug (usually plural: {{{{}}}}. Why hug just once?) |
| :-\| | Unimpressed |
| :D | Cheesy grin (or, 8 in place of : for glasses) |
| >:-( | Furious |

These are the ones I see most often online. There are scores of others. I've seen :-# (lips are sealed), :-& (tongue-tied), :-[ (pout), :-* (kiss) and :-0 (yell). But my favorite is :-p (sticking out tongue).

## Checking mail you've sent

Occasionally you may want to review mail you've sent to others: "What exactly did I say to Billy Joe that caused him to visit the Tallahatchee Bridge last night?"

Even if you don't file your mail, AOL retains everything you send—Internet mail included—for at least five days. You can review any sent mail by choosing Check Mail You've Sent from the Mail menu. AOL responds by displaying a listing of all the mail you've sent recently. Choose the mail you want to know about from that list, then click the Read button to review what you've read (see Figure 3-13).

Figure 3-13: You can reread any mail you've sent by using the Check Mail You've Sent command.

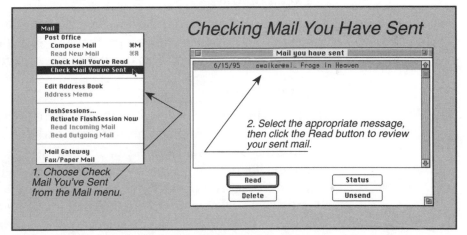

### Online only

The Check Mail You've Sent and the Check Mail You've Read commands are only available when you're online. This mail is stored on AOL's machines, not yours; you have to be online to access data stored there.

As you're reading your sent mail, you can select and copy it, then paste it into other documents. This works especially well for re-minder notices, clarifications and nagging. It may save you some typing as well: you may need to send a message that's almost a duplicate of one you sent four days ago. Rather than retyping text from the old message, just reopen it using Check Mail You've Sent under the Mail menu, copy the sections you need, and paste them into a new message window. Alternatively, you can forward the entire message (including its headers and any comments) by using the Forward button.

## Buttons in the Sent Mail window

A number of buttons appear across the bottom of the Check Mail You've Sent window pictured in Figure 3-13; each serves a specific purpose.

### The Read button

Select a piece of mail from the list, then click the Read button to read that message. Double-clicking a particular piece of mail does the same thing. This function was discussed a few pages back.

### The Status button

The Status button tells you when the recipient (or recipients, if the mail was sent to more than one address) read the message. Though the time displayed will be accurate for mail sent to other AOL members, it won't be for Internet mail. AOL posts Internet mail within a few seconds after you press the Send button, but when is it actually "sent"? When it's posted? When it's routed to the recipient's country, or domain? When you select a piece of Internet mail and click the Show Status button, AOL will display the message "Not Applicable."

### The Unsend button

The Unsend button applies only to mail that has been sent to another AOL member. Once mail is posted on the Net, there's no way to bring it back.

### The Delete button

This button simply removes the selected piece of mail from your Sent Mail list. It does not affect the message's destiny: AOL will still deliver it (and probably already has, by the time you find your way to this button). It's really a feature for people who get lots of mail and prefer to keep their Sent Mail lists short.

## Reading new mail

The third option on the Mail menu—Read New Mail—refers to mail you've just received. I don't use this menu item. To me, mail is like Christmas morning: I can't wait to get to it. Immediately after hearing that I have mail, I click the You Have Mail button (pictured in Figure 3-2) and start unwrapping my presents.

### Time is money

Reading mail while you're online isn't the best use of your time. You can read your mail, reply to it and forward it all while you're offline. You can even have all of your mail transfer occur in the wee hours of the morning, when system traffic is light and data transfer is fast. These are FlashSession features, and FlashSessions are discussed in Chapter 9.

Nonetheless, there are those who don't share my enthusiasm. That, I suppose, is why AOL provides this menu option. When it's chosen, America Online presents the New Mail window (Figure 3-14).

Figure 3-14: Reading new mail can be accomplished with the You Have Mail button in the In the Spotlight window, by pressing Command+R or by choosing Read New Mail from the Mail menu.

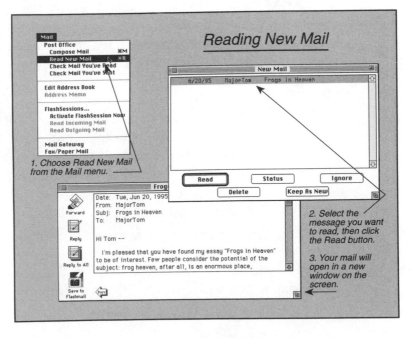

Though Figure 3-14 shows only one unread piece of mail, a number of pieces may appear here. If more than one shows up, they'll appear in the order in which they were received at America Online. The oldest mail will be at the top, the most recent at the bottom. In other words, to read your mail in chronological order from oldest to most recent, read your messages from top to bottom.

### Buttons in the New Mail window

A number of buttons appear across the bottom of the New Mail window pictured in Figure 3-14. They can be confusing at first:

### Read

This button displays the selected piece of mail on the screen for reading. It's the default button: double-clicking an entry on the list does the same thing.

### Ignore

This option will move a piece of mail directly into your Mail You Have Read list without the need of your actually reading the selected piece of mail.

### Keep As New

Clicking this button will return the selected piece of mail to your New Mail list, even though you have already read it. It will remain there until you Read or Ignore it.

### Delete

This feature allows you to permanently remove a piece of mail from your new-mail mailbox. It will not appear on the Mail You Have Read list either (I'll discuss the Check Mail You've Read command in a few pages). Compare this button with the Ignore button mentioned earlier.

### Printing & saving mail

You can print or save any piece of mail that occupies the frontmost (active) window by choosing the appropriate command from the File menu. If you choose Print, AOL displays the standard Macintosh Print dialog box. Click the OK button to print.

If you choose Save or Save As (in this context they're the same command), AOL responds with the traditional Macintosh Save As dialog box. Give your mail a name and put it wherever you please.

Alternatively, you can select and copy any text—mail included— appearing on your screen. Now you can open any text file on your disk (or start a new one via the New command under the File menu) and paste your mail into that file. You can also paste copied AOL text into other Macintosh applications' files if you wish. There are a number of ways to file mail, however, and I'll describe the best of them shortly.

## Forwarding mail

Once you have read your mail, you can forward it, reply to it or throw it out. Each of these options is accomplished with a click of the mouse. To forward a piece of mail, click the Forward button pictured in Figure 3-14. America Online will respond with the slightly modi- fied compose-mail window that appears at the center of Figure 3-15.

The center window pictured in Figure 3-15 is where you enter your forwarding comment and the address of the person who is to receive the forward. The new recipient then receives the forwarded mail with your comment preceding it. America Online clearly identifies forwarded mail by including a line at the top of the mes- sage that declares it as forwarded mail and identifies the person who did the forwarding (see the bottom window in Figure 3-15).

## Replying to mail

You'll probably reply to mail more often than you forward it. Actu- ally, all the Reply icon does is call up a compose-mail window with the To: and Subject: fields already filled in with the appropriate information (see Figure 3-16). Aside from these two features, a reply is no different from any other message. You can modify the To: and CC: fields if you wish, and discuss any subject that interests you in the message text. You can even change the Subject: field or remove the original recipient's screen name from the To: field, though this somewhat defeats the purpose.

Figure 3-13:
Forwarding mail is as
easy as clicking an
icon, identifying the
recipient and typing
your comments.

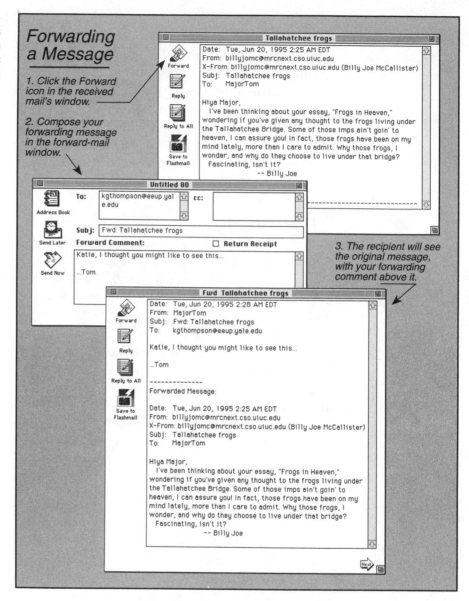

## Forwarding a Message

*1. Click the Forward icon in the received mail's window.*

*2. Compose your forwarding message in the forward-mail window.*

*3. The recipient will see the original message, with your forwarding comment above it.*

Figure 3-16: The reply
window. The Subject:
and To: fields are
already completed for
you.

| | |
|---|---|
| **Untitled 1** | |
| **To:** | billyjomc@mrcnext.cs o.uiuc.edu |
| Address Book | **cc:** |
| Attach File | **Subj:** Re: Tallahatchee frogs |
| | **File:** ☐ **Return Receipt** |
| Send Later | Good to hear from you, Billy. Those frogs are keeping you busy, aren't they? |
| Send Now | -- Tom |
| Help | |

---

### Quoting in your reply

Some people get mountains of mail and don't remember everything they've said. You might be responding to something someone e-mailed to you a week ago, and even though their message is right in front of you at the moment, it might be hundreds of messages in their past. If you respond with something like "Yes. Next Thursday at 2:00 would be good," they might have to search laboriously through their mail filing system (assuming they have one) to discover what provoked your response.

To avoid such a situation, it's a common courtesy to quote the significant part(s) of the message you're replying to. A typical quote might look like this: "In a message dated 5-12, you said >Would you like to have lunch soon and discuss the contract?" Following that, your message of "Yes. Next Thursday at 2:00 would be good." makes a great deal more sense.

There are a number of quoting utilities available online. Sign on, press Command+K and specify the keyword: FileSearch. For your file-searching criteria, specify QUOTING. Read over the file descriptions before the download to find the one that suits you best.

### Replying to all

Look once again at the lower window in Figure 3-14. Note that there are two reply icons, including one marked Reply to All. Reply to All allows you to reply to everyone who was sent a message, including any CC: addressees. In other words, you have your choice of replying only to the original sender (Reply button) or to everyone who receives a message (Reply to All button).

> *Note: Reply to All does not reply to blind CC: addressees. The rule here is: Reply to All replies to all whose screen names are visible in the Mail window. If you don't see a name (which would be the case if someone received a blind carbon copy), that person will not receive your reply.*

### Checking mail you've read

We all forget things now and again: "What did I promise to get my mother for Valentine's Day?" That's why AOL provides the Check Mail You've Read option under the Mail menu. When you choose this command, AOL responds with the Mail You Have Read window (see Figure 3-17).

---

**Replying with a copy of the original**

Some people get lots of mail. Steve Case, for instance, gets hundreds of pieces a day. For Steve's benefit, I always include a copy of his original message when I reply. I do this to help him remember the subject of our discussion. Rather than copy and paste his message into a reply window, I use the Forward button. I then send the forwarded mail—along with my forwarding comments—back to the sender. This little trick also works when you want to reply to a very old message the sender may not recall.

Considering that a copy of the original message gets sent with the reply, using the Forward button is an inefficient way of handling mail. It also can make for extremely long messages if forwards are allowed to build upon forwards. Don't overdo it.

Figure 3-17: The Mail
You Have Read
window lists all mail
you have read, just in
case you forget.

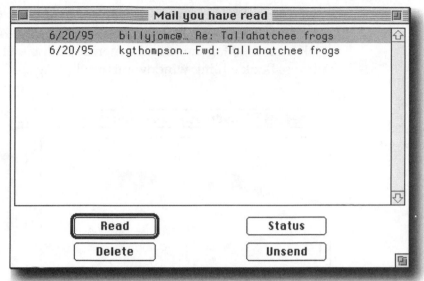

There are no surprises here. Double-click any message in the window to reread it. Mail that's been reread in this fashion can be forwarded and replied to just like any other mail.

## The Address Book

America Online provides an address book just like the address book next to your telephone. In effect, AOL's book is a cross-reference, listing people's real names and their corresponding e-mail addresses. My recommendation is that you use the Address Book, even if you only have a name or two to put there now. Internet addresses are tricky; you're not going to want to type them very often. Typing them is too much work and it's too much of an opportunity for errors.

### Adding a name to the Address Book

No one memorizes Internet addresses. Internet addresses are eccentric composites of alphabet, punctuation and symbol characters—for example, **speterman@lemming.uvm.edu**. Addresses like this are eminently forgettable. That's why America Online provides an Address Book.

Of course, before you can use the Address Book you have to put some addresses there. It's easy. Online or off, choose Edit Address Book from the Mail menu and America Online will provide the Address Book editing window pictured in Figure 3-18.

Figure 3-18: The Address Book Editor window allows you to create, modify and delete members' names and screen names.

To add an entry to your Address Book, click the Create button. AOL provides the editing form pictured in Figure 3-19.

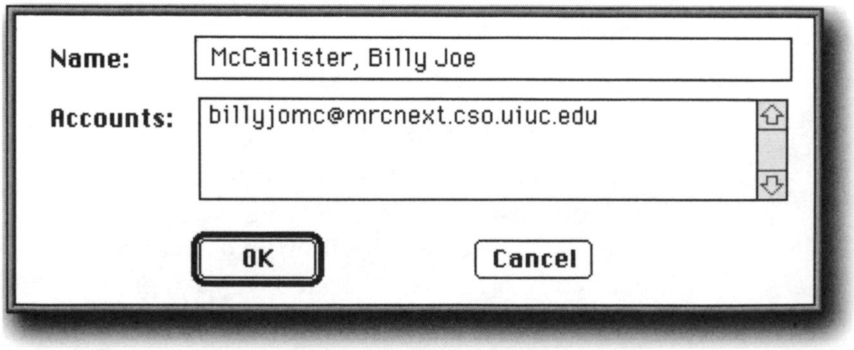

Figure 3-19: The Address Group editing form.

Place the person's real name in the Name: field, then place their
Internet address in the Accounts: field. The next time you choose
Address Book from the Mail window, the new name will appear
there (see Figure 3-20).

Figure 3-20: The
Address Book
now contains the
new entry.

Now you are ready to use the Address Book whenever you prepare mail. Look again at Figure 3-1. Do you see the icon in the upper
left corner marked Address Book? If your Address Book is current,
you can use it to look up addresses and plug them into the To: and
CC: fields of the Compose Mail window. Whenever a Compose Mail
Form is displayed on your screen, all you have to do is click that
icon. From then on, it's only a matter of clicking the mouse.

**Multiple accounts**

If you look again at Figure 3-19, you'll notice that there's room for multiple addresses in the Accounts field. In fact, the word *accounts*, not *account*, appears. You may wonder why.

Imagine that you're participating in an online discourse on frog heaven with three other esteemed theologians. Nearly every piece of mail on the subject has to be sent to all three of them. In this situation, you might want to create an entry in your Address Book called Froggers, and list all three addresses—with commas or returns between each address—in the Accounts field. Once you have done so, all you have to do is select Froggers from your Address Book to send mail to them all.

## Attaching files to messages

Because there's no universal standard for attaching files to e-mail on the Internet, you can't directly send files (or receive them) via Internet mail.

If you want to send a file—text, graphics, data, sound, animation, or programs—to another person on the Internet, you'll have to send it as text in the body of an e-mail message, not as an attachment to e-mail. The process—called *uuencoding*—is described in Chapter 5, where newsgroups are discussed. Though most encoded files appear in newsgroups, a number of us send them via e-mail, therefore a few comments follow:

- Internet e-mail is limited to pure ASCII text. If a file is to be sent using Internet e-mail, it must first be converted to pure text. This may seem anachronistic: how can you send a picture of a frog, for example (or the sound of a frog) as text?

- Simple: you use a program that converts files into text—often called a *uuencoding* program. I'm fond of UUTool by Bernie Wieser at Octavian Micro Development. It's freeware, and it's available at America Online. Sign on and use the keyword: FileSearch, then search using the criterion: UUTool (the Keyword command is under the Go To menu). Download this application, install it on your Mac and refer to its user manual file for instructions on using it.

&#9650; Remember that AOL e-mail is limited to about 28k in length. This means that files converted to text cannot exceed 28k. This is a severe restriction. Fortunately, UUTool (mentioned above) can segment a long file for sending in smaller chunks.

   &#9650; The recipient also needs software to convert the text back into a file. If the recipient is using a Mac, UUTool offers a command to join several files into one.

Although the convert-to-text-and-back process sounds a little bit like a sow's ear, it is in fact a technique that's been employed for years on the Net. It works flawlessly when it's done right, and thousands of people do it every day. My friend Jim and I often exchange architectural drawings in this way.

## Managing your mail

I do almost all of my business via e-mail. I also have a number of friends who live far away, and I use e-mail to keep in touch with them. Jim and I swap architectural drawings via e-mail. When e-mail becomes something other than a casual dalliance, a system for filing it becomes strategic.

### Mail-filing strategies

A while back I mentioned that e-mail to me is like packages on Christmas morning. I look forward to it with great anticipation. I descend into a pit of depression if a voice doesn't say "You've got mail!" when I sign on. Consequently, I have developed a cadre of online friends, and correspond with them regularly. This means that I get a lot of mail.

I send and receive 20 or more pieces of mail a day. With that much mail coming in, finding a place to file that mail is critical. I need fast, convenient, electronic access to it. I copy and paste messages frequently, so a paper filing system just won't do. I am also an environmentalist, another reason why paperless e-mail appeals to me. My e-mail filing system is the bedrock of my online activities.

You might be facing the same need. Because of the Christmas-morning quality of AOL's e-mail system, lots of people get lots of mail, and lots of people need to be thinking about a filing system. Now's the time to bring the subject into the open.

### Saving everything as Flashmail

Though I'll discuss FlashSessions in Chapter 9, you've no doubt noted the Save to Flashmail icon in the received mail window (review Figure 3-4, if necessary). If you click this icon, AOL files your mail in a file with your screen name on it. It's normally found in the Online Mail folder inside the America Online folder on your hard disk. There will be a file there for each screen name on your account.

Mail saved this way can be reviewed online or off by choosing Read Incoming Mail from the Mail menu. It remains available for review until you delete it. (AOL adds a Delete button to the reviewed mail's window when mail is accessed this way.)

This method is extremely convenient, but it has a few flaws:

- It's effective only if you keep a small number of messages on file. Mail stored this way can't be categorized, and the list eventually becomes too long for convenient access (or for the software's 28k limit).

- While filing mail you've read this way is easy, filing mail you've *sent* isn't (unless you send carbon copies to yourself).

- Incoming mail from FlashSessions (I'll discuss FlashSessions in Chapter 9) is filed here, and mixing new FlashSession mail with old mail can become confusing and troublesome.

Nevertheless, if you don't intend to file much mail, if you carbon-copy yourself when necessary, and if you don't intend to use FlashSessions, this might be the most convenient method of them all.

### The Online Mail folder

I mentioned the Online Mail folder a few paragraphs back. America Online's Installer program creates this folder on your hard disk when you install the software. This is a potential location for mail storage. It is never more than a folder away from the America Online application itself, so you won't spend much time searching for it, and it consolidates all of your mail into one place for convenient backup.

This folder has to be organized in some way. Probably the simplest strategy is to save all your mail in your Online Mail folder as it arrives, piece by piece. Every time you read a new piece of mail, choose Save As from the File menu and save the mail in the folder.

While this might work if you don't get much mail, it regresses to anarchy after a dozen or so files have accumulated. A Finder screen of such a scenario appears in Figure 3-21.

| Name | Size | Kind |
|------|------|------|
| About bees' knees | 2K | AOL |
| Customer Service re... | 11K | AOL |
| Donny Beck 6/3 | 10K | AOL |
| Frogging in Alabama | 3K | AOL |
| Nessie | 8K | AOL |
| NM Sunset.GIF | 18K | GIFC |
| Old stuff | 7K | AOL |
| Steve Case 4/02 | 7K | AOL |
| SteveC re chapter 3 | 4K | AOL |
| Stock info | 2K | AOL |
| To Tom deBoors | 8K | AOL |
| To Tom Williams | 12K | AOL |
| Travel tips for NM | 4K | AOL |
| Vases.PICT | 84K | docu |
| Weather for 7/12 | 3K | AOL |

*Online Mail*

### A single-file strategy

Note that all of the strategies mentioned from here on require an understanding of the Macintosh Cut, Copy and Paste commands. If you are not familiar with these commands, either review them in your Macintosh's manual or buy a copy of *The Little Mac Book* (see the Bibliography at the back of this book). If you're new to the Mac, this book is invaluable.

If your mail is infrequent, a single file might prove beneficial. Instead of a Mail *folder*, try a Mail *file* instead. (Use the New Memo command under AOL's File menu to create a new file.) Each time you receive a piece of mail, read it, then select and copy it. Use the Open command under the File menu to open your Mail file, scroll to the bottom, paste and save. You can store 50 or more pieces of mail this way before the file becomes so large that it's unwieldy. Advantages to this method include the following:

- Only one file needs to be managed; only one file must be opened to access all your past mail; only one file needs to be backed up.

- Mail appears in chronological order.

- Comments and replies appear in context—there's no need to search your disk for the mail that provoked SuzieQ to say "You yahoo! I hope your stack overflows!" If you've been consistent, the offending statement is nearby—probably just above Suzie's malediction.

- On the other hand, AOL limits the size of text files to about 28k. If your Mail file exceeds this amount, AOL won't be able to store it. This is a severe limitation.

### File the header too

Most of the filing strategies described here rely on the storage of not only received mail but mail you've sent as well. All you need to do is copy each piece of mail you send and paste it into the appropriate file. Here's a tip: choose Check Mail You've Sent from the Mail menu and open the mail to be copied from there. Mail retrieved this way contains AOL's header information—date, time, CC:'s and blind CC:'s—the retention of which should be considered a necessity in any mail filing system. If you simply copy text from the message field of a Mail window before you send it, your file won't contain all this information.

### A date-based strategy

Alternatively, consider a date-based strategy. This method is essentially the single-file strategy with a file for each month of activity. A greater volume of mail can be accommodated this way, and old material can easily be copied to a floppy for archiving (shown in Figure 3-22).

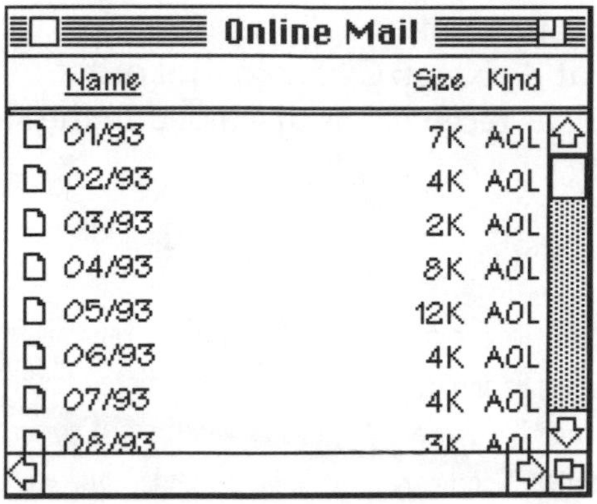

Figure 3-22: The date-
based strategy
accommodates a
greater volume of mail.

```
┌─────────────────────────────────────┐
│ ▤□▤▤▤▤▤ Online Mail ▤▤▤▤ 卫│
├─────────────────────────────────────┤
│  Name              Size  Kind       │
├─────────────────────────────────────┤
│ 🗎 01/93            7K  AOL  ⬆       │
│ 🗎 02/93            4K  AOL  ▢       │
│ 🗎 03/93            2K  AOL          │
│ 🗎 04/93            8K  AOL          │
│ 🗎 05/93           12K  AOL          │
│ 🗎 06/93            4K  AOL          │
│ 🗎 07/93            4K  AOL          │
│ 🗎 08/93            3K  AOL  ⬇       │
│ ⬅                         ➡ 卫      │
└─────────────────────────────────────┘
```

## A people-based strategy

I receive too much mail for the single-file method, and I never
remember dates. The strategy I use is people-based. Inside my Mail
folder are dozens of files, each named after a person with whom I
regularly correspond (see Figure 3-23).

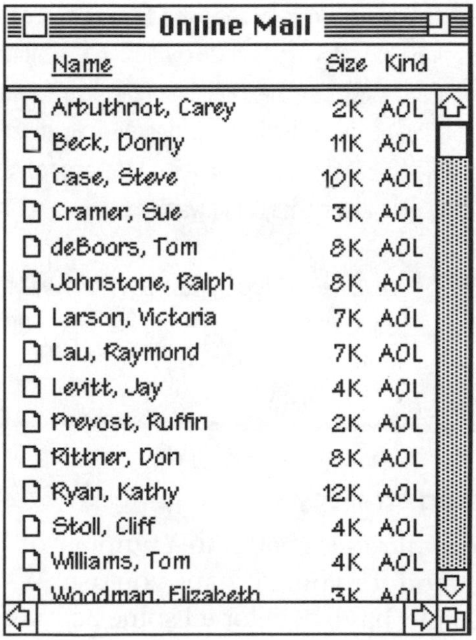

Figure 3-23: The list of
files in my Mail folder,
arranged and sorted
by name.

```
┌─────────────────────────────────────┐
│ ▤□▤▤▤▤ Online Mail ▤▤▤▤ 卫 │
├─────────────────────────────────────┤
│  Name                Size  Kind     │
├─────────────────────────────────────┤
│ 🗎 Arbuthnot, Carey    2K  AOL  ⬆   │
│ 🗎 Beck, Donny        11K  AOL  ▢   │
│ 🗎 Case, Steve        10K  AOL      │
│ 🗎 Cramer, Sue         3K  AOL      │
│ 🗎 deBoors, Tom        8K  AOL      │
│ 🗎 Johnstone, Ralph    8K  AOL      │
│ 🗎 Larson, Victoria    7K  AOL      │
│ 🗎 Lau, Raymond        7K  AOL      │
│ 🗎 Levitt, Jay         4K  AOL      │
│ 🗎 Prevost, Ruffin     2K  AOL      │
│ 🗎 Rittner, Don        8K  AOL      │
│ 🗎 Ryan, Kathy        12K  AOL      │
│ 🗎 Stoll, Cliff        4K  AOL      │
│ 🗎 Williams, Tom       4K  AOL      │
│ 🗎 Woodman, Elizabeth  3K  AOL  ⬇   │
│ ⬅                          ➡ 卫    │
└─────────────────────────────────────┘
```

Each person's file contains all the messages I've sent to and received from that person in chronological order. Again, I include mail I've sent as well as received, as discussed in the sidebar.

---

### Searching text files

At the moment, my Online Mail folder contains over 2mb of data, representing thousands of pieces of mail. Just yesterday, a reader sent me a piece of mail saying, "Thanks, Tom." That's all it said. It was sent by someone with the AOL screen name GeorgeD12. No offense intended, George, but I get a lot of reader mail, and I had no idea why I was being thanked.

I really hate to throw away mail like that. Maybe I did something really nice for George. Maybe George sent the mail to the wrong person. Maybe he meant to tell me to jump in a lake. I had to know.

The solution is a text-searching program. Each text-searching program does essentially the same thing: I tell the program what to look for and where to look, and it looks inside of every file for whatever I'm after. Many of them conduct their work in the background while I work on something else. I told my favorite program of this type—Search Files by Robert Morris—to look for the word *George* in my Online Mail folder, and I went back to work on my manuscript. Sure enough, a few minutes later (yes, minutes, not seconds: most of these programs amble rather than scramble) my Mac beeped and there was a list of all files with the word *George* in them. Sure enough, GeorgeD12 was there in my FANMAIL file. I had forwarded a message for him to a member whose screen name he didn't know. He didn't want me to jump in a lake after all.

A number of these programs are available online at AOL. Use the keyword: FileSearch, then the criterion: Text Search. Pay the shareware fee if you find a shareware program that's useful to you.

---

### A subject-based strategy

If your online mail relates better to a number of subjects, this might be a better method for you. Perhaps you use AOL to plan your travels. You might have developed some acquaintances in **rec.travel.cruises**, a travel-related newsgroup. You might be receiving confirmations from EAASY SABRE, AOL's travel reservations service. Or you might be clipping travel articles from the World

Wide Web. If this is the case, you might develop a number of files for each of your destinations.

These strategies can be combined, of course, and they aren't the only ones. There are no doubt scores of others. What I'm trying to do is convince you of the importance of filing your mail. Decide upon a method, set it up to your satisfaction, and maintain it faithfully. You'll become a better citizen of the e-mail community if you do.

## Moving on

As you can see, AOL's e-mail facility is impressive, and it's the ideal companion for Internet mail. It holds your mail for you, even after you've read it. It allows you to send courtesy copies. Perhaps best of all, it rarely costs you any more than your monthly AOL membership fee.

Very impressive indeed.

While we're discussing electronic mail, there's another subject that might be of interest to you: mailing lists. If you're hungry for e-mail, mailing lists will satisfy your craving. They're abundant and diverse. Subscribing to a single list can generate 10, 20, even 30 or more pieces of incoming mail every day. You'll never suffer from the empty-mailbox blues again. If you want to know more, all you have to do is turn the page.

# Chapter 4

# MADAME, YOUR LIST IS SERVED

I'm fond of analogies. In describing Carol Channing's eyelashes, critic Rex Reed once said they were as long ". . . as shish kebab." Shakespeare once paralleled love to ". . . sunshine after a rain." And novelist Tom Robbins once described a character's hair as being ". . . . straight and red as ironed ketchup." Analogies can be poignant, whimsical, bitter or sweet—but good ones always vitalize a narrative.

It follows, then, that I would search for an analogy to describe the Internet's mailing lists. I think I've found one.

Electronic mail distribution lists (more commonly called "lists," or "mailing lists") have a lot in common with Rush Limbaugh and Ed McMahon.  They're like Rush Limbaugh's talk radio in that they reach thousands of people and everyone's invited to participate. They're like Ed McMahon's sweepstakes letters in that they arrive in the mail, indiscriminate, in great volume, seemingly unbidden.

It's not Shakespeare, but it'll do.

Lists can be entertaining, enlightening, provocative—or a combination of all three. They can become as unruly as a fourth-grade class on the day before summer vacation. They can squander your time like a regret. They can provoke your ire, kindle your passions, or pique your intellect. Lists serve many purposes but one thing's for sure: you'll never want for mail again once you learn about Internet mailing lists.

**Virtual Visigoths**

Speaking of sweepstakes letters, let's spend a moment contemplating chain letters. Chain letters on the Net are about as welcome as Visigoths at the gates of Rome. Not only are electronic chain letters a nuisance; they clobber "bandwidth," the Internet's most precious resource. Furthermore, they're a violation of AOL's Terms of Service and can result in the termination of your account, especially if you post or forward a chain letter on the Net and a number of Netters write to AOL with complaints. Don't even think of starting one, and if you receive one online, do not reply. Contrary to folklore, forwarding an electronic chain letter is *bad* luck—immediate, caustic and merciless.

## The oracle

In Chapter 3 you sent mail to a computer in Oregon. In response, it sent back a provocative quotation for your thoughtful consideration.

You're wiser now. Chapter 3 is behind you. Now we can automate the process of receiving mail. Now we can receive provocative e-mail by asking for it only once. Here's how:

- Sign on to America Online, then choose Compose Mail from the Mail menu.

- Complete the Compose Mail form, using the example shown in Figure 4-1 as a guide.

Figure 4-1: The completed mail form, ready for sending. **Note:** AOL has wrapped the address in the To: field: there are no returns or spaces in it.

| | |
|---|---|
| **To:** | oracle-request@cs.indiana.edu |
| **cc:** | |
| **Subj:** | Subscribe |
| **File:** | ☐ Return Receipt |

SUBSCRIBE Usenet Oracle Tom Lichty

Address Book • Attach File • Send Later • Send Now • Help

- 🔺 Notice that I've placed **oracle-request@cs.indiana.edu** (the address of a computer at the University of Indiana) in the To: field.

- 🔺 This mailing list pays attention only to the Subject: field, so the word "Subscribe" is important here. (This isn't the case with all mailing lists. Be sure to read this entire chapter.)

- 🔺 The message field is functionally ignored by this particular list, but it's a common courtesy to include your real name there. Anonymity is tolerated but rarely appropriate on the Internet.

- 🔺 Click on the icon marked Send. Sign off, if you wish, after the message is sent. Don't remain online waiting for a reply.

Actually, the USENET Oracle mailing list is a *digest* (more about digests later). To reduce the load on the Internet, many lists are mailed only once a week or once a night: all of the messages to the list are stored during that period then mailed in an archive as one e-mail message. The Oracle is a weekly digest: it may take as long as seven days before you receive your first Oracularity. Oracles are like that. Be patient.

**The Oracle**

The USENET Oracle follows the ancient tradition of oracular consultation and reply. Hercules consulted the Delphic Oracle; King Cepheus consulted the Oracle of Ammon (who told him to chain his daughter Andromeda to the rocks of Joppa: some oracles are more malevolent than others).

There's a twist, however: in exchange for a reply, the USENET Oracle often asks a question in return. Your e-mailed reply is reviewed by the Oracle "priesthood"; if it's worthy, it becomes an "Oracle" posting itself. Befitting of the Internet anarchy, the Oracle is actually members of the list, asking and answering questions among themselves. The priesthood maintains the quality and timbre of the Oracularities, but the members are the source.

You'll have to wait, now, for at least a few hours while your request is being processed. You may have to wait a full day. Eventually, however, you'll receive a confirmation (Figure 4-2) congratulating you on your membership in this most exclusive of societies.

Figure 4-2: Though not all lists send them, this list sent confirmation a few hours after I sent the request to subscribe.

```
                    You are now subscribed

 Forward    Subj: You are now subscribed
            Date: 94-03-31 14:51:11 est
            From: oracle-request@cs.indiana.edu
            To:  MajorTom
 Reply
            You are now subscribed to the Usenet Oracularities as:

            majortom@aol.com
 Reply to All
            Should you ever wish to unsubscribe, send mail from this
            account to oracle-request@cs.indiana.edu with the word
            "unsubscribe" in the subject.  Send mail to
            oracle-admin@cs.indiana.edu if you want to talk to a real
            person instead of the automated subscription program.

 Save to
 Flashmail     Prev                                          Next
```

**A confirmation file**

Take time to read confirmations, for they often contain instructions on how to work with the list (as does the one pictured in Figure 4-2). I save my confirmations and file them. You'd be surprised how often you need to refer to this kind of information, and having it on file means that you can copy and paste addresses. This eliminates a lot of errors.

Because of the bewildering ways e-mail gets sent on the Internet, many lists now ask you to perform an additional step (also called a confirmation) before you are added to the list. Follow the instructions in these confirmation requests exactly; you won't be allowed to join otherwise.

Within the week, your first message from the Oracle will arrive. More will follow, automatically, whenever the Oracle feels inspired to pontificate (Figure 4-3).

Before you submit questions to the Oracle, read up on your Oracle etiquette by sending e-mail to **oracle@cs.indiana.edu** with the word *Help* as the Subject. You can remove your name from the list by sending e-mail to **oracle-request@cs.indiana.edu** with the word *Unsubscribe* as the Subject. All of this and more is mentioned in the confirmation.

Figure 4-3: The Oracle speaketh—every week or so.

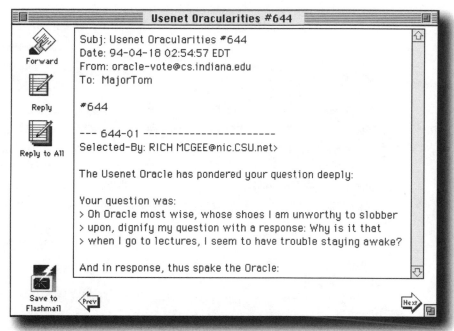

## What is a list?

The USENET Oracle isn't exactly a perfect paradigm for mailing lists. Though you can submit messages to the list, the messages themselves are broadcast anonymously, and only after they're edited by the priesthood.

Not many lists behave this way. And none of the others has a priesthood.

In its basic configuration, an Internet mailing list is, quite simply, a vehicle by which messages sent to the list are broadcast to all members of the list, complete with the sender's identity. Unlike the USENET Oracle, most lists are run by machines which simply route everything sent to them—in the form of e-mail—to the entire list membership. The messages sent through these mailing lists vary widely, so that some lists are riveting, some wearisome, some mesmerizing one day and humdrum another.

But one thing's for sure: they generate a *lot* of mail.

**Digests & Indices**

Here's the best tip of this entire chapter: look for mailing list *digests*. A digest is a summary of a list's activity for a time period—a week, usually. The digest is mailed only once during the summary period in lieu of the list itself. Some digests simply consist of all of the list's messages for the period, mailed at once. Others are edited and more like a "best of" collection. Their infrequency and pithy content offer an ideal way to evaluate and become familiar with a list without wading through scores of messages every day.

Some mailing lists offer a periodic *index*. The index is a list of the messages posted for the period. After reviewing the index, you can then request the individual articles directly from the server.

An effective mailing-list strategy is to subscribe to a list's digest or index for a while, lurking until you get to know the nature of the people and the topics they discuss. Once you've become familiar, you can elect to subscribe to the list itself, or cancel the digest and move on to another potential.

To see if a digest or index is offered for a particular list, read the list's description carefully (descriptons are discussed in the next section of this chapter). To see a list of all of the digests or indexes currently available, use the keyword: MailingLists, click the Search Mailing Lists button, then specify DIGEST or INDEX as your search criterion.

## Finding a list

Yes, there's a list of lists. There are a number of them, actually, and they're available in several ways.

### Using AOL's list-searching database

America Online offers what may be the most comprehensive list of lists available today—and, best of all, it's searchable (Figure 4-4). The list mechanism is remarkably fast, and it allows you to cut and paste list names and addresses into e-mail forms—a significant convenience when you consider the complexity of most lists' addresses and the Internet's intolerance for improperly addressed mail.

Figure 4-4: AOL's search mechanism is fast and convenient.

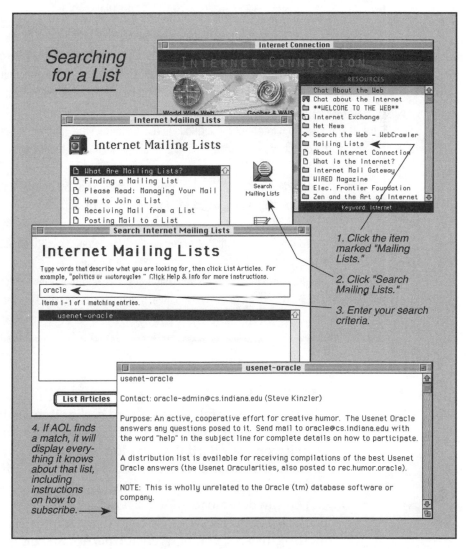

AOL has accumulated an extensive list with an intricate web of keywords that makes this database ideal not only for searching but for browsing as well. If you've a subject about which you'd like to talk with others, try searching AOL's database for it. Chances are you'll find a list or two that will serve your needs.

**Community project**

AOL's list may be one of the most comprehensive available on the Net today, but keeping it that way is a task that should never be asked of a single individual.

AOL's Listmaster David O'Donnell writes: ". . . AOL members can help keep our Mailing List Database the best of the Net by sending information on lists not already in it. . . . . If members can provide the same information as would be found in an already extant entry, we can add the new list quickly."

If you discover a list that's not included in the database, write it up in the same fashion as you see used in the others in the database, then mail it to the screen name: ListMaster.

An alternative to searching AOL's database is to download a "list of lists" and use a word processor to search through it. A word-processor search on the word "camel," for example, would find not only the Camel-List (which discusses camel research—an important consideration in Saudi Arabia, where the list originates), but Camelot as well. Free-form searching like this can sometimes prove rewarding.

There are many lists of lists on the Net, and there are ways to download them to your hard disk, where they're available online or off—perfectly suited for browsing. Read on.

## AOL's list of lists

The very same database discussed earlier is available as a text file, suitable for searching via a word processor. It's a *very* large file, but once it's on your hard disk, exploring it is free. This is the best list of lists available to the AOL member because it's written with the AOL member in mind and many of the instructions are specific to AOL.

You can download AOL's list of lists via anonymous ftp (FTP— File Transer Protocol—is discussed in Chapter 7) at **ftp.aol.com/pub/ mailing-lists**, or via the Web at **ftp.//ftp.aol.com/pub/mailing lists**.

## The Internet List of Lists

On a more global level, consider the Internet List of Lists (LoL), which was originally published by Rich Zellich when there was no Internet, just ARPANET, and the LoL was about three pages long. Now it's nine hundred pages long and measures almost a megabyte. It's updated periodically and available via a number of methods.

### The LoL via FTP

The LoL makes its home at SRI, a California-based research institute that operates the Network Information Systems Center. It's available via anonymous FTP at **sri.com** in the *anonymous.netinfo* directory. Look for the file Interest-Groups.txt. This is the quickest and easiest way of obtaining the list, though it's a sizable download: it's nearly a megabyte, remember.

---

**Periodic updates**

Once you invest in acquiring AOL's list of lists or the LoL, you probably won't want to download them again anytime soon. The solution is to subscribe to the New-List list, where the arrival of a new list is broadcast as soon as the list goes online. Though we'll discuss subscribing in a few pages, all you need to do is search the online database (following the sequence illustrated in Figure 4-4) using the criteria: new AND nodak. (You could just search for "new list," but you would have to hunt through over 200 matches. Since New-List is run from North Dakota (**nodak.edu**), this search is more efficient.) Once you locate the entry for the New-List list, follow the instructions there for subscribing.

This mailing list is echoed to the USENET newsgroup **bit.listserv.news-list** (newsgroups are discussed in Chapter 5). You may find that participating in the list via the newsgroup will be a more rewarding experience than reading e-mail. Use the keyword: Newsgroups, then click the Expert Add button and supply the newsgroup name (**bit.listserv.news-list**) when asked.

### The LoL via e-mail

Remember again that this list is almost a megabyte long, and a megabyte of mail is a little disconcerting, even when you expect it. By the time it reaches you, the LoL will amount to 30 pieces—maybe more—of lengthy e-mail which will have to be reassembled into one file again before you can use the list conveniently. The FTP method described above, in other words, is a better method than the one that follows.

That said, here's how to get the LoL via e-mail: send e-mail to **mail-server@sri.com** with **send interest-groups** in the body of the message. Put anything you like in the Subject: field, then send the mail. Within a day or two you'll receive your reply. Since AOL can't accommodate e-mail messages any longer than 28k, the megabyte-length LoL will be cut up by AOL's host machines and sent to you as about 30 pieces of 28k e-mail. You will have to use a word processor—one that can accommodate megabyte-length files—in order to reassemble the pieces.

### The LoL as a book

The LoL is available as a book as well, published by Prentice Hall under the title *Internet: Mailing Lists* (see the Bibliography). The book is available in many bookstores and can be ordered directly from Prentice Hall by calling 515-284-6751. Be sure to look for the most recent edition.

## Where do lists come from?

Mailing lists are maintained on computers all over the country. There's no central "list machine." The USENET Oracle is maintained at the University of Indiana.

### Moderated lists

Lists are maintained either by a machine or by a person. Those maintained by people are termed "moderated."

Moderated lists can be just as anarchistic as unmoderated lists, but moderators usually weed out troublemakers and keep the discussions on the topic (a much-appreciated process called "noise control"). A description for a moderated list appears in Figure 4-5.

Figure 4-5: The
description of the
moderated Folk_music
mailing list.

> ## A Moderated List
>
> *FOLK_MUSIC@NYSERNET.ORG*
>
> Subscription Address: LISTSERV@NYSERNET.ORG
> Owner: Alan Rowoth <alanr@nysernet.org>
> Last Update: 3/23/94
>
> Description:
>   Folk_music is a moderated discussion list dealing with the music of the
> recent wave of American singer/songwriters. List traffic consists of tour
> schedules, reviews, album release info and other information on artists like
> Shawn Colvin, Mary-Chapin Carpenter, David Wilcox, Nanci Griffith, Darden
> Smith, Maura O'Connell, Don Henry, and others.
>
>   All questions, requests for information, etc., should be sent to the moderator.
> Submissions are accepted by mail to <folk_music@nysernet.org> or by fax at
> 812.555.2766.

Though the description shown in Figure 4-5 plainly states that the list is moderated, not all descriptions do. The presence of this moderator guarantees a low-noise list—in writing, no less!

If you want to know more about a list, look for instructions detailing avenues for help, or send e-mail to the person listed as the contact in the list's description.

## LISTSERV & Majordomo

Many lists are simply maintained by a machine, and that requires a program. *LISTSERV* is a computer program first written by Eric Thomas on behalf of the many list managers who wanted to get away from the drudgery of mailing-list administrivia. We're talking about volunteers, remember: few people are paid to manage a list.

LISTSERV isn't the only list-management software available. LISTSERV runs primarily on IBM mainframes, *Majordomo* runs on many others. These two programs are functionally similar.

Deciding whether to use LISTSERV (or Majordomo) vs. maintaining a list by hand is a matter of attitude. Some list managers prefer the hands-on approach; some don't. The list itself rarely reflects this attitude in terms of quality: sterling examples exist among automated lists, just as they do among people-managed lists.

Sometimes you can tell by its address if a list is automated. If the first word of a list's address is Majordomo or LISTSERV, you know it's automated. If the first word is something else, you'll have to read the description to find out.

### BITNET

Remember that the Internet is a collection of independent networks. Some of these networks interconnect with other networks solely via the Internet, but many exist independently of the Internet: their connection to the Internet isn't their only connection, to them the Internet is just another door in a room full of doors.

Such is the case with BITNET (an acronym for "Because It's Time Network"). BITNET actually predates the Internet. It started as an academic network, and its protocols and commands are vastly different from those of the Internet. Because of this, BITNET doesn't have much of a presence on the Internet, with one significant exception: e-mail.

### Mailing lists vs. newsgroups

If you're familiar with newsgroups (we'll discuss them in Chapter 5), perhaps you've noticed the similarity between newsgroups and mailing lists. Indeed, many mailing lists are newsgroups in e-mail form, provided for the convenience of those Netters who have nothing but e-mail access to the Net. The Oracle is one.

Some say mailing lists offer content of higher quality. A number of newsgroup users would refute that, of course. The operative difference is presentation: using AOL, the mailing lists are "in your face": it's hard to ignore e-mail when a voice reminds you that "You have mail!" every time you sign on.

The qualitative difference, however, depends on the content, not the medium. Not all newsgroups are duplicated as lists, and not all lists have a corresponding newsgroup. Both offer fertile ground for stimulating conversation. You'll have to explore them both to realize the Net's full potential.

Most of the machines running the LISTSERV mailing-list program are connected via BITNET. This doesn't amount to much as far as we're concerned, but you'll see **.bitnet** or **.bit** often in mailing-list addresses, and that's why.

## List addresses

A mailing list address looks much like any other e-mail address; however most mailing lists offer two of them: one for the list itself and another for administrative purposes. There's a significant difference; failure to observe that difference can be embarrassing.

### Subscription addresses

Most lists offer a subscription address for administrative tasks: signing up, resigning from the list, help—the kind of communication that isn't intended to be published but is sent in anticipation of a personal reply. Some lists that are available in digest form offer two of these addresses: one for the "regular" list, and another for the digest version of the list.

Often—though not always—the word *request* is included in the subscription address and excluded from the posting address. Though not all subscription addresses include the word, those that do should never be used for postings.

The online database of lists may or may not provide both the subscription address and the posting address for each list. Read the entry carefully to be sure that you don't send your subscription request to the post address or vice-versa! If you send a subscription request to the posting address, it may be forwarded to everyone else on the list. This is one of the quickest routes possible toward becoming a "Net weenie."

Look at the database entry for the NHCTEN mailing list pictured in Figure 4-6. The "contact" address listed there is the subscription address. Don't send a posting to this address! Subscribe to the list first (or, if one's available, the digest), read it passively for a couple of months, then post if you wish. By then you'll be familiar with the list's etiquette, tone and personality. Posting to a list without first becoming familiar with it might make you feel like the man who attended a Christian convention in the nude: he thought the invitation read "Sun Worshippers," when it actually read "Son Worshippers . . . ."

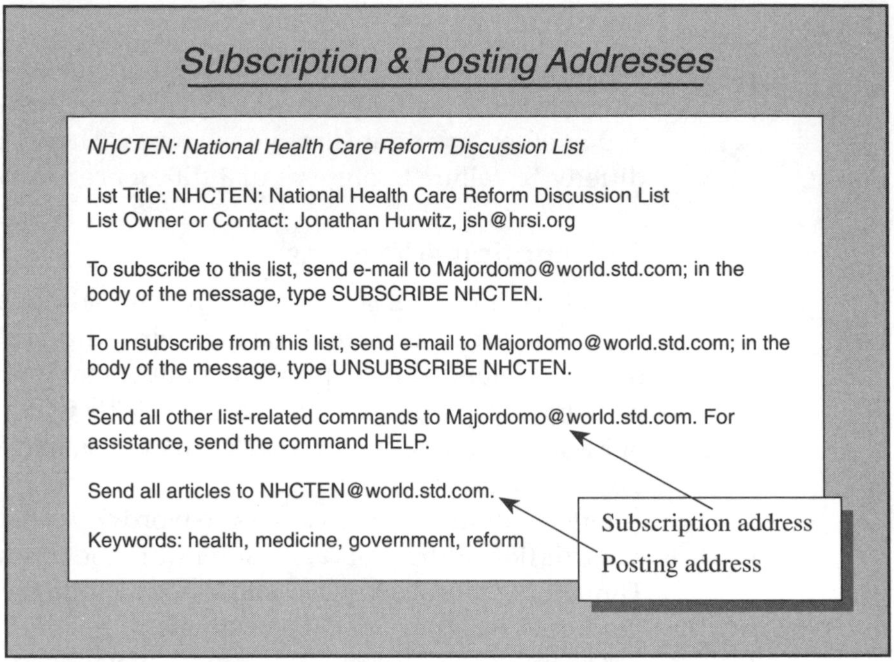

Figure 4-6: A typical database entry offers the subscription and posting addresses.

## Subscription & Posting Addresses

*NHCTEN: National Health Care Reform Discussion List*

List Title: NHCTEN: National Health Care Reform Discussion List
List Owner or Contact: Jonathan Hurwitz, jsh@hrsi.org

To subscribe to this list, send e-mail to Majordomo@world.std.com; in the body of the message, type SUBSCRIBE NHCTEN.

To unsubscribe from this list, send e-mail to Majordomo@world.std.com; in the body of the message, type UNSUBSCRIBE NHCTEN.

Send all other list-related commands to Majordomo@world.std.com. For assistance, send the command HELP.

Send all articles to NHCTEN@world.std.com.

Keywords: health, medicine, government, reform

Subscription address
Posting address

### FAQs

Nearly every mailing list and newsgroup periodically posts its list of Frequently Asked Questions, or FAQ. Typically, FAQs are posted every month or so, but if you're impatient you can probably find the one you're after in the **news.answers** newsgroup (newsgroups are discussed in Chapter 5, "Newshounds Anonymous"). AOL automatically subscribes you to this newsgroup; become familiar with it.

If you intend to post a message in either a newsgroup or a mailing list, read the appropriate FAQ first. Nothing irritates a Net user more than having to suffer through a question that's been asked hundreds of times before.

### Posting addresses

A posting address is the actual address to which you post messages intended for the general list readership. You'll receive the posting address when you become a member of the list if it's not in the database entry. The message of acceptance shown in Figure 4-2 went on to say that I should send messages to **oracle@cs.indiana.edu**. Note that this is not the subscription address that appears in Figure 4-1(**oracle-admin@cs.indiana.edu**). Though some subscription addresses include the word "admin" or "request" in the address, many do not, including many of those administered by the automated list servers.

## List activities

You can subscribe, get help, read, respond to or resign from a list. Here's how.

### Subscribing to a list

To subscribe to a list, consult the online database for the subscription address, which should be placed in the To: field of a Compose Mail window. (You'll find the Compose Mail command under the Mail menu.) Read the list's description before you do this: sometimes list names don't fully or accurately describe their content. The online database will include instructions regarding how to subscribe. Follow them to the letter, being doubly sure you're sending to the subscription, not the posting, address.

Technically speaking, there are two broad categories of lists: those administered by people and those that are automated. If you follow the database directions, subscribing to a list shouldn't be a problem, and it won't make any difference whether the administrator is a person or a program.

Generalities, however, can be made. Most human administrators prefer that you place the word *Subscribe* in the Subject: field of your mail message. Repeat the subscribe request in the message field and include your real name there as well. Most administrators won't pay much attention to the message field, but it's a common courtesy to include your real name nonetheless. When you're done, sign on and send the message. Expect a reply within a couple of days.

**No guarantees**

There's no guarantee that you will be allowed to join any particular list. Some of them restrict access. Though mailing lists use less system overhead than newsgroups, they do tend to increase loading on the moderators' machines. In other words, the number of people that can be added to a list may be limited by machine resources as well as by other criteria.

The LISTSERV and Majordomo programs ignore the Subject: field, though AOL's software requires something there. The word *subscribe* will do. The message field, however, must contain the word *subscribe*, the name of the list and your real first and last names. Remember that the names of automated lists usually begin with the words *majordomo* or *listserv*.

If you're unsure, assume that all lists are handled by a person, and address your subscription request accordingly. No one likes being treated like a machine, but few machines mind being treated like a human.

Figure 4-7:
Subscription requests
for human and
LISTSERV-administered
lists.

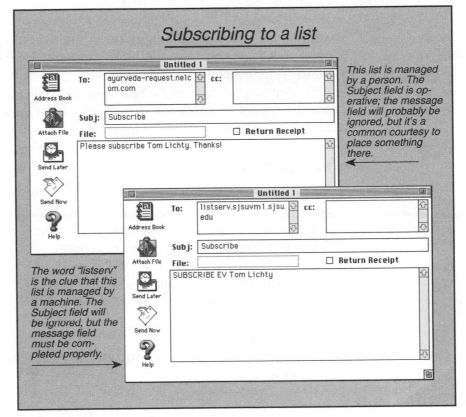

## Getting help

Most automated lists include the word *help* in their vocabularies of commands. To find out what any particular machine can do, send mail to its subscription address and include the word *help* in the message field. The subject field will be ignored, but AOL requires something there, so repeat the word *help* in that field too.

Lists administered by humans may or may not offer help. Typically, your welcoming message will contain a mailing address for questions pertaining to the list. Be sure to send your request to the indicated address, and put the word *help* in the subject field.

### Reading a list

Though the database listings are the ultimate authority with regard to subscribing, getting help and resigning from a list, reading a list to which you've already subscribed is no different than reading any other e-mail: just click on the You've Got Mail icon on AOL's Spotlight screen (or press Command+R), or choose Read New Mail from the Mail menu. Consult Chapter 3 for more details on the subject of e-mail.

### Responding to a list

Sending mail for publication to the list membership amounts to nothing more than choosing Compose Mail from the Mail menu, placing the list's posting address in the To: field, and completing the Subject: and message fields as you see fit.

Alternatively, you can click the Reply button when a particular piece of mail-list mail is on your screen, and compose your reply normally. Remember, however, that mail composed this way will carry the subject line "Re: XXX" (where the XXX's represent the subject of the message to which you're responding). Don't click the Reply button, in other words, unless you really intend to reply to the mail on your screen.

### Reading mail off-line

Digests like the Oracle are often lengthy. If you anticipate the receipt of a lengthy piece of mail (list or not), consider AOL's FlashMail feature. FlashMail is mail you save on your disk as it's received. You read it later, offline, when you're disconnected from AOL.

Though I'll discuss FlashMail in Chapter 9 ("FlashSessions & the Download Manager"), it's appropriate that I mention the subject briefly here as well.

Peculiar as it may sound, don't read your mail normally (by choosing Read New Mail from the Mail menu). Instead, when you're ready to sign off, choose Activate FlashSession Now from the Mail menu. When the Activate FlashSession Now dialog box appears, click the Sign off when finished check box, then click the Begin button. AOL will take it from there, downloading all of your mail onto your hard disk, then signing off.

Once you're offline, choose Read Incoming Mail from the Mail menu. Each of your pieces of mail will appear there, as if you were reading them online (see Figure 4-8). Read them leisurely: the clock's not running.

Figure 4-8: AOL's FlashMail feature allows you to read mail offline.

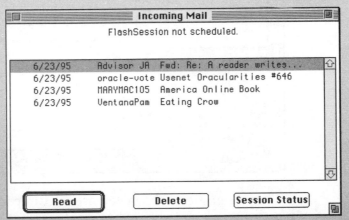

When you're finished reading a particular piece of mail, file it if you wish, then click the Delete button available at the bottom of the mail's window. This clears the read mail from your FlashMail box, so you won't see it there again.

## Removing your name from a list

Once again there's a difference between human and machine-administered lists. Be sure to send your request to the subscription address and place the word *unsubscribe* in the Subject: field.

Automated lists usually require the words *signoff* or *unsubscribe* in the message field, followed by the list name. You needn't include your name in the signoff command, but remember to always put something in AOL's Subject: field.

Figure 4-9: Two typical examples using the unsubscribe command.

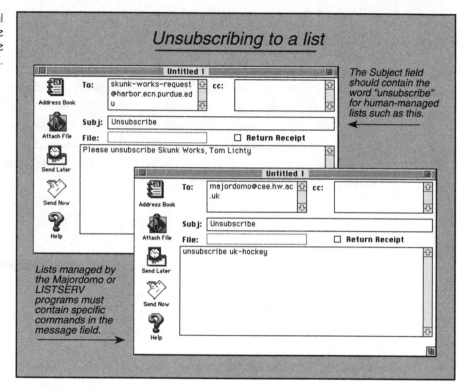

Most significant, however, are the directions contained in the greeting you probably received when you first joined the list. That's why I suggest you keep these greetings on file—for every list to which you subscribe—so that you may consult them when it's time to unsubscribe.

## Moving on

Many people love mailing lists because they love receiving mail. Others prefer something less passive. Most mailing-list activity takes place offline, and some people prefer their interaction on a more immediate level.

An alternative to the mailing list is the newsgroup. Newsgroups are more immediate, and their content is often more spontaneous. They're the home of flame wars, diatribes and fulminations (among other things). To many, they *are* the Internet. To learn more, turn the page . . . .

# Chapter 5

# NEWSHOUNDS ANONYMOUS

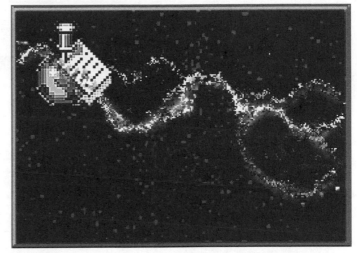

**N**ose to the ground, the newshound sniffs in eternal pursuit of information. Newshounds devour data with a John Candyesque appetite: pugnacious, voracious and occasionally pernicious. Other newshounds follow different paths, their appetites no less glutton-ous, their destinies no less vaporous, and their lairs no less inflated with their fervor.

I'm being a little severe, I know, but newsgroups are like choco-late: while there are people who are capable of self-discipline, most of us become addicted after a bite or two.

For better or for worse, newshounds are proliferating at an amaz-ing rate. According to statistics from the Network Information Center in Amsterdam, 2,900 host computers per day are being connected to the Internet in Europe and Russia alone. At least that many more are connecting in the U.S. and the Pacific Rim. This is indeed fat city for newshounds.

(Among other things, hounds are discussed in **rec.pets**, **rec.pets.dogs**, **alt-tv.muppets**, **alt.pets.chia** and my favorite: **alt.smouldering.dog.zone**. And if fat is your concern, try **alt.food.fatfree**.)

Figure 5-1: The keyword: Newsgroups opens the door to the Internet's most popular attraction.

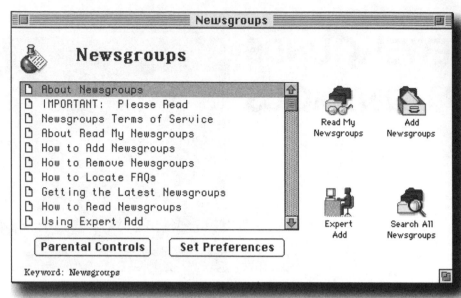

## The learning curve of Sisyphus

Don't let the magnitude of the Internet overwhelm you. The current (spring, 1995) count of nearly 20,500 newsgroups isn't stifling, it's liberating: it's a vast new territory for exploration. Electronic Frontier Foundation cofounder John Barlow once wrote: "On the most rudimentary level there is simply terror of feeling like an immigrant in a place where your children are natives—where you're always going to be behind the eight-ball because they can develop the technology faster than you can learn it. It's what I call the learning curve of Sisyphus. And the only people who are going to be comfortable with that are people who don't mind confusion and ambiguity.... We've got a culture that's based on the ability of people to control everything. Once you start to embrace confusion as a way of life, concomitant with that is the assumption that you really don't control anything. At best it's a matter of surfing the whitewater."

## The best of the Internet

With over 20,000 newsgroups and scores more arriving every week, how can you be sure you'll spend your newsgroup-reading time wisely? Frankly, you can't. Almost every newsgroup has its share of "noise": inappropriate (and sometimes inarticulate) messages that contribute nothing to the value of the group itself. One newsgroup that's no exception—but fun to read—is **alt.best.of.internet**. We'll start this chapter with a little exercise that explores the process of subscribing to that newsgroup.

▲ Begin by signing on and pressing Command+K. Enter the keyword: Newsgroups to get to the newsgroups area quickly.

▲ When you already know the name of the newsgroup you want to add to your personal list (as you will in a moment), click the Expert Add button (see Figure 5-2).

Figure 5-2: Adding the
**alt.best.of.internet**
newsgroup to your
personal list.

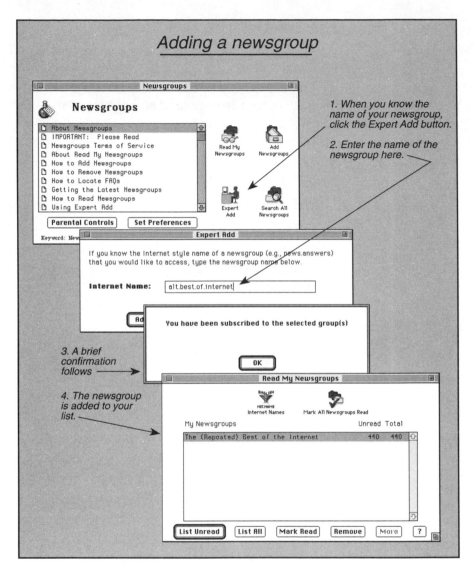

▲ Enter the name of the **alt.best.of.internet** newsgroup as shown in Figure 5-2.

▲ After a confirmation, the newsgroup will be added to your personal list of newsgroups. (In the interest of clarity, the illustration at the bottom of Figure 5-2 shows only one newsgroup. Your list will no doubt offer others.)

🔺 Double-click the name of the new newsgroup to read its messages (Figure 5-3).

Figure 5-3: You can read newsgroup messages, respond to them, or copy and paste them into other text documents.

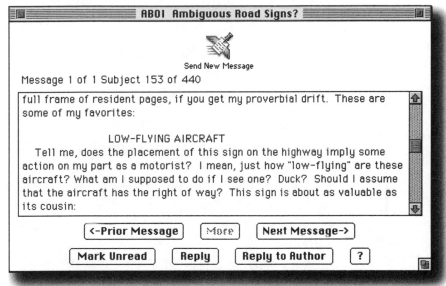

## What are newsgroups?

Now that you've sampled their wares, it's appropriate that we discover what newsgroups really are. Actually, you shouldn't have much trouble with this: newsgroups are similar to mailing lists in that they're a free exchange of ideas, opinions and comments—confined, usually, to a specific field of interest. You visit a newsgroup, read the messages that are there, reply to those that inspire a response, post new messages when you have a new topic to propose, and come back another day to see what responses you've provoked.

Unlike mailing lists, no mail is involved with newsgroups. Most activity occurs while you're online, including reading and responding to messages. Thus, some will say that newsgroups are more immediate, more interactive and more conversational than mailing lists. Newsgroups or mailing lists: for most it's a matter of preference. You will probably want to dabble in both of them.

**Windows humor**

The message below is a typical example of the wit you'll come across in newsgroups, found in **alt.best.of.internet**. As a Macintosh user, you might find the content befitting.

Subject: ABOI: Is Windows a Virus?
From: tangent@uclink2.berkeley.edu (Hai N Tang)
Date: 23 Jun 1995 01:03:02 GMT
Message-ID: <3sd3s6$rsm@agate.berkeley.edu>

Is Windows a virus?
No, Windows is not a virus.  Here's what viruses (viri?) do:
1. They replicate quickly — okay, Windows does that.
2. Viruses use up valuable system resources, slowing down the system they do so — okay, Windows does that.
3. Viruses will, from time to time, trash your hard disk — okay, Windows does that, too.
4. Viruses are usually carried, unknown to the user, along with valuable programs and systems. Sigh... Windows does that, too.
5. Viruses will occasionally make the user suspect their system is too slow (see 2) and the user will buy new hardware. Yup, that's with Windows, too.

Until now it seems Windows is a virus but there are fundamental differences: Viruses are well supported by their authors, are running on most systems, their program code is fast, compact and efficient and they tend to become more sophisticated as they mature.

So, Windows is *not* a virus.

One thing's for sure: few newsgroups have anything to do with the news. Newsgroups aren't groups assembled to discuss the "MacNeil/Lehrer NewsHour" or *USA Today*; this is an anarchy: there are no restrictions whatsoever on newsgroup topics. That's why there are more than 20,000 of them.

The Internet doesn't have a monopoly on discussion areas like newsgroups. America Online has hundreds of them, though AOL prefers to call them message boards. CompuServe has forums, GEnie has bulletin boards and Delphi has round tables. They're all the same thing, and they all exist to satisfy our passion for discourse. Accordingly, newsgroups are arguably the most popular resource on the Internet.

And they *are* an Internet resource, meaning they're outside of AOL's sphere of influence. No one polices the Internet other than the Internet's tenants themselves. Newsgroup subject matter and use of language are appropriate to the Internet anarchy. In a way, AOL is performing a service similar to that of the telephone company when it comes to newsgroups: AOL is just the medium, not the message. The picture in Figure 5-4 was uuencoded and posted to **alt.binaries.pictures.furry**. Encoding is discussed later in this chapter.

Figure 5-4: GROOVIN.GIF, drawn by Bill Fortier and posted to the **alt.binaries.pictures. furry** newsgroup.

## Newsgroup names

That hirsute image in Figure 5-4 was posted to **alt.binaries.pictures. furry**, a newsgroup where computer graphics of furry things are posted for the rest of us to enjoy.

The graphic, however, isn't our topic for discussion. The newsgroup's name is. Let's take a moment to dissect it.

Unlike e-mail addresses, newsgroup names go from the general to the specific as you read from left to right. Thus, in the name **alt.binaries.pictures.furry**, the term *alt* is the most general; the term *furry* is the most specific.

Properly speaking, seven "official" categories of newsgroups exist in the Internet, along with scores of "alternative" ones. One of these categories always appears at the very beginning of a newsgroup name:

comp    These newsgroups discuss computer science and computers in general, including hardware, software; and computer news, including **comp.sys.mac.advocacy** for the debate of Macintosh-related topics, and **comp.sys. mac.announce**, for announcements of importance to Macintosh users.

news    Groups concerned with newsgroups themselves. These include **news.newusers.questions** and **news.announce. newusers**. You are automatically subscribed to these groups. Please read them: it's the best way to become familiar with newsgroups.

rec    Recreation, including hobbies and the arts.

sci    Discussions of scientific research other than computer science.

soc    Social issues. That's a very broad term, and so is this category. Topics range from **soc.women** to **soc.men**. (As you might expect, everything in between is available too.)

talk    Debate and controversy ranging from the ridiculous (**talk.bizarre**) to the sublime (**talk.environment**).

misc    Anything that doesn't fit into the categories above.

In addition to the seven conventional categories listed above, there are at least half a dozen alternative categories. For our purposes, the alternative categories aren't much different than the conventional categories, but their inclusion among the accessible newsgroups differs from site to site: some Internet sites carry them, some don't. They include the following:

alt    Bizarre things are posted here, but you'll also find groups that simply have elected to bypass the bureaucratic process of formal inclusion in the seven categories above.

Most alt groups, however, are alternative (and typically antic) in nature. Try **alt.barney.dinosaur.die.die.die** or **alt.swedish.chef.bork.bork.bork** to see what I mean.

bit   Redistributions of the more popular BITNET LISTSERV mailing lists mentioned in the previous chapter.

biz   Business-related groups.

clari   The ClariNet system consists of commercial news systems such as UPI and AP. The stock exchanges are here as well. As you can imagine, this is a commercial resource that subscribers pay for. If you'd like a sample, try **biz.clarinet.sample**.

The second part of our newsgroup name—*binaries*—identifies this group as one where binary, rather than textual, information is posted. Binary information is usually composed of computer programs (you'll find a lot of binaries in the *comp* newsgroups), but computer graphics are a close second. We'll discuss binary postings later in this chapter.

The third part—*pictures*—distinguishes this newsgroup from other binary newsgroups, especially the programming newsgroups in *comp*.

The fourth part—*furry*—identifies the nature of the pictures. There are cartoons on the Net, and ASCII pictures (remember the Christmas tree graphics composed entirely of X's?), and a number of others.

Most newsgroup names are self-explanatory once you've learned the conventions. The best way to get to know the conventions is to browse through the List of Active Newsgroups. I'll tell you how to get it later in this chapter.

## USENET

You'll hear a lot about USENET as you discover newsgroups. In fact, newsgroups are often referred to (correctly) as "USENET newsgroups." Because of the popularity of newsgroups, many people believe the Internet *is* the USENET. Others—sanguine in their knowledge that the Internet consists of many networks—proclaim that the USENET is the network that newsgroups run on. Neither is correct.

**Circular acronymonics**

Actually, anarchy prevails even in the face of order. In fact, not all newsgroups participate in USENET. Many are accessed only through gnUSENET, a peculiar circular acronym, meaning "GnUSENET is Not USENET."

USENET consists of those sites that agree to exchange newsgroups. Most of USENET uses the Internet as the "delivery truck," but there are other carriers as well. The difference between USENET and the Internet might be compared to the difference between your newspaper and the carrier who delivers it. There's considerable debate on this distinction, but it's somewhat like arguing whether your newspaper carrier rides a bike or pedals it. The important thing is the message, not the medium.

**An encyclopedia a day**

With more than 20,000 newsgroups actively exchanging dozens—sometimes hundreds—of messages every day, USENET generates an enormous volume of Internet traffic. It's estimated that 50 megabytes of newsgroup messages are generated daily, nearly the equivalent of the entire Encyclopedia Britannica. America Online endeavors to store a couple of months' worth of USENET traffic at all times, available for perusal at our convenience. The storage requirements for this feature are, well, encyclopedic; the social implications are abstruse; and—perhaps most significant—the trivia quotient is titanic.

## Finding newsgroups

You probably don't want to subscribe to 20,000 newsgroups. That's a bit like standing under an avalanche to get some ice for your tea. Participating in more than a half dozen newsgroups would exceed the limits of human tolerance. Finding half a dozen personally appropriate newsgroups, then, is a high priority for us all.

### Searching AOL's list

Naturally, there's a list of currently available newsgroups, and, naturally, it's posted in a newsgroup (more about that later), but that list now exceeds a quarter of a megabyte in size. What we really need is some form of database mechanism—preferably one that's convenient and free—by which we can search the list.

Take a look at Figure 5-5. Note specifically the Add Newsgroups and Search All Newsgroups buttons highlighted there. These are your entry points to AOL's list of newsgroups.

Figure 5-5: The Add Newsgroups and Search All Newsgroups buttons allow you to perform online searches of the more than 20,000 newsgroups available worldwide.

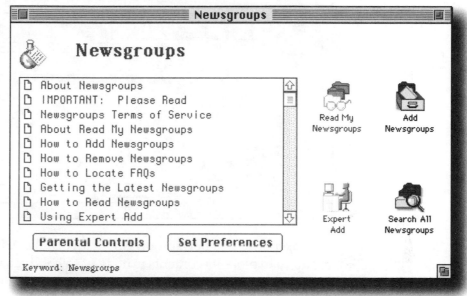

The Add Newsgroups button doesn't perform a search per se; it's more like navigating through a number of menus (Figure 5-6). Its most useful feature is its ability to display actual messages from within a newsgroup without your having to subscribe to the newsgroup itself.

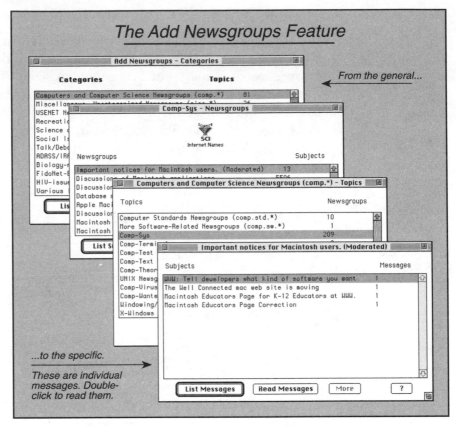

Figure 5-6: The Add Newsgroups feature allows you to peek at a group's messages without having to add the group to your list.

Subscribing to a newsgroup isn't irrevocable. Adding a newsgroup to explore its contents is no way to conduct a scouting expedition, however. Think about it: to explore a newsgroup by adding it, you first have to add a newsgroup to your list, read a message or two, then remove the group from your list when you decide it's not to your liking. The Add Newsgroups feature eliminates the need to go through those hassles for each sampling.

Instead, you can search the list using the Search All Newsgroups button pictured in Figure 5-5. This button leads to a searchable online database of newsgroups that's not only complete but also remarkably fast (Figure 5-7).

Figure 5-7: The Search All Newsgroups button allows you to conduct an online search for newsgroups that interest you.

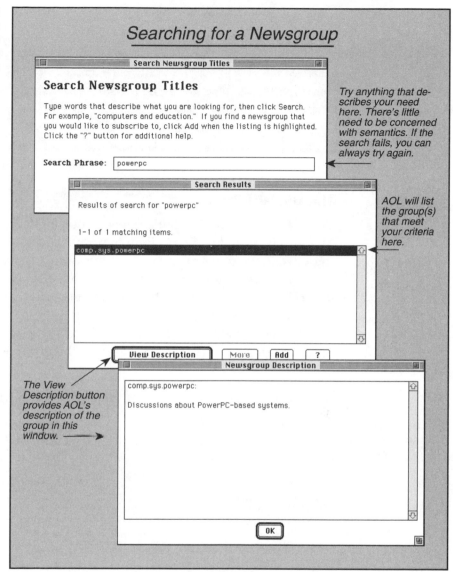

Searching for a Newsgroup

**Search Newsgroup Titles**

Type words that describe what you are looking for, then click Search. For example, "computers and education." If you find a newsgroup that you would like to subscribe to, click Add when the listing is highlighted. Click the "?" button for additional help.

**Search Phrase:** powerpc

*Try anything that describes your need here. There's little need to be concerned with semantics. If the search fails, you can always try again.*

**Search Results**

Results of search for "powerpc"

1-1 of 1 matching items.

comp.sys.powerpc

*AOL will list the group(s) that meet your criteria here.*

**View Description**    More    Add    ?

*The View Description button provides AOL's description of the group in this window.*

**Newsgroup Description**

comp.sys.powerpc:

Discussions about PowerPC-based systems.

OK

**Follow the scent**

The Search All Newsgroups feature stops short of offering individual messages for browsing, however. You might try using the Search All Newsgroups button to find the name of a specific newsgroup or two, then use the Add Newsgroups button to sniff out individual messages before actually adding them to your list. No better strategy exists for the newshound on the scent of a hot group.

## The USENET list

The list of currently available newsgroups (actually, there are several of them) is posted periodically in a number of newsgroups, including **news.lists**, **news.groups**, **news.announce.newusers**, **news.announce.newgroups**, and **news.answers**. The newsgroup that reliably includes all of the lists is **news.answers**. If that group isn't already on your personal list, add it then search for the "List of Active Newsgroups" (something you will have to do by just scrolling through subjects of the messages in the group—see Figure 5-8).

Figure 5-8: The List of Active Newsgroups appears regularly in the **news.answers** newsgroup.

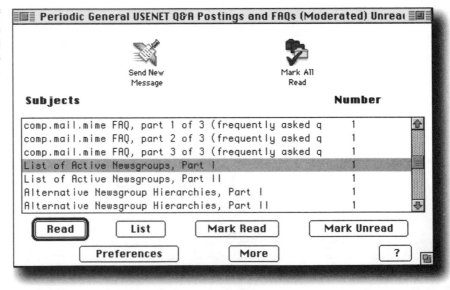

## Logging Messages

Many of us prefer to log our newsgroup messages, then read and reply to them offline.
This is especially true for lengthy messages such as the newsgroups list mentioned in
the text. The AOL software offers a feature, called *logging*, that suits this purpose well.
To log a newsgroup session, choose Logs from the File menu and follow the sequence
for opening a log file illustrated in Figure 5-9. Once the file is opened, each newsgroup
message (actually, any article you read online) will be logged—recorded in the file
you opened. You must cause each message to appear on the screen, but you don't need
to read the messages online; you don't even need to scroll them to the end.

Figure 5-9:
Choose Logs
from the File
menu to log
newgroups
messages.

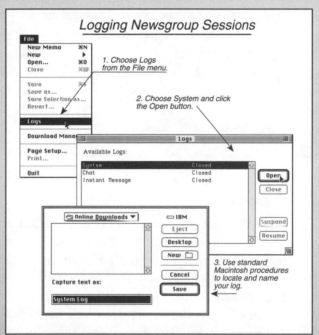

When you've read all the messages that interest you, choose Logs again from the
File menu, then close the log file before you sign off.

After you've signed off, choose Open from the File menu and open the log file
(unless you changed it, the log file will be named System Log, with the date appended).
Now you can read your newsgroup messages at your leisure: the clock's not running.
You can choose New from the File menu, if you wish, and compose replies in the new
document. When you sign back on, you can post your replies by copying and pasting
them into newsgroups reply windows. We discuss posting and replying to messages
later in this chapter.

## Adding newsgroups to your list

Over time you'll add and remove newsgroups from your personal list. A few will remain, but others will come and go. Newsgroups are like friends and acquaintances in that way. Some will remain on your list indefinitely: they're the friends. Others will drift in and out of your life: they're acquaintances. Because of this transience, it's appropriate that we discuss adding and removing newsgroups here.

### A strategy

Before we continue, a word about enthusiasm. Newsgroups are like a quart of ice cream: you're gonna want the whole thing, but that's not necessarily what's best for you. A single, active newsgroup can take 45 minutes out of your day, every day, and bury you with unread messages if you miss two or three days while you're away pursuing your nonvirtual life. If you're subscribing to a newsgroup for the first time, subscribe to only one. Live with it for a couple of days. Then, if you have time for more, subscribe to another. This is the best strategy: one at a time. If you eat all of the chocolates in the bowl at one sitting, you're going to live to regret it.

### Expert add

Now that you've found a newsgroup that piques your interest, add it to your list. You can do this either by using the Add Newsgroups technique I mentioned earlier or by using the Expert Add button. If you already know the name of the newsgroup, however, use the Expert Add feature to add it to your list.

Let's say you're interested in desktop publishing. You've searched the newsgroups and discovered the one you want to try: **comp.text.desktop**. You now want to add it to your list. The sequence discussed below is illustrated in Figure 5-10.

1. With the main Newsgroups window open, click the Expert Add button. The Expert Add window will appear, as shown at the top of Figure 5-10.

2. Type the name of the newsgroup. Capitalization isn't important but spelling and punctuation are. Be exact. **Note:** there are *never* any spaces in a USENET newsgroup name. It's "comp.ai," never "comp. ai."

3. Click the Expert Add window's OK button. A confirmation will appear: OK it as well.

4. Close the Expert Add window and click the button marked Read My Newsgroups in the main Newsgroup window. Your newly added newsgroup will appear; you can read its messages by double-clicking the newsgroup's name.

Figure 5-10: Use the Expert Add process when you already know the names of the newsgroups you want to add.

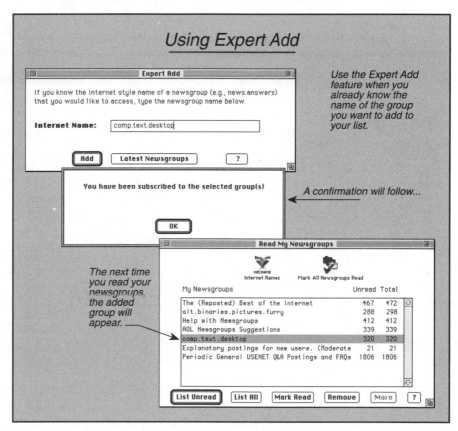

**Internet Names**

If you look again at the bottom window in Figure 5-10 you will see the Internet Names icon. Use this icon whenever you want to see the actual Internet name of any particular newsgroup. The newsgroup discussed in the text appears as **comp.text.desktop**, the proper newsgroup name, in the Read My Newsgroups window. Others are more obtuse: AOL provides descriptive names for some groups, as shown in Figure 5-10. To see the Internet-style names of your newsgroups, click the Internet Names button that's also pictured in Figure 5-10. You can choose between English-style or Internet-style newsgroup names in your Read My Newsgroups window by setting a preference. (Preferences are discussed throughout this chapter.)

### Reading messages

Once you've added a newsgroup to your list, you'll probably want to read its messages. Though a moment ago I suggested that you double-click the **comp.text.desktop** newsgroup's name to read it, this might not be your best strategy.

Note that the group has 320 messages, of which 320 are unread (which is appropriate: I just added the group to my list). If I simply double-click the group's name, I'm going to see the first thread (more about threads later) of those 320 messages, which will probably be a couple of months old. Moreover, even after I read the first message of that thread I'll still have 319 remaining to be read.

### Mark All Read

Starting a newsgroup journey with 320 unread messages is like starting with "Abalone" in your cookbook when what you really want to look up is the recipe for "Zucchini." Under these conditions you might consider eliminating those unread messages and waiting a day for new ones to appear, then start reading the newsgroup. Look again at the lower window in Figure 5-10. There's an icon marked Mark All Newsgroups Read there, and it appears to be just what you're looking for.

*Watch out!* The Mark All Newsgroups Read button in the Read My Newsgroups window updates all messages in *all your newsgroups* as read. This is rarely your intention.

*Note:* I call the Mark All Newsgroups Read button the "vacation button." When I'm away from my newsgroups for a period of time, the quantity of messages that accumulates is overwhelming. Catching up with my mail is difficult enough: catching up with my newsgroup messages seems downright hopeless. That's when I use this button. It's a bit like cutting in line, but who's to reprimand you for it?

Instead, double-click the newsgroup's name to produce that group's window (see Figure 5-11), *then* click the button marked Mark All Read. (Note the syntax: one button is labeled Mark All *Newsgroups* Read; the other is labeled Mark All Read—it's subtle, but it makes a difference.) AOL will then update all of the messages as read *in that newsgroup only.* This is usually your intention.

Figure 5-11: Updating all messages in a specific newsgroup as read.

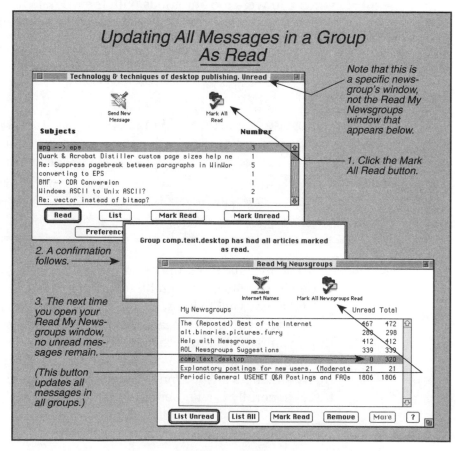

### Mark Read/Unread

Look again at the top window in Figure 5-11 and note the Mark Read and Mark Unread buttons there. These buttons are similar to the e-mail buttons with the same names.

The *Mark Read* button simply removes a message from your list of unread messages, without your having to actually read it. This is especially convenient when you encounter your favorite newsgroup's monthly FAQ posting and you know the FAQ by heart (perhaps you're the one who wrote it!). You don't want to spend time online receiving the FAQ just to get it off your unread list, so you simply click Mark Read and *poof!* it's gone.

The *Mark Unread* button applies to those occasions when you read a message and want to read it again the next time you sign on, or when you were too ambitious with the Mark Read button. When you click it, Mark Unread simply places the selected message back on your list of unread messages.

### List all

Updating a group's messages as read or marking a specific message as read doesn't eliminate the marked messages forever. You can always read old newsgroup messages—whether you've read them or not—by clicking the List All button pictured at the bottom of Figure 5-11.

Clicking this button will produce every message AOL is holding for that newsgroup, regardless of whether it's read or unread.

All of this talk about updating unread messages may give you the wrong impression. Though I'll mention it again in a few pages, you should always get to know a newsgroup before posting a message of your own there. If that means reading 320 messages, then read them. But if you're in no hurry to post, take your time, get a fresh start and become acquainted with your newsgroup at a leisurely pace. Haste rarely enhances any journey. To quote Robert Louis Stevenson, "To travel hopefully is a far better thing than to arrive."

### Reading the header

I include this section for the incurably curious reader. Reading headers is like reading the ingredients list on a bottle of aspirin. You really don't have to do it, but if you're one who indulges in fine print, here's your pharmacopoeia. Refer to Figure 5-12 as we discuss headers.

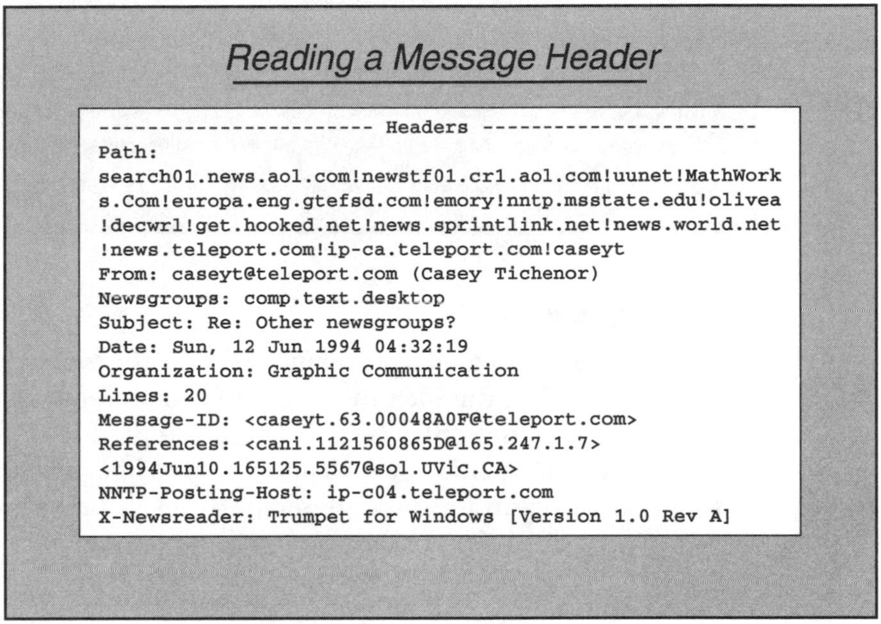

Figure 5-12: A typical newsgroup message header.

## Reading a Message Header

```
---------------------- Headers ----------------------
Path:
search01.news.aol.com!newstf01.cr1.aol.com!uunet!MathWork
s.Com!europa.eng.gtefsd.com!emory!nntp.msstate.edu!olivea
!decwrl!get.hooked.net!news.sprintlink.net!news.world.net
!news.teleport.com!ip-ca.teleport.com!caseyt
From: caseyt@teleport.com (Casey Tichenor)
Newsgroups: comp.text.desktop
Subject: Re: Other newsgroups?
Date: Sun, 12 Jun 1994 04:32:19
Organization: Graphic Communication
Lines: 20
Message-ID: <caseyt.63.00048A0F@teleport.com>
References: <cani.1121560865D@165.247.1.7>
<1994Jun10.165125.5567@sol.UVic.CA>
NNTP-Posting-Host: ip-c04.teleport.com
X-Newsreader: Trumpet for Windows [Version 1.0 Rev A]
```

**A matter of preference**

Headers, it seems, are like dinner salads: some prefer them first, some prefer them with the main course, and others prefer them not at all. Like a good restaurant, AOL recognizes our idiosyncrasies and leaves the matter up to us. Though the newsgroups preferences are discussed later in this chapter, take a moment to review Figure 5-1 and note the Set Preferences button there. Among other things, this control allows you to determine the placement of your newsgroup message header: above the message, below the message, or not at all.

You should begin by placing the headers at the top. Don't spend a lot of time reading them, but once you get used to the style of these headers, try placing them at the bottom of the messages, or not using them at all. Header placement is a matter of preference, after all, but not until you've sampled each of the alternatives.

### The path

Newsgroup messages bounce all over the Net before arriving at AOL. The path identifies the route taken for a particular message to get from the source (which appears at the end of the path statement) to the destination (which appears at the beginning). Intermediary networks and routers are separated by exclamation points (!). (Reading paths is for the esoterically disadvantaged.)

### From

Here's the sender's e-mail address. Most newsreader software also posts the sender's real name (in parentheses) as well, a pleasant courtesy. AOL posts your screen name here when you originate a message. The From: line is repeated at the top of AOL's presentation of the message.

### Newsgroups

This one is worth checking out. Most newsreader software allows senders to post to multiple newsgroups, and if they do, the Newsgroups line will identify all the groups to which the message was posted. At the moment, responding with a flame to a message that has been posted in 20 newsgroups will *not* flame all 20 newsgroups, but AOL is considering a "cross posting" feature, and when the feature is in place, you could torch USENET like a Luddite torching looms in Nottinghamshire. Regardless of whether AOL adds the cross-posting feature, it's always best to know which newsgroups are involved whenever you read a posted message.

### Subject

This line is also repeated at the top of the message. If there's a Re: ahead of it, it's a response to a prior message.

### Date/time

Also posted at the beginning of the message. Times are local to the organization that maintains the connection to USENET—AOL in our case.

### Organization

The name of the organization with which the sender is affiliated. This is an optional header item and may not appear in all messages.

### Lines

The length of the message. This information indirectly identifies the length of the message, thus AOL also posts it at the top of the message. This is an optional header item and may not appear in all messages.

### Message-ID

Message ID's are unique. Use this ID when you're replying to the message. We'll discuss replying later in this chapter.

### References

If the post is in response to another post, the ID of the message that provoked the response is identified here. This is an optional header item and may not appear in all messages.

### NNTP-Posting-Host

This is the USENET posting host where the message originated. This is an optional header item and may not appear in all messages.

### X-Newsreader

This is the software the poster used to originate the message. This is an optional header item and may not appear in all messages.

### Reading the thread

Whenever someone responds to a message, the message and its response form the beginning of a *thread*. Some threads can become quite lengthy, composed of scores of messages. By threading messages, AOL's newsgroup software eliminates the need to sift through hundreds of messages, looking for a response (if one exists) to a particular posting. Threading not only tells you if any responses exist, it also gathers the original and all of the responses together, regardless of how much they may be separated by time or distance. It's easy to tell if a thread exists for any particular message: just look at the Number column of the group's window (see the top window in Figure 5-13). If the number exceeds 1, you're seeing a thread.

Once you open a message, AOL takes additional measures to be sure you don't lose your way among the threads. The "counter" that's visible in Figure 5-13's lower three windows tells you not only which message you're reading within the newsgroup but which message you're reading within a thread as well.

Figure 5-13: Observe the onscreen information when you're reading threads.

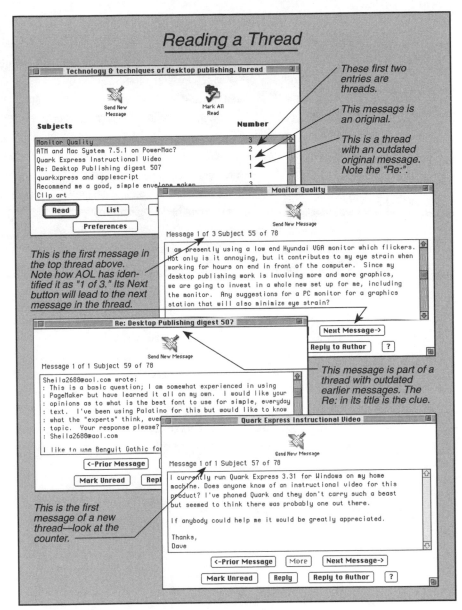

**Reading a Thread**

Technology & techniques of desktop publishing. Unread

Send New Message    Mark All Read

| Subjects | Number |
|---|---|
| Monitor Quality | 3 |
| ATM and Mac System 7.5.1 on PowerMac? | 2 |
| Quark Express Instructional Video | 1 |
| Re: Desktop Publishing digest 507 | 1 |
| quarkxpress and applescript | 1 |
| Recommend me a good, simple envelope maker | 3 |
| Clip art | |

Read    List    Preferences

These first two entries are threads.

This message is an original.

This is a thread with an outdated original message. Note the "Re:".

**Monitor Quality**

Send New Message

Message 1 of 3 Subject 55 of 78

I am presently using a low end Hyundai VGA monitor which flickers. Not only is it annoying, but it contributes to my eye strain when working for hours on end in front of the computer. Since my desktop publishing work is involving more and more graphics, we are going to invest in a whole new set up for me, including the monitor. Any suggestions for a PC monitor for a graphics station that will also minimize eye strain?

Next Message->
Reply to Author    ?

This is the first message in the top thread above. Note how AOL has identified it as "1 of 3." Its Next button will lead to the next message in the thread.

This message is part of a thread with outdated earlier messages. The Re: in its title is the clue.

**Re: Desktop Publishing digest 507**

Send New Message

Message 1 of 1 Subject 59 of 78

Sheila2688@aol.com wrote:
: This is a basic question; I am somewhat experienced in using
: PageMaker but have learned it all on my own. I would like your
: opinions as to what is the best font to use for simple, everyday
: text. I've been using Palatino for this but would like to know
: what the "experts" think, even
: topic. Your response please?
: Sheila2688@aol.com

I like to use Benguit Gothic for

<-Prior Message
Mark Unread    Repl

**Quark Express Instructional Video**

Send New Message

Message 1 of 1 Subject 57 of 78

I currently run Quark Express 3.31 for Windows on my home machine. Does anyone know of an instructional video for this product? I've phoned Quark and they don't carry such a beast but seemed to think there was probably one out there.

If anybody could help me it would be greatly appreciated.

Thanks,
Dave

<-Prior Message    More    Next Message->
Mark Unread    Reply    Reply to Author    ?

This is the first message of a new thread—look at the counter.

**Delayed responses**

With more than 20,000 newsgroups on the Net, megabytes of messages are generated each day. In the interest of storage space, each newsgroup site establishes a time limit on the retention of USENET messages. At the moment, AOL's limit is about 30 days—one of the most generous on the Net. Occasionally, however, someone working at a site that's even more generous will post a response to a message that's beyond AOL's message-retention time limit. More often, a thread will exceed two months' duration. In either case, the original message will no longer be found on AOL's disks.

   When this happens, a response will appear as an original message. These situations are easy to identify: just look for the prefix Re: (for regarding) ahead of the message. Typically, the message that started the thread will be quoted in the response, so catching up with the thread won't be a problem.

Unfortunately, it's easy to lose track of a thread when you're reading newsgroup messages. You read the first message, then click the Next Message button, then read a few more, clicking the Next Message button in between each one. When you've finished the thread, however, the Next Message button remains active. When you've read all of the messages in a thread, the Next Message button indicates the availability of the next message in the newsgroup, not the next message in the thread. If you're not watching the counter or the message titles, this can become confusing.

### Kill lists

Eventually, AOL will offer a feature that allows you to exclude messages from people you specify, or exclude messages with certain words or phrases in their subject lines. This feature has been a tradition for a long time on the USENET, where it's known as a "kill list."

The nomenclature aside, kill lists aren't as discriminatory as you might think (though they can certainly be used that way). A number of newsgroups use subject-line codes to identify the content of threads. The newsgroup **rec.arts.tv.soaps**, for example, uses the abbreviation DOOL for "Days of our Lives," and GH for "General Hospital." If you're not a "General Hospital" fan, include "GH" in your kill list and exclude General Hospital threads from your reading list. Newsgroups with conventions such as this regularly post announcements identifying the kill codes and their meanings.

You can get a peek at AOL's kill feature—even before it's introduced—by clicking the Preference button in any newsgroup's window (Figure 5-11's top window is an example). Note that kill lists are associated with specific newsgroups, not USENET as a whole. You can have (and will want) different kill lists for different groups.

## Posting messages

For the most part, people are attracted to the Internet because of its dialog. The Internet isn't the morning newspaper, news on the hour, or even "General Hospital." The Internet not only encourages dialog; when it comes to newsgroups, it *is* dialog. It stands to reason, then, that you can post your own messages to newsgroups as well as read those posted by others.

## FAQs

Before you litter the USENET with your comments, however, you'd best get to know the natives. And in most newsgroups, the natives are singularly intolerant of redundancy.

Imagine yourself as a member of the newsgroup **alt.devilbunnies**, fighting imaginary bunny rabbits who kill people and eat their victims' toes. (I'm not making this up: **alt.devilbunnies** *does* exist, and eating toes is what the bunnies do.)

Each day, two or three messages interrupt your thread with the question, "What's a Fudd?" Over time, your limits of patience may be reached. You might become tempted to eat *their* toes.

The answer is a FAQ: a list of Frequently Asked Questions (see Figure 5-14). Many newsgroups post them; if your newsgroup offers one, you should read it before you post to that group.

Figure 5-14: A number of FAQs appear regularly in the **news.answers** newsgroup. Search here before posting.

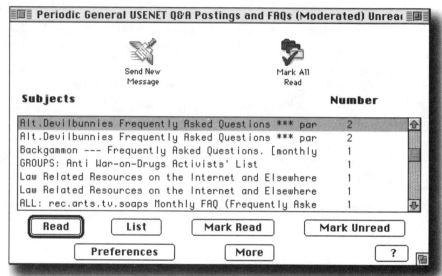

FAQs are usually re-posted every couple of months or so—more frequently for large active groups. Though each newsgroup posts its own FAQ within the group periodically, the mother lode of FAQs is the **news.answers** newsgroup pictured in Figure 5-14. If AOL hasn't already done so for you, join **news.answers** (AOL may title it "Periodic General USENET Q&A Postings and FAQs") and search it (in its entirety, which will take a while) for a FAQ relating to any newsgroup to which you intend to post. Failure to do so will result in flames capable of incinerating cement.

**FTP is better**

The best way to find FAQs is via FTP. Most of the published FAQs are stored at **rtfm.mit.edu**, an FTP site that AOL mirrors (stores locally). The process of downloading a FAQ is demonstrated in Chapter 9 (see Figure 9-17); FTP is discussed in Chapter 7, "Getting the Goods."

## Responding

Newsgroup discussions are impulsive things. When we're compelled to respond to a posting, we usually want to do so *right now*. This is good: it provokes a conversational exchange, a colloquial alternative to the formality of e-mail.

As you might expect, AOL offers a "right now" feature—the Reply button pictured in Figure 5-15.

Figure 5-15: The Reply button is the easy way to respond to a newsgroup posting.

```
┌────────────────────────────────────────────────────────┐
│ □          Good book for PHOTOSHOP                   ⌐│
│                                                          │
│                        Send New Message                  │
│  Message 1 of 2   Subject 42 of 68                       │
│  ┌────────────────────────────────────────────────┐ ▲  │
│  │ I've checked the FAQ's, etc., and didn't see any  │    │
│  │ recommendations for good photoshop books.         │    │
│  │                                                    │    │
│  │ What are the best books on 3.0, specifically for  │    │
│  │ the Mac?                                           │    │
│  │ If you didn't have a single one, which one would  │    │
│  │ you get first?                                     │    │
│  │                                                    │    │
│  │ I'm looking for one that is covers the basics, but│    │
│  │ also goes into depth on most subjects. Although I │    │
│  │ don't know a lot of photoshop techniques,         │    │
│  │ I know the Mac inside and out, and I've spent a   │    │
│  │ lot of time using                                  │ ▼  │
│  └────────────────────────────────────────────────┘    │
│      [ <-Prior Message ]  [ More ]  [ Next Message-> ]  │
│                                                          │
│   [ Mark Unread ]  [ Reply ]  [ Reply to Author ]  [ ? ]│
└────────────────────────────────────────────────────────┘
```

The Reply button semi-automates the process of replying to a newsgroup article by filling in the Send To: and Subject: fields for you (see Figure 5-16).

Figure 5-16: The Response form appears when you click the Reply button.

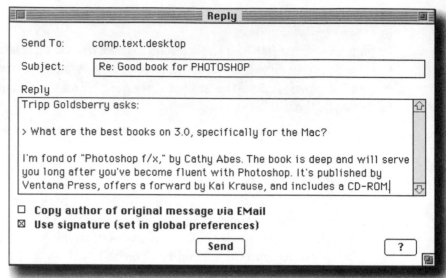

🔺 Your response will be offered to all of USENET, available to all who subscribe to that newsgroup. Your response will not be sent as e-mail to the individual to whom you're responding. (I'll discuss replying by mail later in this chapter.)

🔺 Word your text appropriately, be succinct, and be prepared to back up any claims you make.

🔺 It is customary to quote the text that provoked your response (see the "Quoter" sidebar that follows). Don't overdo it however: quote only the salient portions of the original message.

## Quoter

Newsgroup response postings are traditionally preceded by the text that provoked the response. Over the years, a convention has developed whereby each line of the quoted text is preceded by a greater-than sign (>). This means, however, that you must break each line of the quoted text manually, and insert the > sign as well—a laborious process at best.

Enter Quoter, a nifty little piece of freeware that does the job for you (shown in Figure 5-17).

Figure 5-17: Quoter takes the drudgery out of quoting USENET articles.

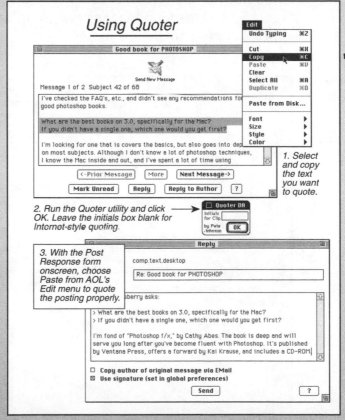

Quoter was developed by Pete Johnson just for occasions such as this. It hardly takes up any memory, it's perfectly compatible with your AOL software, and, best of all, it's free. Use the keyword: FileSearch, then search using the criterion: Quoter. Documentation is included with the software.

While it's customary to quote when you're responding, it's not customary to quote using AOL's traditional << quote quote quote >> format. The Internet has developed its own format (with the > sign at the beginning of each line) and newsgroups are a part of the Internet. Therefore, the use of Quoter or something similar is highly recommended. Whatever method you use, be consistent.

### Posting with a new subject

Not all of your posts will be responses. You may come up with a subject of your own and begin a new thread. For this purpose, AOL offers either of the two Send New Message buttons pictured in Figure 5-18. One's found in the newsgroup's window; the other appears in every message window.

Figure 5-18: Use the Send New Message button to post a message that's not a response.

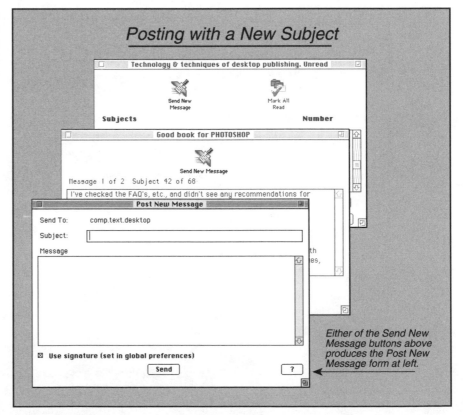

⚠ Stay on the subject addressed by the group. Don't post a Macintosh hardware question, for instance, in the **comp.os.mac.apps** newsgroup. Instead, use **comp.os.mac.hardware**.

⚠ Use a descriptive Subject line. Subject lines such as "Me too" rarely inspire attention.

*Tip: I always complete the Message field first then go back to fill in the Subject field. It seems there's always a phrase I can pluck from the message that serves well as a subject, but I never consider it until I complete the message itself.*

⚠ *No commercials!* Commercial activity on the USENET is one of the most controversial topics out there. Originally, USENET was noncommercial to the core.

Although some accommodation to commercial activity has been made recently, the vast majority of newsgroups neither want nor appreciate commercial activity. As a responsible citizen of USENET, you should honor these guidelines. Where are the guidelines? Read the FAQs.

⚠ Need I mention chain letters? They're as out of place on the Net as they are in the U.S. Mail, where they're against the law.

⚠ Sign your message. No one likes to scroll up (or down) to the header to find your name or e-mail address. Use your full real name, not just your screen name. (See the "Signatures" sidebar for more about signing messages.)

**Signatures**

You'll usually see a signature at the end of a newsgroup posting. Most newsgroup software (including AOL's) automates the process of including one. A signature is a short (four lines or fewer, ideally) disclaimer at the end of a message identifying the sender, the sender's affiliation (all of the early Netters were associated with some military or educational institution, you'll remember), and the sender's e-mail address(es).

Here are some signature pointers:

- Cook up a signature for yourself. Spend some time at it, but don't make it too flashy. Signatures people appreciate the most are succinct and informative.
- Be sure to include your real name as well as your screen name in its Internet format (with **@aol.com**).
- Once you have a signature you like, use the keyword: Newsgroups and click the Set Preferences button in the main Newsgroups window (review Figure 5-1). Place your signature in the box at the bottom of the Preferences window.
- If alignment is important, use a word processor to format your signature using Courier or some other monospaced font where all of the characters are the same width. Once you have the layout you want, select and copy your signature, use the keyword: Newsgroups, click the Set Preferences button, then *paste* your signature in the box at the bottom of the Preferences window.
- Turn on the Use Signature feature shown at the bottom of Figure 5-17 and Figure 5-18. Use your signature for all of your postings.

**Posting anonymously**

There may be occasions when you want to post a message to a newsgroup (or receive replies) anonymously. Interestingly, there is no built-in way to do this on the Net. Instead, you must employ the services of one of the anonymous servers offered. "Employ," I suppose, is a poor choice of words, as these servers rarely charge anything for their services.

The **anon.penet.fi** anonymous server is the best known and most frequently used of the genre. Upon request, the server automatically allocates an ID for you. You may then use this ID in all your subsequent anonymous posts or mailings, and any mail sent to your anonymous address gets redirected to your real address.

In the anonymization process all headers indicating the true originator are removed, and an attempt is made to remove any automatically included signatures as well.

To find out more, send e-mail to **daemon@anon.penet.fi** with the word *help* in the message field.

## When e-mail makes more sense

Whenever you're about to respond to a newsgroup article, ask yourself: "Would e-mail be better?" Many replies are better suited to e-mail. Not that they contain sensitive material or personal information (although they may). The argument for e-mailed replies is usually more mundane than that: many replies are simply questions, requests, advice, suggestions or just hellos. The point is, don't clutter the Net with material that's best relegated to e-mail.

Think of talk radio: would you rather your comment be broadcast to a vast audience, or would a phone call serve the purpose more effectively?

To reply to the author of a newsgroup posting, click the Reply to Author button pictured in Figure 5-19.

Figure 5-19: The Reply
to Author button is
often a more
appropriate alternative
than posting a reply to
the entire newsgroup.

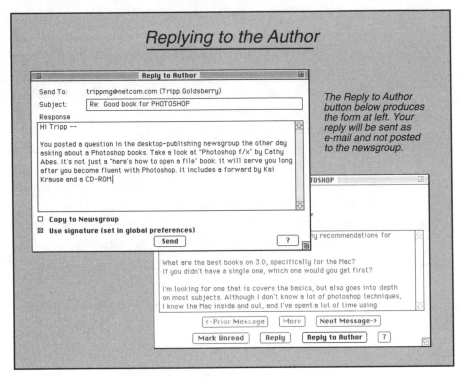

## Binaries

The newsgroup is a textual medium. Nontextual data—programs, spreadsheets, graphics, sounds—won't transfer from one machine to another via newsgroups without some uncommon maneuvering.

Impetus for the transfer of nontextual (binary) data arose early in the history of the USENET. In its early days, many (perhaps most) of the machines on the Net ran the UNIX operating system, and UNIX programmers wanted to exchange UNIX files with one another. For many of them, newsgroups were their only common link.

Though things have changed—UNIX isn't as dominant as it once was—the need to exchange binary information with other people on the Internet has not, and for many of those people, e-mail and newsgroups are their only common access to the Net.

Enter *uuencoding*: the conversion of binary information to textual data and back again. The term stands for *UNIX-to-UNIX encoding*, but it's used by all systems now. Uuencoding is how binary information—graphics in particular—is shared via newsgroups.

## Decoding binaries

Decoding uuencoded material can be a monumental task. Not only must binary postings be decoded but because many of them are posted in multiple segments, these segments must first be concatenated (combined) before they can be decoded. Once decoding is complete, the data must be displayed (or heard, if sound is involved, or run, if the binary is a program).

None of which should concern you. Your AOL software not only decodes uuencoded newsgroup postings, it also concatenates *and displays* them (or plays them, if they're sound or video). All you have to do is watch. Refer to Figures 5-20, 5-21 and 5-22 as we examine the process, step by step.

Figure 5-20: Selecting a binary posting for download.

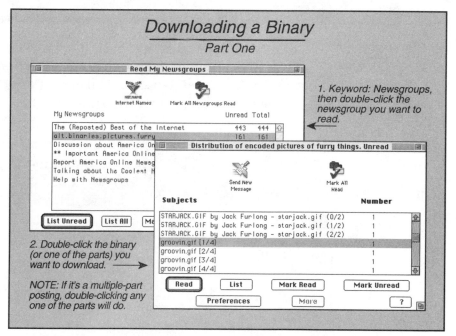

▲ Note the appearance of the binary postings in Figure 5-20. The files are listed with DOS-style filenames, including the filename extension. The extension identifies the file's format (GIF, in this case). These aren't really filenames at all, they're the Subject line of the post, thus they're the poster's doing. Observe the protocol for a while before you post your own material: the format of the Subject line, in particular, is important.

⚠ Note also that the Subject lines for the postings displayed in
Figure 5-20 indicate that these are multiple-part postings, the
total number of parts for each image, and which part each
posting represents. (Part one of four is indicated [1/4]; part
two is [2/4], and so on.)

**Help with binaries**

Note the "Help with USENET encoded-binary files" newsgroup in the Read My Newsgroups window pictured in Figure 5-20. This is a local newsgroup (it only appears on
AOL; its Internet-style name is **aol.newsgroups.help.binaries**) and it's patrolled by
the Internet Connection's CyberJockeys. If you have any trouble with encoded files, this
is the first place to visit.

As the text within Figure 5-20 indicates, it makes no difference
which part of a multiple-part posting you select first: if you choose
to download the file, AOL will find all of the parts, then concatenate
and decode the posting without your intervention.

Figure 5-21: The
automatic-detection
process.

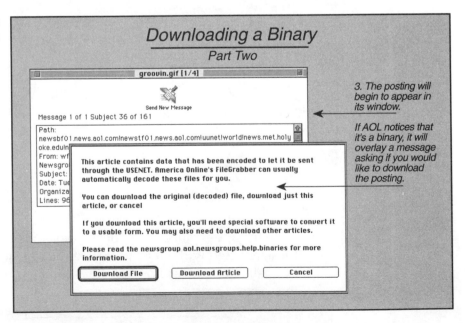

In the background, whenever AOL feeds a USENET posting to
you, it looks at the posting's content and attempts to find a binary

header. This is typically a single line appearing near the top of the message that reads "begin 644 xxxxxxxx.xxx" (the number is not always 644, and the x's represent the file's name and extension). If AOL finds a binary header, the overlay you see pictured in Figure 5-21 appears.

If you click the Download File button, AOL will search the newsgroup for all of the parts of the file (assuming it's a multiple-part posting), download the postings into AOL's machines, decode the posting, and feed the file (not the postings) to your machine. It will also display the file, if it's in a format that AOL can display. (The display feature is optional and can be suppressed: read the Preferences appendix in this book for more.)

If you click the Download Article button, AOL will download the individual posting (not all of the parts) onto your hard disk. You will have to repeat the process for each of the remaining parts if it's a multiple-part posting.

If you click the Cancel button, the overlay will disappear and you'll see the first 1,000 bytes of the post.

Figure 5-22: The download commences and the graphic is saved and displayed.

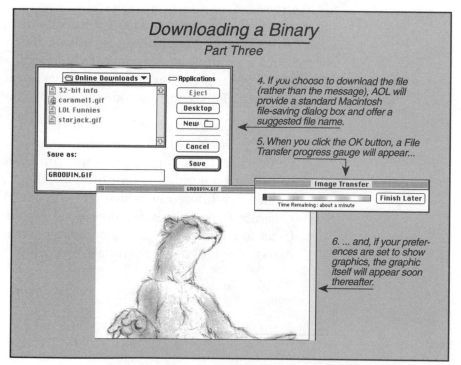

Note that the graphic is both displayed *and saved* during the process illustrated in Figure 5-22. You will be able to close the graphic's window and open the file later, using either the AOL software or any other software that's appropriate for the binary's format.

⚠ Note also that the Finish Later button is available in the center window in Figure 5-22. If you intend to download a number of postings during a particular session, consider this option. When you've finished the session—but before you sign off—choose Download Manager from the File menu, *then* download the files. AOL will download—as a batch—all of the files you've marked for downloading later. This it can do unattended or even in the background as you read your mail or browse the Web. The Download Manager is discussed in Chapter 9.

## When things go wrong

The binary decoding/viewing/saving process doesn't always work as described here. Binaries are posted by people on the Internet, and the Internet embraces a wide range of people—especially in terms of experience. Some binary postings, in other words, might be corrupted, and when they are, the fault is usually the fault of the person who did the posting. So you're going to have to engage in a little damage control. Following are some typical problems and solutions.

⚠ The most common error is a *missing part* of a multiple-part posting. This is usually caused by mismatched subject lines. In Figure 5-23, for example, note that both **threesom.gif** and **saltlick.gif** are multiple-part files, but their Subject lines are capitalized differently, which will cause AOL's software to generate an error. *Solution*: download the postings as messages (refer to Figure 5-21 again, if necessary), then concatenate and decode the files using third-party software.

Figure 5-23: Mismatched subject lines in multiple-part postings will trigger an error when you're trying to download the postings as files.

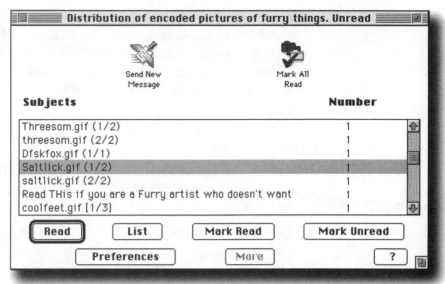

 What's the best third-party software? Check with the CyberJockeys in the **aol.newsgroups.help.binaries** newsgroup. They're always familiar with the latest software for this purpose.

 You'll occasionally run across a binary with a *missing binary header*. As I mentioned earlier, the binary header is usually a single line within the message body that reads "begin nnn xxxxxxxx.xxx" (where "nnn" is a three-digit number, and the x-ed portion is the filename and filename extension). If that line is missing, your AOL software won't recognize the posting as a binary and won't offer to download it. No error message will appear. *Solution*: you can try to read the message normally, then choose Save from the File menu and save the message on your hard disk. Once you're offline, you can open the file, add a header yourself (just above the first coded line in the message), resave the message, then use third-party software to decode the file. The header should have been added automatically, however, so the remainder of the message is probably corrupt as well. The corruption probably occurred at the poster's end, and there's not much you can do about that.

⚠️ The most frustrating error is a *corrupted file*. A corrupted GIF graphic will sometimes appear with repeated parts of the image, or bands of the image shifted right or left, or colored bands running across the image. Corrupted files aren't uncommon in the binary newsgroups, and there's not much you can do about them.

## Posting binaries

Naturally, you can post binaries as well as receive them. You will have to use software other than AOL's to encode the file, however. Here are brief step-by-step instructions:

⚠️ Spend some time downloading and decoding binaries before you post any of your own. USENET is particularly intolerant of people who post binaries without first becoming familiar with the medium. In this way, posting binaries is a bit like learning to drive a car: you wouldn't venture out in traffic alone without first observing others, would you?

⚠️ Obtain suitable encoding software. Encoding software will take any binary file on your hard disk (graphics, sound, video) and convert it to an encoded text file suitable for posting in a newsgroup. The software should be able to create multiple-part text files.

**UULite**

As I write this, the most popular Macintosh software for encoding and decoding USENET binaries is UULite, by Jeff Strobel. UULite is shareware and it's capable of concatenating, decoding, and encoding binary files. To obtain your copy of UULite, go online and use keyword: FileSearch to conduct a file search. Specify "UULite and Strobel" (without the quotation marks) as your search criteria.

By the time you read this, there might be something better. To find out, visit the **aol.newsgroups.help.binaries** newsgroup. Consult the FAQ that's posted there before you post a question.

⚓ Encode your file, using a file limit of no more than 26k by making it AOL compliant (see Figure 5-24). There's a reason for this: many newsgroup readers (AOL's included) simply use the text-editing routines that are built into the Macintosh (TeachText exemplifies these routines). It makes sense: if the text-editing tools are already within Macintosh, why re-invent the wheel? That editor, however, can only handle files up to 28k in size. Strip 2k from that figure to allow for USENET message headers, and you have 26k remaining.

Figure 5-24: UULite's Encoding Preferences window offers an America Online compliant setting.

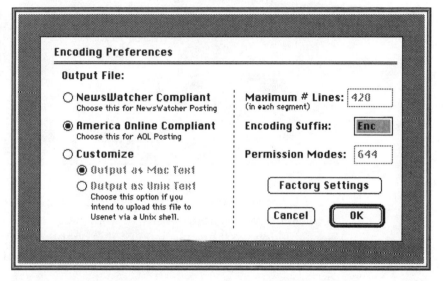

⚓ You will now have a text file (or a series of them) on your disk representing the binary you want to post. Most encoding software will add a filename extension such as ".uue" or ".enc" to the encoded text files and offer the option to add a descriptive phrase ahead of the encoded material (shown in Figure 5-25).

Figure 5-25: Choose a
file for encoding.

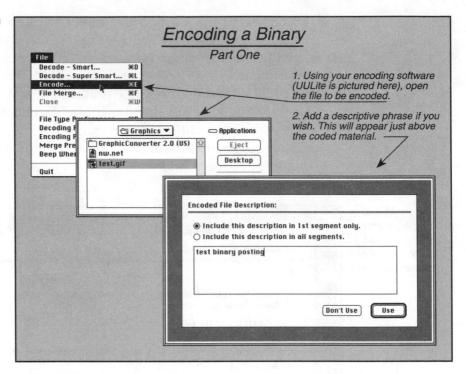

Once you've encoded the file, run your AOL software, sign on, and visit the appropriate newsgroup. The **alt.test** newsgroup (which we'll discuss later in this chapter) is the place to test your wings, and that's what we're showing in Figure 5-26.

Figure 5-26: Select the appropriate newsgroup and prepare to send a new message.

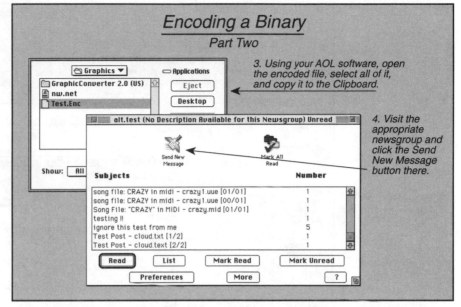

🔊 The actual posting process is as simple as copy-and-paste. Begin by opening the encoded file you created a moment ago, selecting all of it and copying it to the Clipboard. The Select All and Copy commands are under the Edit menu.

🔊 Now click the Send New Message button illustrated in Figure 5-26, and paste the text that's on the Clipboard into the Post New Message form that appears in Figure 5-27.

Figure 5-27: Paste and send the new message. It will appear on the newsgroup later.

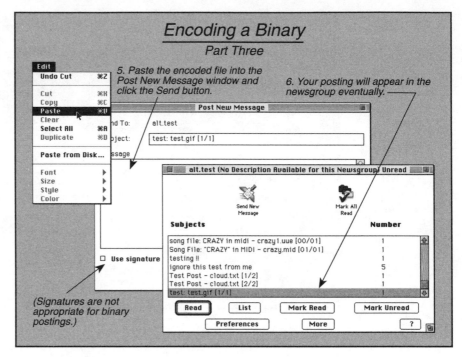

👆 Post the message by clicking the Send button displayed in Figure 5-27.

How soon your message appears in the newsgroup is a matter of network traffic and newsgroup policy. Remember, some newsgroups are moderated, and it might take the moderator a few days to review your submission and add it to those in the newsgroup.

## Parental controls

Newsgroups aren't exempt from aberrance. In fact, when you consider the degree of anonymity and the variety of cultures that are represented on USENET, it's a wonder that routine interchange occurs at all.

All of which is a polite way of saying that there's stuff here that might not be suitable for every user on your account. Rather than censor the Internet, AOL prefers to empower you with *Parental Controls*: the option to declare what portions (if any) of the USENET are available to each of your screen names. It's a just and appropriate strategy: this is a matter of moral sensibility; it's no place for Big Brother, but it *is* a determination that we as individuals should be able to make, should we choose to do so.

### More Parental Controls

Parental controls for USENET are not the only parental controls AOL offers. Other parental controls pertain to AOL on a local (rather than Internet) level, including blocking Instant Messages and selective blocking of AOL's chat rooms. To learn more, use the keyword: Parental Controls.

Parental Controls are the privilege of the person identified as the "master account name"—the account name that you chose when you first signed up with America Online. You, as the master account member, determine how the other members on your account can access USENET, and though the Parental Controls button appears in the Newsgroups window for all users of your account, only the master account name can use it. Only if you're signed on using your master account name will this button lead to the controls pictured in Figure 5-28.

Figure 5-28: Parental Controls provide control over USENET access.

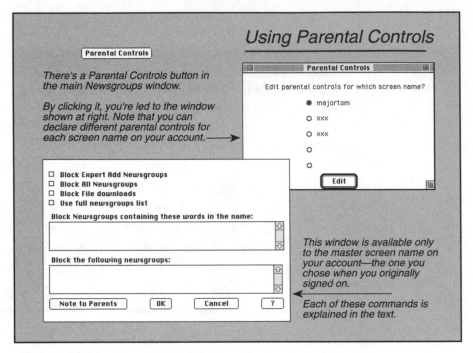

Let's take a moment to examine the options you see displayed in Figure 5-28:

- *Block Expert Add Newsgroups* turns off the Expert Add feature. Expert Add allows members to add newsgroups to their lists by typing or pasting newsgroup names directly into the software (review Figure 5-10). Blocking the Expert Add feature eliminates the potential of adding newsgroups using this technique, no matter how familiar you might be with USENET.

- *Block All Newsgroups* does just what it says. It's extreme but undeniably effective.

- *Block File download* does *not* block the reading or saving of binary postings, but it does disable the AOL software's ability to automatically decode and display binary-encoded graphics. Note that the default setting for account names other than the master is on.

- *Use full newsgroups list* reveals the names of all current newsgroups when the Add Newsgroups button is pressed. As I write this chapter, 138 newsgroup names appear in the alt.sex.* hierarchy when "Use full newsgroups list" is turned on. When the feature is turned off (the default), only two appear.

- *Block Newsgroups containing these words in the name* allows you to identify general categories of newsgroups for exclusion. Blocking newsgroups with the word *alt* in their names, for example, eliminates the entire alt hierarchy.

- *Block following newsgroups* allows you to identify specific newsgroups for exclusion. Remember that new newsgroups are being added to the USENET every day, and that a number of what you might consider to be offensive postings are cross-posted to multiple newsgroups regularly. This control is best used to block a specific newsgroup or two, rather than a category of them.

## Removing a newsgroup from your list

There's a practical limit to the number of newsgroups you'll want to participate in. Time is an important factor: surely you've got a life outside of the Net . . . .

You'll also want to try a "trial subscription" once in a while, and sometimes the trial will prove unfruitful.

No matter what the reason, removing a newsgroup is easy. Simply select (in the Read My Newsgroups window) the newsgroup to be removed (see Figure 5-29), and click the Remove button. AOL will confirm the deletion; when you click OK, the newsgroup will be removed from your list.

Figure 5-29: Removing
a newsgroup from
your list is almost as
easy as changing your
TV channel.

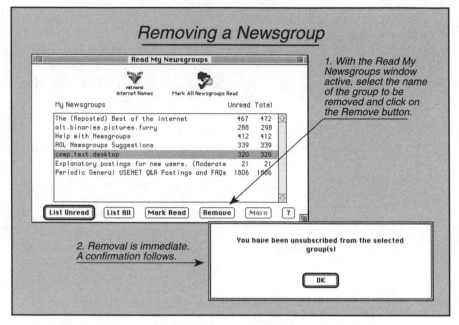

Removing a newsgroup from your list isn't necessarily forever—you can always add it back if you want. If you do, however, be aware that in the process AOL will lose track of the messages you've read. You'll either have to reread all those you've read or use the Mark All Read button pictured in Figures 5-13 and 5-14.

## Testing & getting help

Newsgroup posting is a little like entering a cool pool: some jump right in; others prefer to adjust gradually. (Self-confidence is elusive for some of us.) If you're a member of the latter group, there's help.

### Testing

Most newsgroups, you'll remember, are broadcast throughout the Net. This is not the place to experiment. If you're insecure about your ability to post to a newsgroup, experiment using the **alt.test** or the **aol.newsgroups.test** groups. That's what they're for.

- First you'll have to add the group to your list. Use the Expert Add feature we discussed earlier. Try it with the **alt.test** newsgroup. Once the group is added to your list, double-click its name in the Read My Newsgroups window (see Figure 5-30) and allow its window to open.

- With the **alt.test** group's window active, click the Mark All Read button. Believe me, this is one group you're not going to want to read.

- Now click the Send New Message button and compose a message. Someone might just read it, so keep it simple: the word *test* will do. You might also try out your signature here if you have one. Send the message and sign off.

- After an hour or two, sign back on and read the **alt.test** group. Your message should be there—along with a few others, perhaps—waiting for you.

Once you're confident in your ability to post and read your own messages on USENET, remove the **alt.test** group from your list. Like a bubble bath, it's appropriate at times—but not every day.

Figure 5-30: The **alt.test** newsgroup exists so that you can send test messages through USENET and observe the results.

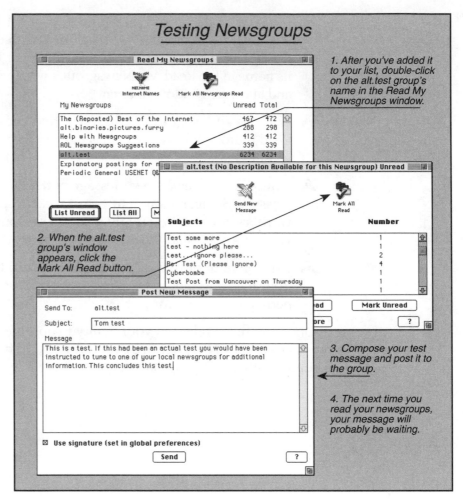

**Testing Newsgroups**

1. After you've added it to your list, double-click on the alt.test group's name in the Read My Newsgroups window.

2. When the alt.test group's window appears, click the Mark All Read button.

3. Compose your test message and post it to the group.

4. The next time you read your newsgroups, your message will probably be waiting.

### Autoresponders

A number of machines constantly monitor the **alt.test** newsgroup for activity, and automatically respond—unless they're instructed to do otherwise—to any test postings to that group. The responses arrive in the form of e-mail.

Consequently, don't be surprised if you receive four or five e-mail messages after you post a test.

Figure 5-31:
A reply from
an auto-
responder at
the University
of Florida in
Gainesville.

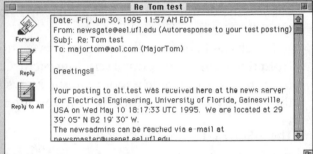

```
                            Re  Tom test
  Date:  Fri, Jun 30, 1995 11:57 AM EDT
  From: newsgate@eel.ufl.edu (Autoresponse to your test posting)
  Subj:  Re: Tom test
  To: majortom@aol.com (MajorTom)

  Greetings!!

  Your posting to alt.test was received here at the news server
  for Electrical Engineering, University of Florida, Gainesville,
  USA on Wed May 10 18:17:33 UTC 1995.  We are located at 29
  39' 05" N 82 19' 30" W.
  The newsadmins can be reached via e-mail at
  newsmaster@usenet.eel.ufl.edu
```

This autoresponder observed my test and sent me the e-mail message in Figure 5-31 soon after I posted my article in the **alt.test** newsgroup. I received similar responses from Switzerland, Israel, Korea, South Africa and lovely Leeds, West Yorkshire, England.

Read these messages: not only will they tell you when and how your message was received (observe the Path statement in the header), but how to suppress the autoresponder's messages in the future.

## Getting help

Help is never far away when you're using newsgroups via AOL. A number of methods are available for accessing help, either from AOL, from other members or from the Internet community at large.

### Online help

Look again at Figure 5-30: Do you see the question-mark buttons? Those little question marks lead to the help files that are stored on AOL's hard disks. Those pictured in Figure 5-30 aren't the only ones: nearly every newsgroup window pictured in this chapter offers a similar question-mark button.

The good news is that because these help files are stored at AOL (and not on your hard disk), they can be changed whenever the Internet staff wants to change them. These help files, in other words, are always reflective of the changes made in response to suggestions from users or changes in the Net itself.

The bad news is that you have to be online to access them, and for that you pay.

Here's a tip: print 'em. Whenever a help window is open, all you have to do is choose Print from the File menu and you'll have a hard copy of the online help file that's currently open. You can print them all in this manner if you like.

**Note:** The help files discussed in this section are also available from the main Newsgroups window pictured in Figure 5-1. They're organized into a single window in the Newsgroups window, so they're easy to access—especially if you intend to print them.

### The USENET Terms of Service

The staff at AOL has prepared an extensive USENET Terms of Service (TOS) document, just for AOL members. It should be required reading before you're allowed to post to newsgroups; but failing that, here's my most adamant request of this chapter: *read that document!!* It could save you from considerable embarrassment down the line.

You can find the USENET TOS in the main Newsgroups window (review Figure 5-1 if necessary) where it's called "Newsgroups Terms of Service." The time spent reading it is free.

### Peer assistance

I'm a firm believer in peer assistance. AOL members are usually your best source of help because they can empathize: they understand your needs. Experts are often too far removed from your situation (and have too many other things to do) to help you the way other members can.

In other words: if you have a question, ask around.

You might start with the Internet Connection message boards. Use the keyword: Internet, then double-click the Internet Connection Message Board listing in the main window. Though the contents of all boards change, this one will no doubt always offer a USENET Newsgroups interest area, where you can post questions and receive replies from others who've experienced a similar situation.

Another source of peer assistance is the Internet Connection's conference room. This is where the Cyberjockeys are stationed, ready to answer your questions in real time. The room isn't available 24 hours a day, however. For the current schedule, use the keyword: Internet and click on the Conference Room button. The conference room isn't staffed 24 hours a day; check with one of the Cyberjockeys for the current schedule.

### aol.newsgroups.help

Finally, be sure to remain subscribed to the **aol.newsgroups.help** newsgroup. This is the most active available location for newsgroup assistance available, and it's local, it's not broadcast throughout the Internet. Your questions are seen only by fellow AOL members and your responses will come from fellow AOL members.

## Netiquette

In her "Dialog Box" column in the August, 1994 issue of Windows magazine, Eileen McCooey makes the following observation about electronic communications: "The timid turn truculent, shrinking violets issue impassioned declarations, and sticklers for propriety show an alarming lack of discretion . . . . Would you commit yourself to paper so cavalierly?"

She's right. Haste seems to be the byword of electronic communications: typos are commonplace, the familiar voice is assumed (no matter how unfamiliar the reader may be), proofreading is anathema.

Nowhere is the etiquette of online conduct more critical (or more abused) than in newsgroups. When a faux pas is committed, it's usually by a newbie—someone like you or me. This is a community, after all: one with a particularly stalwart camaraderie and an intense adherence to an iconoclastic propriety. These folks are a little offbeat, in other words, but so were the Native Americans who used to make a ceremony of giving trout to the first streamlined trains that crossed the country.

The faux pas with Native Americans 250 years ago are legion. A mini-course in netiquette, then, may save us from a return to these bad habits. Here are some pointers that might be of assistance:

- Give back when you take. Newsgroups in particular are a two-way medium. If you download binaries, upload a few. If you read a group regularly, start contributing. Help newbies. The Internet is a community, and it will stay that way as long as we all share.

- There are people on the other end of the line: people with emotions and feelings. Honor them.

- Honor yourself as well. You are known on the Net by what you write. Project the image you want others to see.

- Brevity is admirable; verbosity is disfavored. If you say what you have to say succinctly, your words will carry greater authority and impact.

- Read before writing. Add something to the conversation, don't simply repeat what's already been said. The only way to do that is to read the group's FAQ if there is one, and to read the entire thread to which you're responding. By reading before you write you'll have a better sense of the tenor and conventions of the newsgroup to which you are posting.

- Quote the messages you're responding to. Edit the quoted material in the interest of brevity (and indicate when you've done so), use the quoting fashion described in this chapter, and always acknowledge the person you're quoting.

- Contribute something. Some people speak simply to be heard; the same people post simply to see their material online. Don't contribute to the tedium: look for a new perspective, ask a probing question, make an insightful comment. If none come to mind, wait for another opportunity. There are plenty of opportunities on the Net; we all have something worthy to contribute eventually.

- Use help. If the help files described in this chapter don't answer your question, post a message in **aol.newsgroups.help** or MHM. Lots of people are willing to help you if you ask.

**Emily PostNews**

Brad Templeton originally created Emily PostNews a number of years ago; Steve Summit keeps her alive today. Emily is a satirical document, providing witty examples of what not to do when using newsgroups. Here's an example:

"Q: What sort of tone should I take in my article?

A: Be as outrageous as possible. If you don't say outlandish things, and fill your article with libelous insults of net people, you may not stick out enough in the flood of articles to get a response. The more insane your posting looks, the more likely it is that you'll get lots of followups. The net is here, after all, so that you can get lots of attention.

If your article is polite, reasoned and to the point, you may only get mailed replies. Yuck!"

Emily PostNews is posted every couple of months in the **news.answers** newsgroup. She may be satirical, but she's effective at conveying the spirit of the newsgroup community without being condescending. Be sure to read her.

## Moving on

No brief chapter, this. Newsgroups arguably represent the most bountiful potential on the Net, and their orthodoxy is unyielding. They warrant a commodious tome.

The tome, however, has ended, and it's time to move on to something entirely different. A brave new world awaits you as we next explore AOL's latest foray in the Internet. The World Wide Web is the subject of the next chapter: just turn the page.

# Chapter 6
# WEB WALKING

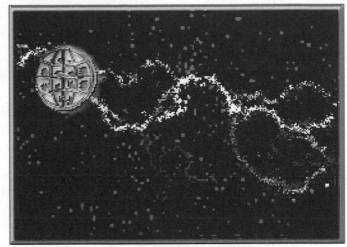

Mitsui Sokubei Takatoshi was a 17th-century samurai. Mitsui, however, preferred to make money, not war. Rebelling against his noble caste, he pursued alternatives to the martial arts—income opportunities in particular. Seeking a product with interest to all his people, he chanced upon sake, and Mitsui's sake establishment opened to an eager clientele in 1616.

Mitsui's wife, Shuho, soon discovered that patrons would pawn their valuables for a drink of sake. Opportunism apparently ran in the family, for Shuho's ideas eventually spawned Mitsukoshi, which, by offering a variety of pawned goods at a single location, became Japan's largest department store chain.

Mitsukoshi, the Royal Exchange, Bon Marché, Wanamaker's, Marshall Field, Macy's—they all achieved success with one primary merchandising strategy: offer a variety of goods, conveniently located under one roof, in comfortable, familiar surroundings.

If you've read this book from the beginning, you may now feel overwhelmed by the quantity and variety of the Internet's goods. As it has been presented thus far, the Internet is about as welcoming and comfortable as, well, a samurai on a bad hair day. Apply the department store strategy to FTP, newsgroups, Gopher and WAIS, however, and you have the World Wide Web—an elegant, convenient, comprehensive presentation of Everything Internet. The Web (as it's called) is our topic for this chapter.

**Nomenclature**

As we begin this discussion of the World Wide Web, a few terms require interpretation.

▲ The meaning of the word *browse* in this context isn't much different from its meaning in other contexts. You browse art galleries, bookstores, markets and shops. You browse *TV Guide* and the movie listings in the Sunday paper. You browse the Web in the same way, casually strolling through cyberspace, stopping occasionally to examine an article here or an object there. The Web's emphasis on multimedia—graphics, sound, and video in particular—not only makes browsing easy, it makes it seem almost magical.

▲ A *Web browser* is software designed to browse the World Wide Web.

▲ A *Web page* is a document presented within the browser's window. Web pages can contain links, text, graphics, sounds or videos—or a combination thereof.

▲ A *link* is an area within a Web page that when clicked on brings up another page. Links are usually highlighted underlined text, but links can be areas of a graphic as well.

▲ A *URL (Uniform Resource Locator)* is an address. There's a URL for each page or file available on the Web. There are millions of them, and they can originate from anywhere on the Internet: Germany, Denmark, AOL—even your own hard disk. Because they come from all over the world, their addresses are lengthy and specific. The URL for Mirsky's Worst of the Web (a good place to see how the Web should *not* be used) is **http://turnpike.net/metro/mirsky/Worst.html**.

▲ *HTTP* stands for HyperText Transfer Protocol, the Internet protocol used to transfer hypertext documents. Appearing at the beginning of a URL, "http" tells the browser to expect a hypertext Web document.

▲ *HTML* is for HyperText Markup Language, a descriptive computer language that's used to create Web pages.

## The secretary of commerce

Our chapter-opening department-store analogy is appropriate on another level: commerce. The Web's initial growth was fueled by its glamour. Until the Web's introduction, 99 percent of all Internet activity was textual. The Web brought an immediate and glorious change to that, with pictures, sound, and video around every corner. No wonder the Netters were attracted to it.

Glamour, however, is fleeting. What's fueling the Web's continuing ascent is commerce. Very quickly, the Web is becoming a fertile medium for commercial activity. In a world jaded by fifty years of television, both the entertainment industry and its audience are primed for something different, something less passive and more accessible. No advertiser worth his storyboards can ignore the Web's advertising potential.

Where there are advertisers, there is money. And where there is money, there is content—lavish content. Hundred-thousand dollar Web pages are becoming commonplace (try **http://www.sony.com**). Every major advertising agency—from Chiat/Day (**http://www. chiatday.com/web**) to Winkler McManus (**http://www.winkler-mcmanus.com**) has a home page now and is producing Web content for major clients.

Figure 6-1: A portion of the Chiat/Day advertising agency's home page at **http:// www.chiatday.com/ web**.

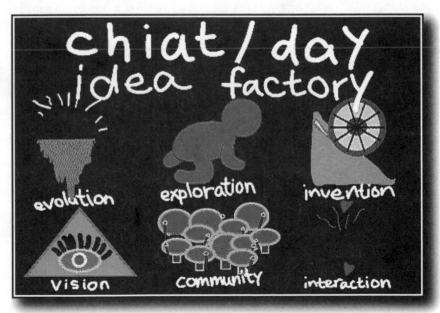

© Chiat/Day inc. Advertising

With all of this money and talent comes compelling content. With compelling content comes an expanding audience, and with an expanding audience comes the impetus for even more money and the discovery of even better talent. The Web isn't a *web* at all: it's a spiral, and it's spiraling outward like the Milky Way, flinging stellar enticements our way with all the energy of nuclear fission. The critical mass that's behind it all is commerce.

## Hypermedia

From Mitsui's 17th century department stores, let's jump ahead 300 years and meet another opportunist. In 1965, Ted Nelson began promoting the notion of *hypermedia*: an information retrieval system that could provide access to disparate information using a familiar, convenient computer interface. Nelson's idea floundered for 20 years until the mid-1980s, when Apple Computer introduced HyperCard. Later, Microsoft's Windows Help system promoted hypermedia as well. In all cases, documents are associated by embedded *hot links* (or just *links*). Links are usually identified by a change in type style or color; when you click one, another document appears, with more links, leading to more documents with even more links. I've simplified matters a bit for the sake of clarity: links can be sounds, graphics, videos and, in the near future, even virtual reality environments (see Figure 6-2).

Figure 6-2: Links provide a nonlinear pathway to the infinite potential of the World Wide Web.

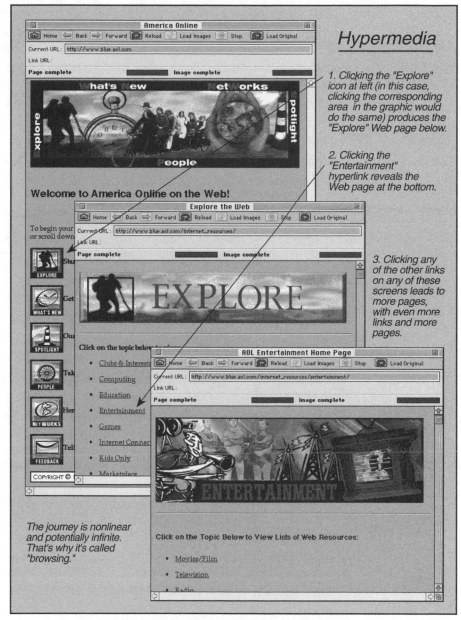

Applying hypermedia to the first paragraph of this chapter, we might find the word "Mitsui" highlighted. By clicking that word we might invoke an encyclopedia at the National Archives in Washington, DC, where we discover a biography of Mitsui Sokubei Takatoshi that might contain the highlighted term "department store." Clicking that link might invoke an article from the UK, where merchandising magnates of the early 20th century are discussed. One of those magnates might be David May, and a click on his name produces myriad references to the word "May," including, perhaps, a drawing of the German battleship *Bismarck*, which was sunk on May 27, 1941. The word "Bismarck" could lead us to Los Angeles for a sound clip from Johnny Horton's pop music of the 1960s, and from there we might be attracted by an animation of Dr. Seuss's *Horton Hears a Who*, and from there . . . .

**A Nerkle a Nerd and a Seersucker, too!**

Speaking of Dr. Seuss, I find the Web's jargon—indeed, all of computerdom's jargon—to be a bit like a Seuss book. Case in point: the word *nerd* first appeared in 1950 in Dr. Seuss's *If I Ran the Zoo*: "And then, just to show them, I'll sail to Ka-Troo And Bring Back an It-Kutch a Preep and a Proo a Nerkle a Nerd and a Seersucker, too!" The nerd is pictured as a small humanoid creature looking comically unpleasant—think of Don Knotts as the landlord in "Three's Company." The word was picked up by preschoolers and passed on to their older siblings who, by the mid-1950s, had made it a universal term for their "square" contemporaries.

## CERN

Now let's consider the European Particle Physics Laboratory (CERN) in Geneva, Switzerland. It was there, in 1989, that the CERN physicists dreamed up the *World Wide Web*. The Internet had become unwieldy. The physicists wanted to access the Net's data but they wanted to remain physicists as well, not cyberjockeys. They formulated a number of goals, the loftiest of which was to create an environment in which information of any type from any source could be accessed in a simple and consistent way.

"Information (goods) of any type from any source" and "simple and consistent" almost define Mitsui's department store strategy from the 17th century. The environment selected by the scientists at CERN was that of hypermedia, where nonlinear associations prevail—just the stuff particle physicists are made of.

Combine the department store approach with the versatility of hypertext, and you have the World Wide Web. The Web combines text, graphics, sound and video from all over the world onto one screen, with hypertext's point-and-click convenience and efficiency.

Perhaps best of all, CERN's physicists believed that the World Wide Web should not be confined to the scientific community or even the existing Internet community: it should be available to everyone. Accordingly, they put both the client software (the software that runs on our machines) and the server software (the software that runs on AOL's machines) in the public domain. It was free to all, and the rest is history.

---

### Mosaic & the Web

A linguistic clarification is appropriate here. The client software—the Web browser—that grew out of the CERN project is named *Mosaic*. Mosaic was developed at the National Center for Supercomputing Applications (NCSA) at the University of Illinois, Urbana-Champaign. NCSA is funded by the National Science Foundation—a federally funded agency—thus its products are free.

Mosaic is a trademark for a family of Web-browsing software. It bears the same relationship to the Web as a Ford does to a highway. There are Chevys and Toyotas and Chryslers on the highway as well. Netscape, for example, is a popular Web browser from Netscape Communications Corporation, a private company. There's a browser called InternetWorks, too, from BookLink Technologies, a company that AOL acquired in early 1995. Significant portions of the InternetWorks product are integrated into the AOL client that's running on your machine. Many say it's the best of the Web browsers; AOL hopes you agree.

The important thing is not to make the error of using *Mosaic* and *The World Wide Web* synonymously—a common error. That would be like referring to a highway as a Ford. They're not the same thing.

---

The Web took off like sake sales on a Saturday night. Compared to everything before it, the Web was easy to use, it was *very* graphical, it looked familiar to all Mac and Windows users and it was free. During 1993, its third year online, Web traffic increased 2,500 percent; few have tried to keep track of its growth since.

**A one-way medium**

For the most part, the Web is a one-way medium. You won't be "posting" to the Web in the way you post to newsgroups, though a degree of interactivity is planned for the future. Some Web sites prompt for data input, but rarely is that data seen online. At present, America Online offers only a browser. Soon, however, you'll be able to put your own World Wide Web page online through AOL. Keep watching for an announcement at keyword: Web.

## Hot Lists

Before we begin browsing the Web, we need to take a side trip. Browsing the Web is like collecting seashells: "Oh, I gotta have that one," and "That one, too!" Pretty soon, your hands are full. By then you need a bucket. "Collectible" URLs—ones that you want to return to—accumulate like seashells. And like seashells, they'll need to be stored somewhere: you're going to need a place—a "bucket"— to keep these references in. That's what Hot Lists are for.

You can open a Hot List by choosing Hot Lists from the Services menu in the browser window. From there, select either the Main Hot List or any other list you may have created. More on creating new Hot Lists later.

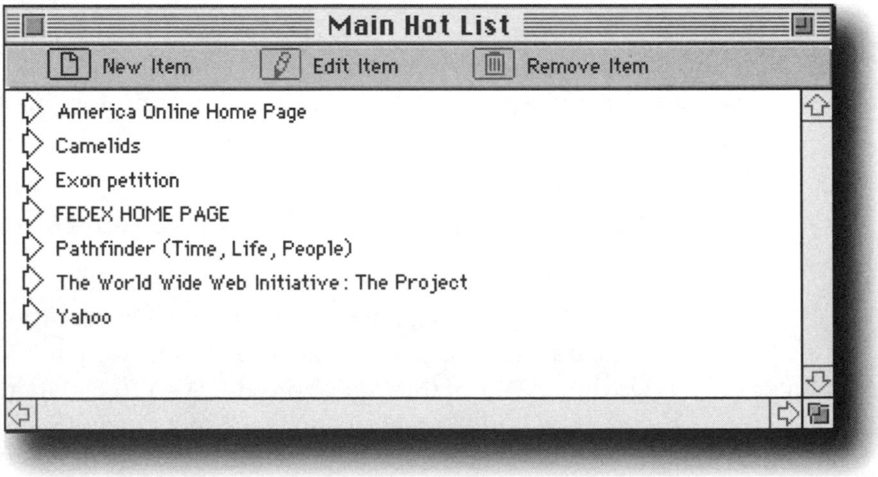

Figure 6-3: My Main Hot List. You can fill yours any way you please.

Main Hot List

New Item    Edit Item    Remove Item

America Online Home Page
Camelids
Exon petition
FEDEX HOME PAGE
Pathfinder (Time, Life, People)
The World Wide Web Initiative: The Project
Yahoo

## Adding pages to the Main Hot List

If you want to "mark" a page by adding it to your Main Hot List, simply select Add to Main Hot List under the Services menu or press Command+Option+H and there it will appear (see Figure 6-4). If your Main Hot List window is open on your screen, you can also drag the URL directly over and drop it on the window. To go to one of the pages, just double-click it.

Figure 6-4: Adding pages to your Main Hot List is simple.

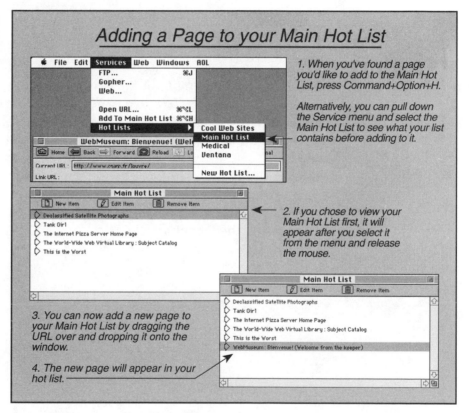

## Modifying a page in a Hot List

You can change the name or the URL of a page in a Hot List by first selecting it, then clicking the Edit button in the Hot List window. You will want to edit the title given to pages marked with the drag & drop method because it uses the URL rather than the page's name—URL addresses alone aren't known for being easily recognizable. Be careful when you modify URLs: they're easy to invalidate.

### Organizing your pages in Hot Lists

Figure 6-4 shows the easiest way to add a favorite place, by adding it to your Main Hot List, but it's messy. When they're added, pages appear in your Main Hot List in alphabetical order without regard to type or topic. This might work for four or five pages but not hundreds—and hundreds is what you'll have, soon enough.

The solution is *categories*. The browser allows you to make new Hot Lists to store your stuff. Once you've made a new Hot List, you can add pages to it.

### Creating a new Hot List

You can create a new Hot List by selecting New Hot Lists... under the Hot Lists menu item in the Services menu. Give your new Hot List a name and save it. To add a page to a Hot List other than the Main Hot List, just open the Hot List you want to place it in, drag the URL from the browser window, and drop it in the Hot List window (see Figure 6-5). Alternatively, you can add them to your Main Hot List using Command+Option+H and then move them over by dragging them to the Hot List window. You can move more than one page at a time by holding down the shift key while selecting and then dragging them over together.

Figure 6-5: Drag and drop the URL to place a page in a Hot List.

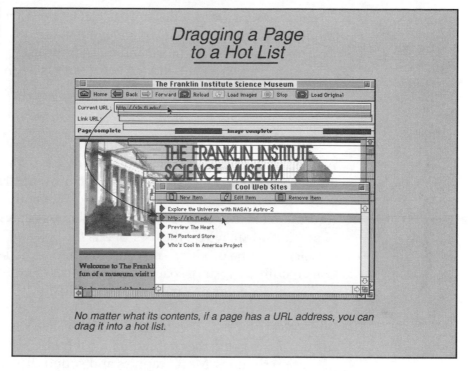

*No matter what its contents, if a page has a URL address, you can drag it into a hot list.*

### Deleting a page or a Hot List

The Remove Item button (refer again to Figure 6-5) deletes whatever is selected from your Hot List window. To delete an entire Hot List, you'll need to actually delete the file that stores the Hot List information itself—you'll find it in the Web Files folder within the Online Browser folder.

**You may pass Go**

If you want to go to a specific page upon entering the Web, paying only lip service to the Main Menu and the Spotlight screen, just add that page to a Hot List.

When you're next ready to sign on—but before you do—open the Browser from your Finder, open a Hot List, find the page you want to go to, and double-click it. AOL will make a beeline for your destination, saving you time and trouble. You can even connect to AOL through the Browser—just select Connect... under the AOL menu.

Maintaining your Hot List entries can be done whether you're online or off. You can't add a page when you're offline, but you can create new hot lists and move and delete entries.

There is no Save command for your Hot Lists. Changes are saved the instant you make them. It's automatic.

## Using the browser

With an understanding of the Hot Lists feature, we can now discuss the process of actually using AOL's Web browser. The latest computer-industry acronym is *oobe* (it rhymes with "ruby"), meaning "out-of-box experience." Software developers eagerly pursue this "Camelot" ideal, where the user opens the box and immediately sets to work with the product—no configuration, installation or instructions required. A bar of soap is a good oobe. Out-of-box experiences are especially elusive in the computer industry.

Unless, perhaps, you consider AOL's presentation of the World Wide Web. The Web as offered by AOL is about as close to an oobe as you'll ever get in the presence of a computer. There are no configuration routines. Most graphics and sound display without additional software. Once you've installed the browser, simply sign on and use the keyword: Web. The browser's window appears with AOL's home page loaded into it, inviting your participation (see Figure 6-6).

Figure 6-6: AOL's Web browser is available whenever you use the keyword: Web or select Switch to Browser under the Windows menu.

### Specifying a URL

It's time to visit a Web site. Naturally, you can click one of the links on the home page pictured in Figure 6-6, but eventually you'll want to venture out on your own. And for that, you'll need to specify a URL. A *URL*, as defined earlier, is a Uniform Resource Locator, or a Web address. In the context of this discussion, a URL is the address of a Web page. You'll encounter URLs all the time: friends will e-mail you with them; you'll read about them in newsgroups. Just this morning I heard one on the radio. URLs are to the 90s what astrology was to the 70s. No longer is it chic to ask "What's your sign?" Hip Web-sters know to ask "What's your URL?" (The acronym "URL," by the way, is pronounced "you are ell." Don't try to make a word out of it.)

### Double-clicking on a page in a Hot List

There are four ways to specify Web addresses (URLs) when you're using AOL's browser. Perhaps the most obvious is to double-click an entry in a Hot List. Assuming you're online when you do this, the browser window will establish contact with the remote site you've specified. Moments later, the site will begin to fill your browser's window.

### Drag & drop

The second alternative: if a browser window is already open and you want to specify another URL, it's best if you open one or more of the browser's Hot Lists. A Hot List can overlap the browser window and provide access to both (see Figure 6-7).

Working in a Hot List, find the URL you want and *drag it* to the browser window in the background. This will load the specified URL into the browser window.

Figure 6-7: By overlapping a Hot List window atop a browser window, you can invoke any page by dragging it to the browser window.

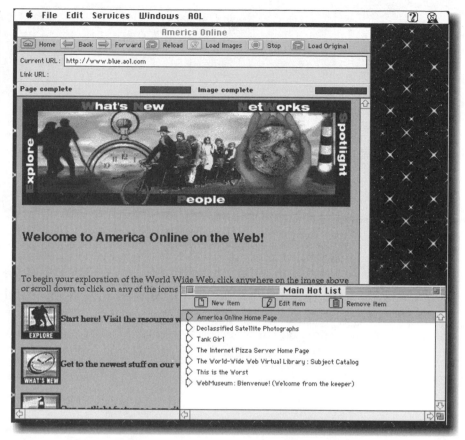

You're not limited to the pages immediately preceding or following the page you're currently viewing. Selecting Recent Items from the Web menu reveals a list of all of the places you've visited during the current session.

### Browser entry

The third method of invoking a URL is to paste or type it directly into the URL text box in the browser window (see Figure 6-8), and press the Return key. This is convenient for those occasions when you're sampling a URL—one, perhaps, that you saw in a magazine or heard about from a friend—and aren't yet ready to commit it to your Favorite Places hierarchy.

Figure 6-8: The browser window's text box allows you to enter a URL directly.

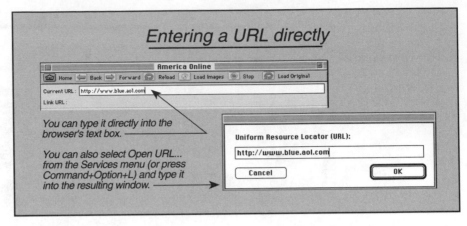

## Menu entry

The fourth method of specifying a Web address is to select Open URL... from the Services menu (or press Command+Option+L), type it in, and press the Return key (refer again to Figure 6-8). This is most useful when you've closed the browser's window, or when you've just opened the browser and haven't yet entered the Web.

**In defense of imprecision**

It doesn't always pay to be specific. At first glance, URLs might seem to depend on exactitude, but imprecision does have its merits.

When you encounter a URL that doesn't work (your software will respond with an error message to the effect that it "can't connect" with the resource), lop a few characters off the right end of the address and see what happens.

Let's say you've read about a really slick recipe for dandelion soufflé, and its URL is **http://www.foobar.com/taraxacum.html** (this is a fictitious URL—don't try it). When you plug that address into AOL's URL text box, you encounter an error. Perhaps the file has been renamed, or removed from the site. Maybe it's in another directory. If you've pasted the URL into the text box, it might be followed by a space, which could invalidate the address.

Try removing from the URL all text that follows the rightmost slash. "**http://www.foobar.com/taraxacum.html**" becomes "**http://www/foobar.com/**". Now try again by pressing the Return key. Lacking a specific document name, AOL's browser will simply attempt to connect to the site and display its directory or a less specific Web page. If the connection is successful, you can always navigate the site's directories and files manually (either by selecting the appropriate link if you receive a hypertext page, or by double-clicking them if you receive a directory) until you find the resource you're after.

Now that you know how to specify a URL, and if you haven't done so already, browse a while. AOL offers an Explore button on its home page (AOL's home page is usually available by clicking the Home button in the browser window) that's a good place to begin. Make note of the time before you do, and allot 15 minutes for this initial foray onto the Web (be careful: browsing is addictive!). Click a few links that interest you, and follow them two or three pages deep. Don't worry about spending your time productively: it's only 15 minutes, and the Web rewards obliquity.

**Maximize!**

Few of the early Web browsers could open more than one window at a time, thus most Web pages are designed with the assumption that they have the entire screen to themselves.

As it comes out of the box, AOL's browser operates in a reduced window, usually much smaller than full-screen. To realize the maximum benefit of the Web pages you're viewing, maximize the browser's window by zooming it. The zoom button is the one in the upper right corner of the browser's window—the one with the smaller square inside of it.

### The home page

The first page you encounter in a Web session is typically referred to as your *default home page*. The default home page that AOL provides might not suit your needs perfectly. You might want to use another, or—if you know how to program with HTML—you might want to use one of your own.

No matter where you are in a Web session, you can always return to the home page by clicking its icon in the browser's window.

Many AOL members aren't aware that the home page can be changed. If you work for General Motors, for example, you might want to specify the GM Web page as your home page. Using Configure... under the Edit menu and then selecting the Web icon, you can specify any Web page as the default page for your installation: just place its URL in the Home Page text box pictured in Figure 6-9.

Figure 6-9: The Home Page text box in the Configure window allows you to specify any Web page as your home page.

```
┌─────────────────────────────────────────────────────────┐
│  ▤▤▤        AOL Internet Configuration         ▤▤▤       │
├─────────────────────────────────────────────────────────┤
│  ▒▒▒▒  ⬆  Home Page:  http://www.blue.aol.com            │
│  ▓▓▓▓                                                    │
│  FTP Client  Page Setup:  Read Links:  ▔▔  Unread Links: ▔│
│                           Text:        ▔▔  Background:  ▔▔│
│   ▒▒                      Text Size:  Small ▼             │
│  General                                                 │
│             Browser Setup: ☒ Display Active URL  ☒ Display Hyperlink URL:│
│   ▒▒                       ☒ Download Images             │
│  Web                       ☒ Open a new window for each user-specified URL│
│                            Expire read links after 15 days.│
│  ⬇         Maximum simultaneous connections for image retrieval: 5│
└─────────────────────────────────────────────────────────┘
```

It's important to note that the home page remains the same regardless of which of the five screen names you use on your account.

## Your own personal home page

If you're familiar with writing HTML, you might want to write your own home page, store it on your hard disk or local network and specify it as your default home page. Web pages stored locally are much faster than those downloaded from AOL, and you can change them whenever you wish.

A few important points:

You can specify a local Web page by using the URL format file:///path\filename.html (insert the path and the filename of your HTML document where shown). If you aren't sure of the path, open it first in your browser and then copy the URL that appears. This file can be located anywhere on your hard disk or on your local network. Take note that it is important to use the .html extension in your page's file name—without it, the browser will display it differently than it would a Web page.

Local pages such as this are not available to other people on the Web; they're "published" only on your machine or your network.

If you want to learn more about writing HTML, investigate the *Beginner's Guide to HTML*, available at **http://www.ncsa.uiuc.edu/General/Internet/WWW/HTMLPrimer.html**.

### Buttons in the browser window

The browser window offers seven buttons, providing additional navigational tools and control over the operation of the browser itself.

### Home

As discussed above, this first button takes you to your home page no matter where you may be in the Web. If you configure your browser to display a page other than the AOL Home Page, choose one with a number of useful links. With that, you'll always have a ready oasis of opportunity close at hand.

### Forward & back

As you're rummaging around the Web, try the Forward and Back buttons (see Figure 6-10) in the browser window. You will often encounter a Web page that's especially fertile. You'll try one of its links, like what you see, and think, "Gee, I'd like to try another." Fine. Click the Back button, go back to the page with the links that interest you, and try another.

Figure 6-10: The Forward and Back buttons in the browser's window allow you to conveniently return to pages you've recently accessed.

Both the Forward and Back buttons refer to the list of pages you've visited during the current session. The Forward button, then, only works if you've back-tracked. Don't confuse the Forward button with the links available on a page: links take you forward into new territory; the Forward button moves you forward on the list of places you have already visited. In other words, you can't move forward on that list unless you have moved backwards within it earlier, via the Back button.

### The blue bars

The blue bars below the URL text box notify you when portions of a Web page have been received at your machine. The first one shows you the browser's progress as it loads the page's textual information. The second one shows the progress of the graphics as they load, and a page with more than one graphic will provoke the second bar for each graphic it carries.

### Graphics

AOL's Web browser offers a concession to those of us with less-than-hypersonic connections to the Web. Because they're rich with graphics, Web pages are frequently slow to display—not instantaneously as if by magic. There's nothing magical about graphics on the Web. Each one has to be downloaded before it can be viewed, and downloading graphics can be time-consuming, even at the fastest modem speeds.

### Two stages

A moment of clarification here: Though it seems so, you're never really connected directly to the Web via AOL. Your "connection" occurs in two stages.

Immediately after you've requested a URL, AOL goes onto the Web and fetches it. AOL's connections to the Web are via multiple T3 communication circuits, each running at 45 million bits per second. Reception of most Web documents takes only moments under these conditions, and as soon as the document is received at AOL, AOL breaks the connection with the site. This is good manners: access to Web sites is a precious resource.

Once the document is received and stored on AOL's disks, AOL transmits it to you. Even if you're using a 2,400 baud modem, the time required to feed the document to you involves no Internet resources: it's all between you and AOL. By the time you receive the document, the original Web site has been freed up for other users.

This two-stage process provides the opportunity for AOL to simplify the document (thus reducing its size and transmission time) before it's sent to you. The degree of simplification is controlled by the Web preferences discussed in this section.

Consequently, you can determine the reception method that's to be used when the browser encounters a graphic. Your browser is set to show graphics by default. To disable this, select Always Load Images from the Web menu and the check mark beside it will disappear. From this point on, AOL will feed you only the text—including the links—of the Web site to your browser. You'll see either a graphic marker or a word where a graphic would normally appear (see Figure 6-11). This is fast, but not really in keeping with the character of the Web.

Figure 6-11: AOL's Home Page with graphics disabled; compare this to Figure 6-6.

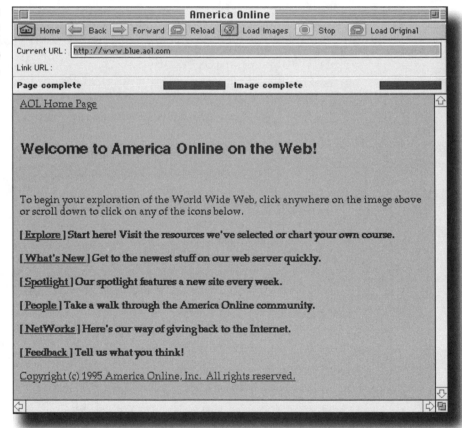

To re-enable graphics, select Always Load Images again. Now AOL's machines will pass the graphic along to you without change. It is probably best that you leave graphics on unless circumstances are unusual. If you sign on during a period of extreme system activity, for example, you might want to turn off graphics.

### The Reload & Load Images buttons

Note the Reload button pictured in Figure 6-12. One of the primary purposes for this button is to allow you to reload a page after you've toggled your graphics on or off.

Like the Reload button, the Load Images button (also pictured in Figure 6-12) is useful for loading images when a page has been loaded without them.

Figure 6-12: Either the Reload button or the Load Images button can be used to reload a page after the graphics have been turned on or off.

Let's say you spot a stunning graphic of a rare designer wallet that you'd love to add to your wish list. You might go to the Web menu, select Always Load Images to enable it, and then click the Reload button. AOL will re-feed the page to you, loading the wallet graphic. (I'm sure most of us can use a loaded wallet . . . .)

### The Stop button

The browser window's Stop button allows you to stop the transmission of a Web page to your browser. You'll want to use this button whenever a page seems to take an unusually long time or when its contents aren't what you'd hoped they would be. Once transmission has stopped, you can try another URL, or go back or forward with the Back or Forward button.

### The Load Original button

If you've stopped a page during loading and decide you'd like to see it in a different light, the Load Original button will load it again from scratch. This means if you loaded a page with full graphics the first time but would prefer not to view them, you can turn your graphics off and click Load Original to see just the text. This button is also useful when you want to refresh your page—some pages are constantly updated, such as the Seattle traffic page which shows a new traffic flow map every five minutes.

**Configuring your browser**

I would be remiss if I didn't elaborate on the browser's configuration options here. Like your AOL Preferences, the Web browser allows you to customize it to suit your style. To configure the browser for the Web, choose Configure from the Edit menu (or press Command+Option+C) and click on the Web icon. A number of useful options are hidden away here—be sure to investigate (refer to Figure 6-9).

Besides offering a place to set your home page as discussed previously, you can also change your text size and your link colors. I suggest keeping your colors as they are, however—some pages refer to links by color and changing them may become confusing.

You can also change whether or not your browser displays the current URL (to show where you are) and the Hyperlink URL (to show where you can go). Both links are very handy if you are doing serious Web surfing, but you may want to turn them off it they get in the way or take up too much real estate on your screen.

If you don't like surprise downloads, you can disable automatic downloading which will occur when you click on a link that references a graphic. In addition, you have the option of having separate browser windows for each URL you type in yourself—useful for keeping a page with several links available at all times.

Expire read links after X days refers to the amount of time the links for previously visited pages appear as read (read links are usually in a different color than unread links). You can also set the number of images that the browser will try to load simultaneously—anywhere from 1 to 16 with the default at 5. Try lowering this number when you have a slow connection.

## Saving pages

Naturally, you can save Web pages that are displayed on your screen. As we pursue this discussion, remember that saving Web documents is limited to the contents of the current (frontmost) window only. If you've been browsing a Web path and you want to save all of the pages you've encountered along the way, you'll have to save each individual page along that path.

AOL offers a variety of formats for saving, depending on your needs and the type of data that's currently displayed.

**Text format:** If you want to save just the text of a Web page, choose Save As... from the File menu. Use this option when you want to keep a copy of the text from a page to read offline at your leisure, or when you need a copy for later reference. Bear in mind that you may need to view text saved from a Web page with a word processor rather than with the AOL software. The Web browser software is capable of displaying more text in a page than the AOL software can read.

**Source format:** This option saves the page as HTML source code. As mentioned earlier, HTML is the HyperText Markup Language that's used to define the appearance and content of Web pages. Typical of many computer languages, HTML consists of numerous commands (called "tags") within a plain-text document. HTML isn't as cryptic as most computer languages, but it takes familiarity with the language to understand everything that's going on.

To save the HTML code of a Web page, choose Save As... from the File menu and select Source from the pop-up menu at the bottom of the window. HTML code is plain text. It contains none of the page's graphics or other nontextual resources, only tags pointing to the locations of these resources. A portion of the HTML code for AOL's home page appears in Figure 6-13.

Figure 6-13: A portion of the HTML code representing AOL's home page.

## HTML Code

```
<HTML>
<HEAD>
<TITLE>America Online</TITLE>
</HEAD><BODY>
<IMG SRC="internet--resources/aol--logo.gif" ALIGN=MIDDLE
ALT="[America Online]">
<p><a href="aolhome.map"><IMG SRC="webhome.gif" ALT="Home
Page" ISMAP></a>
<h1>Welcome to America Online on the Web!</h1>
To begin your exploration of the World Wide Web, click
anywhere on the image above or scroll down to click on any of
the icons below.
<p>
<DL>
<DT>
```

**External files:** Another form of Web "page" consists of a stand-alone graphic (weather maps are a good example—try one of the maps at *The Daily Planet* at **http://www.atmos.uiuc.edu/**). Frankly, these aren't Web pages at all. They're "external media files," available within the Web browser's window. Don't confuse them with the inline graphics that appear within many Web pages: an external file appears in a window by itself—and unlike inline graphics, external files can be saved.

You can tell if you have an external file by the small download window that appears while the graphic is being loaded. To save an external file, choose Save from AOL's File menu while the graphic is in the frontmost window. Most graphics are GIF or JPEG formats, which the AOL software itself can open.

Figure 6-14: The browser will load the file in a small window. When finished, you can click the Save button to keep a copy on your hard drive.

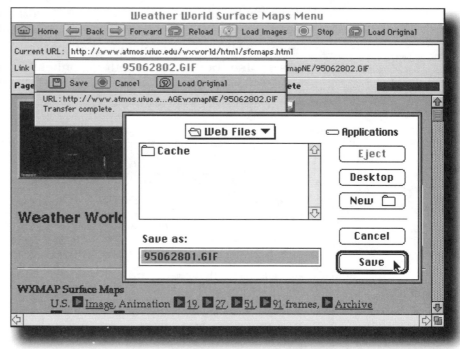

**Sound files:** Sound files are a third form of data you'll find on the Web. AOL's browser understands (and plays) Mac SND, MIDI, AU, and WAV sound files. A sound file will load in a small window like that for an external graphic. Once loaded, you can hear the sound by clicking on the Play button in the window (see Figure 6-15). This audio player window will appear quickly, but watch the numbers at the bottom of the window to determine when the transmission has ended. You won't be able to play the sound until the sound file has been received in its entirety. If you decide you'd rather not wait for the sound to load, click the Cancel button—simply closing the window won't stop the transmission.

Figure 6-15: The audio player window appears when received Web data represents an audio file.

When the file is received—and assuming it's one of the formats AOL and your machine can play back—you can hear the sound through your system by clicking the Play button. You can play it again by clicking the same button.

To save a sound file, click the Save button or choose Save from the File menu.

### They're big

There's no way around it: sound and video files are big. Most are measured in megabytes, and megabytes take lots of time to download.

Well-constructed Web pages identify the size of sound and video files so you'll know what you're getting into before you request the download. Others do not, however, and with those you're taking pot luck. *Caveat emptor!*

**Video files:** Last of all, we come to video files. Online video is an emerging technology, and so is the hardware required to play it. At the moment, your AOL software understands the MPEG format, but there are many others.

When opening an MPEG file, AOL automatically searches your hard disk for an application that can play the animation and opens it. Again, you'll have to wait for the transmission to conclude. Once the file is received in its entirety, you can click the Open button to have AOL open your animation software and see the video in action.

You can also download animation files of other types and save them to disk, to later open and play with compatible software. AOL itself will play QuickTime movies—just open the animation from the File menu and presto!

## The cache

Browsing the Web via a standard phone line can be frustrating. Even at 28.8 kbps, some pages seem to flow with all the viscosity of restaurant ketchup.

The problem is aggravated when you elect to return to a page you've recently visited. Here's information you've already seen; you should be able to see it again without having to spend time online downloading the page a second time.

You *can* see it again, without a second visit to the site to download the page. It's done with a *cache*—an area on your hard disk that automatically records the contents of places you've been (see Figure 6-16).

Figure 6-16: The WWW cache retains pages you've recently visited.

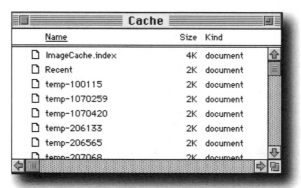

The cache is actually a portion of your hard disk that's set aside to keep a "diary" of the Web pages you've visited. The cache holds as much data as you allow it to. When you request a specific Web page, the browser first looks in the cache. If the page is there, it's retrieved from your hard disk—almost instantly. With the page available on your hard disk, there's no need for the browser to go on the Net or even for AOL to retrieve it. The cache is one of the most important features of the browser, and it can truly make the difference between the tortoise and the hare.

A few comments about the cache:

- Web pages are cached on your hard disk (in the Cache folder in your AOL folder), as well as in RAM.

- You can erase the contents of the cache by deleting the files in the Cache folder. Do this only if you desperately need the disk space. If the cache is purged, all of the pages it was holding for you will have to be retrieved from the Web when you visit them again.

- The cache applies to all five of your AOL accounts, if you're using that many. It's not specific to any one of them. This implies that the cache contains pages from not only your Web browsing but the browsing of everyone else who uses your account as well.

## Problems & solutions

"Why do I keep getting 'Unable to connect' errors when I use the Web?" "Why is the Web so slow?" These are simple questions with no simple answers. There are lots of reasons why you might encounter Internet error messages or a slow Web page. Causes can be divided into three categories: 1) it's the remote site's problem, 2) it's AOL's problem, or 3) there's a problem with something in between.

### Problems with remote sites

Don't think of Internet sites as community property, available to everyone at all times. Most sites are operated by agencies with no mandate to serve the public via the Internet: their participation is voluntary.

Many sites are operated on everyday PCs running multiuser operating systems such as UNIX. There's nothing magical about these setups. They might slow down when as few as 5 or 6 people access them at the same time; they might become unbearable with 10 or more; and they might consequently limit the number of users who can log on concurrently. Other sites refuse anonymous access during certain times of the day. All sites go offline for periodic maintenance.

Some other sites—usually the ones you most want to investigate—are shriveling under tremendous demand. As I write this (spring,

1995), *Playboy* magazine's Web site (**http://www.playboy.com/**) suffers 800,000 "hits" (connections) a day. That's almost 10 hits *per second*. Sites such as this are best avoided during periods of peak usage.

Media attention to the "Information Superhighway" gives the false impression that the Internet is a reliable and instant resource that's as organized and easy to use as the telephone system. Dependability is rarely mentioned; neither is speed. When something goes wrong or when things are sluggish, we're inclined to point the finger of suspicion in the most convenient direction: America Online. Unfortunately, when the remote site is the problem, blaming AOL is like blaming the telephone company for a busy signal.

## Problems at America Online

From the day it went online, the World Wide Web has become one of AOL's most popular features. AOL has dedicated an arsenal of powerful machinery and T3 circuits to serve the Web, but even that armory is put to task when thousands of people are using it simultaneously. Moreover, the telephonic network between you and AOL, and AOL's internal routing system—the system that routes your requests to AOL's various computers—slows down as it reaches capacity. Peak usage periods (typically, 6:00 pm to midnight, Eastern time) are not the best times to access AOL, especially if you're planning to browse the Web.

## Problems with everything in between

On its way from its origin to AOL, and again from AOL to you, Web data must pass through hundreds of connections and regional telecommunications services. As often as not, data must cross political borders and even oceans. It's a perilous journey. If any one of these pathways is running slowly—struggling under an unusual load, for example—transmission is affected. The speed of the others makes no difference, no matter how well they're functioning. Your connection can be plucked from the data stream like a salmon on its way to its spawning ground. There's nothing any of us—AOL included—can do to prevent these circumstances.

## Solutions

Now that you understand many of the roadblocks in your path, a few solutions are in order.

- The mother of all solutions is to confine your Web browsing to AOL's nonpeak times—before 6:00 pm weekdays, Eastern time.

- Consider setting your browser to not load images. With this setting in effect, all graphics on all Web pages will be skipped. Transmission time for Web pages will be vastly improved. You can always change back to load images and reload any page that warrants a more scenic visit. This solution is especially effective if you browse new territory often.

- Look for *mirrors*—duplicates—of popular Web sites on the Web (see Figure 6-17). Many of the most popular sites are duplicated at other sites. Sometimes, the mirror sites are less crowded. Some are located in parts of the world where the difference in local time provides a slack period when you're wanting to browse. Try mirrors: you can always return to the original site (via the Back button) if the mirror is no faster.

- If you have the minimum amount of RAM (8mb) that the browser needs, consider purchasing RAMDoubler from Connectix Corporation. RAMDoubler, used in conjunction with MaxRAM (available online by searching at keyword: FileSearch for "MaxRAM"), can double, triple or even quadruple your memory and give the browser more breathing space.

- Check the amount of memory allocated to the browser by clicking on the Browser's icon in the Finder and pressing Command+I. If you have the available memory, increase the minimum and maximum amounts accordingly and restart your Browser. The memory needed for your browser to run at peak performance will vary from computer to computer—experiment and find out what works for you.

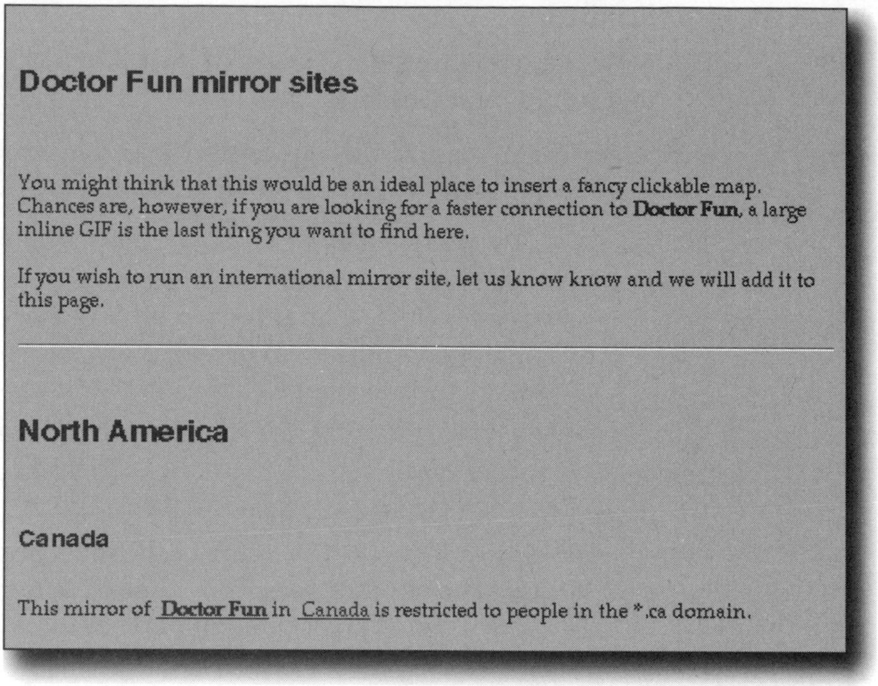

Figure 6-17: The Doctor Fun site (**http:// www.unitedmedia.com/ comics/drfun/**) is popular for its cartoon commentary on life, computing and the Web. Because of its popularity, a number of mirrors are offered.

## Doctor Fun mirror sites

You might think that this would be an ideal place to insert a fancy clickable map. Chances are, however, if you are looking for a faster connection to **Doctor Fun**, a large inline GIF is the last thing you want to find here.

If you wish to run an international mirror site, let us know know and we will add it to this page.

---

## North America

### Canada

This mirror of **Doctor Fun** in Canada is restricted to people in the *.ca domain.

Figure 6-17: The Doctor Fun site (**http:// www.unitedmedia.com/ comics/drfun/**) is popular for its cartoon commentary on life, computing and the Web. Because of its popularity, a number of mirrors are offered.

⚠ Some sites offer statistics on their activity (see Figure 6-18), including their peak access periods. Take note of these statistics, and try to avoid those sites during those periods.

Figure 6-18: The Digital
Picture Archive on the
17th Floor (**http://
olt.et.tudelft.nl/fun/
pictures/pictures.html**)
offers statistics and
usage notes.

*17th floor*

## Welcome to the Digital Picture Archive
## on the 17th floor

This archive contains hundreds of megabytes of gif and jpeg pictures. This site is operational since 1992.

### Before the fun: some serious stuff

Many thousands of people visit this archive every day. Therefore we are faced with heavy network traffic (see the latest traffic statistics for an update on the current status). During rush hours, this server is likely to be slow. We had to implement **access restrictions** to prevent the server from crashing under the heavy load. There's also a

⚙ If you know a site is functioning yet you can't access one of its pages, click the Stop button, do something else for a few minutes, then try the site again. This might give you a more dependable link than the one that wasn't working earlier. The Web is a bit like an automobile in that way: if it won't start, don't keep grinding away. Stop, wait a few minutes, then try again.

⚙ Use the Forward and Back buttons. These buttons access your local cache, where previously viewed Web pages are retrieved from your computer's hard disk—the fastest access possible.

## Moving on

I used to think I was an online junkie. I was jaded. I've been using online services since 1983 and was surfing the Internet when the waves were barely two feet high.

My first encounter with the Web, however, taught me a lesson: be humble. We ain't seen nothin' yet. It's tempting to look at the Web and say "Wow! This is what the Internet is all about! This is the ultimate online experience!" It's not. There's even more to come, of that I'm sure. People are already talking of avatars (visual representations of people on the Web), URLs that are actually little programs that run right on a Web page, and Web sites that offer virtual realities that emphasize interactivity. Someday we'll look back on these early days of the Web and think of them as we think of 300 baud modems today.

In the meantime, however, the Web is our new playground, and it's not a bad place to bide our time. The Web is the best the Internet has to offer, and with its options, caching, and hot lists AOL's browser is one of the best in the business. We're cruising in the fast lane, and we have the perfect vehicle for the task.

# Chapter 7

# GETTING THE GOODS (FTP)

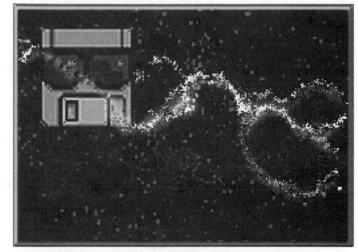

Ironically, almost everything we've discussed up to this point is ancillary to the historical rationale behind the Internet.

The National Science Foundation didn't fund the Internet so that we could exchange e-mail; they didn't fund the Internet so we could exchange wisdom in **alt.sex.fetish.feet** or discuss rock-and-roll via the Concrete-Blonde mailing list. Though e-mail, newsgroups and the World Wide Web have become the Internet's *raison d'être* for many, the Net was originally established to provide a means for scientists to exchange data and computing resources. ARPANET was commissioned in 1969 and existed for ten years before the first USENET Newsgroup connections were established in North Carolina. BITNET—the home of the original mailing lists—was just emerging from its New York incubator when Ronald Reagan launched his second term in the White House. And if the World Wide Web was human, it would just now be teething.

Most significantly, the Internet was founded to serve the need for shared computing resources. Computers were rare and expensive in the 1960s; data was precious. To serve military and academic needs, technology had to be dispersed. One of the mechanisms that emerged to serve the need is the subject of this chapter: FTP.

**Alien in cyberspace**

The military community phased out ARPANET in 1990. By then, Sventek (the international hacker described in Cliff Stoll's *Cuckoo's Egg*) was behind bars, Robert Morris's Internet worm (the first debilitating network virus) was sealed in formaldehyde, and Mitch Kapor had founded the Electronic Frontier Foundation. Nearly half a million hosts were on the Net, hundreds of newsgroups were entrenched, and e-mail volume probably exceeded that of most post offices in the country. The Internet had emerged from ARPANET's belly not unlike Hollywood's Alien: dyspeptic, mischievous and thoroughly antithetical to its progenitor.

## FTP defined

*FTP* is an abbreviation for File Transfer Protocol. FTP is the method by which you download files from other machines on the Net. FTP is two things, actually: it's a protocol, allowing machines on the Net to exchange data (files) without concern for the type of machine that originated the file, the file's original format or even the operating systems of the machines involved. It's also a program that *enables* FTP. Just as the word *telephone* denotes both a device you hold in your hand and a system for international communications, FTP is both the message and the medium.

The term is also used as both noun (e.g., "It's available via FTP.") and verb (as in "FTP to **sri.com** and look in the netinfo directory."). It's hard to misuse the term, in other words. Just don't try to pronounce it: this is one acronym that's always spelled out when it's said aloud.

Unfortunately, FTP was designed long before the days of mice and menus, and its command-line interface seems arcane and unfriendly to members of the GUI (graphical user interface) generation (see Figure 7-1).

Figure 7-1: An FTP session via a dial-up provider, typical of FTP without AOL's convenient interface.

| ftp Dialog | Comments |
|---|---|
| `ncftp>open sri.com` | Using the ftp software available at my dial-up Internet provider's site, I establish a connection with sri.com, a California-based research institute. |
| `CRVAX.SRI.COM MultiNet FTP Server`<br>`Process 3.2(14) at Fri 30-Sep-94`<br>`9:56AM-PDT` | SRI tells me a bunch of things I already knew or didn't care about knowing.... |
| `Welcome to SRI.COM anonymous FTP`<br>`server.` | ..then says hello. |
| `Guest User TLICHTY@AGORA.RDROP.COM`<br>`logged into SYS$USER:[ANONYMOUS]`<br>`at Fri 30-Sep-94 09:56, job`<br>`22a12546.` | My dial-up Internet provider is agora.rdrop.com, where my user name is tlichty. |
| `Directory and access restrictions`<br>`apply` | Being an anonymous user, I'm not afforded the full complement of features at this site. I can't delete or move files, for example. |
| `Logged into`<br>`sri.com.sri.com:SYS$USER:`<br>`[ANONYMOUS]ncftp` | Note that I'm currently in a directory called "Anonymous." |
| `ncftp>cd netinfo` | The phrase "ncftp>" is the prompt. The command "cd netinfo" means I want to change directory to the netinfo directory.  I knew about this directory ahead of time. |
| `Connected to SYS$USER:`<br><br>`[ANONYMOUS.NETINFO].sri.com:`<br>`SYS$USER:[ANONYMOUS.NETINFO]` | Notice that I'm now in the anonymous.netinfo directory. |
| `ncftp>ls` | The ls command means list all files and directories in this directory. |
| `message00`<br>`index.txt`<br>`domains-list`<br>`finding-email-addresses`<br>`interest-groups.txt`<br>`internet-access-providers-us.txt`<br>`...` | SRI responds with a listing. These are all files. Note that the SRI machine is able to use long filenames. |
| `sri.com:SYS$USER:`<br>`[ANONYMOUS.NETINFO]` | A reminder again of where I'm at. |
| `ncftp>get interest-groups.txt`<br>`groups.txt` | The get command instructs SRI to transfer the file "interest-groups.txt" to my machine. I've renamed the file in the process to "groups.txt." |
| `groups.txt: 883560 bytes received`<br>`in 34.04 seconds` | The file transfers across the Net quickly. |
| `ncftp>close` | I close the connection with SRI... |
| `ncftp>quit` | ...and quit the ftp program. |

During the session shown in Figure 7-1, I downloaded the list of mailing lists mentioned in Chapter 4 of this book. The 34-second transfer was from **sri.com** to my provider's site and does not include the time it took to download to my machine.

True to form (and fortunately for us), AOL puts a pretty face on FTP. It connects with remote computers, lists files, changes directories and downloads files—all with a few clicks of the mouse. To make effective use of FTP, you no more need to know about the ultraism of UNIX and the voodoo of VMS than you need to know about the physics of electromagnetic radiation to watch an episode of Roseanne.

## A typical FTP session

Getting acquainted with AOL's interpretation of FTP can best be accomplished by walking through the session pictured in Figure 7-1, using AOL as our Internet connection.

We begin with the keyword: FTP, or by clicking the FTP button in the Internet Connection window. The primary FTP window appears (Figure 7-2).

Figure 7-2: AOL's
primary FTP window is
refreshingly
unpretentious. Use the
keyword: FTP to get
there.

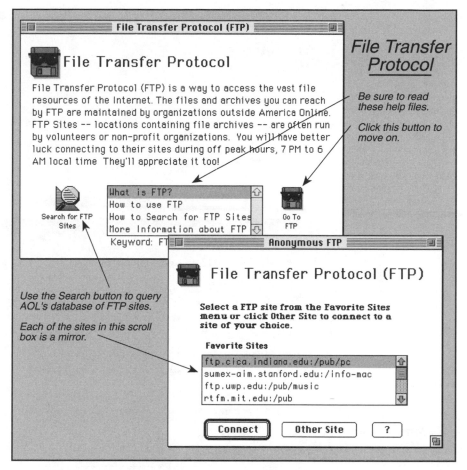

The site we want to visit—**sri.com**—isn't among AOL's Favorite
Sites (we'll discuss Favorite Sites in a few pages), so we click the
Other Site button (Figure 7-3).

Figure 7-3: You must
know the exact
address in order to
successfully connect
to a remote site via
the Other Site feature.

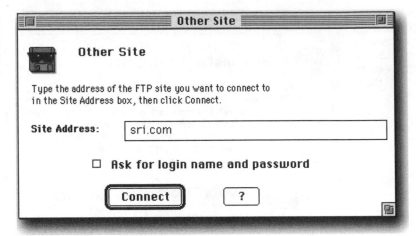

We enter the address for **sri.com**—use the exact address, including capitalization, if any—and AOL establishes the connection, automatically logging us on as Anonymous and using my screen name as the password (we'll discuss passwords and anonymous FTP later in this chapter). The remote machine replies with the same greeting (the first part of which appears in Figure 7-4) that we encountered in Figure 7-1.

Figure 7-4: The remote
host welcomes us as
an anonymous FTP
user.

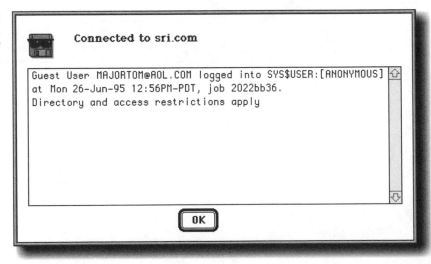

Knowing that we want to visit the *netinfo* directory, we click Figure 7-4's OK button and are rewarded with Figure 7-5's directory listing.

Figure 7-5: AOL's listing of the **sri.com** primary directory is familiar and convenient.

We scroll until we find the NETINFO.DIR directory (indicated by the folder icon) in Figure 7-5's listing, then double-click (Figure 7-6).

Figure 7-6: The netinfo directory offers the file we're after.

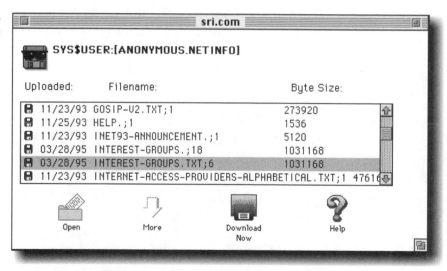

Scrolling again, we find the *interest-groups.txt* file we're seeking and click the Download Now button to download (Figure 7-7).

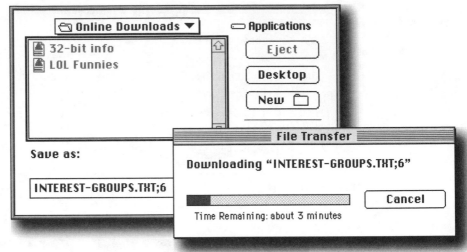

Figure 7-7: AOL asks us to identify the destination for the file to be downloaded then initiates the download sequence when we click the OK button.

At this point, I hope you're saying: "That's so easy as to be self-evident. I wonder why he even bothered to demonstrate the process." Which is my point: AOL takes all of the mystery out of FTP. None of Figure 7-1's arcane commands are necessary; downloading a file from a remote site via AOL FTP is as convenient and predictable as downloading a file from AOL itself. Interpret this exercise as a confidence-builder: FTP has never been easier.

## Anonymous FTP

Here's another situation where AOL simplifies matters. Originally, most FTP sessions occurred between a site and a person at a remote location with an account at that site. The person would log on by supplying an account name and a password, then conduct the appropriate file activities.

The need soon became apparent, however, for less restrictive access. What if a site wanted to post a file for *anyone* to download? A number of publicly funded agencies require such an arrangement. NASA's space images, as an example, are funded by public money; thus the public should have access to them.

The solution is *anonymous FTP*. During an anonymous FTP session, the user logs on to the remote site using the account name "anonymous." The password, typically, is the user's Internet address—a common courtesy so the people at the remote site can determine who is using their system if they wish.

### If you prefer the Web

If you prefer using the World Wide Web for FTP access, you're welcome to. Just use the keyword: Web. Any FTP address can be typed into the Web browser's text box using this sequence: **ftp://[site.address]** (insert the site's address where shown). A number of configuration options exist for advanced users—check Configure... under the Edit menu. Review Chapter 6 for more about the World Wide Web.

When you use America Online, the default user ID is anonymous, and AOL automatically provides your Internet address as the password. This has more than informational value. Anonymous FTP users are subject to certain access restrictions at most remote sites: we can't upload files, we can't delete files, we can't rename files and we can't move files to new locations. Only users with private accounts are provided this full level of access. Anonymous users can view only publicly accessible directories and download only unrestricted files residing in those directories.

Fortunately, the number of sites with anonymously accessible directories is prodigious, and the number of unrestricted files within these directories is downright megalithic.

### Honor thy neighbor

Before you engage the services of a remote computer for a 45-minute download, make note of that computer's location and the time of day at its location. Most Internet sites are operated by businesses or educational or governmental institutions. Most of their employees work during the day, rather than at night. It's therefore common courtesy to give priority to a site's chartered users during daylight hours. The machines at some sites do this automatically by limiting the number of anonymous log-ins during certain parts of the day, but others do not. If local users find it difficult to gain access to their site, they can rightfully petition for restrictions on anonymous FTP access. If they do, we all lose another resource. Play fair: determine a site's local time before you download, and return at another time if necessary.

## Favorite Sites

Some FTP sites are as lush as a rain forest in spring, verdant with potential. Others are more like Death Valley in August. Unfortunately, it takes just as much time to discover the Death Valley sites as the rain forest sites. In other words, there's plenty of potential for misadventure here.

Save yourself the trouble. The Favorite Sites pictured in Figure 7-2 are lodes worthy of mining. They've been selected on the basis of interest and reward; none will let you down.

### Mirrored sites

Some sites are so popular that America Online has elected to mirror them locally. A mirrored site is one that is replicated on AOL's hard disks. Everything available via anonymous FTP at the remote site is copied to AOL's disks—even the directory structure is the same. When you access a mirrored site, you're accessing a copy of the site—at AOL—not the original. Mirrors are usually updated within a matter of hours after the original changes.

Why bother? Reliability, for one reason. Mirrored sites are always available, regardless of the status of the original or the network connections to and from it. Availability is another: there's no restriction on the maximum number of anonymous users AOL's mirrors can accommodate simultaneously. Mirror connections are established more quickly, files are transferred more effectively and network traffic is reduced when mirrors are used.

How do you tell if a site is a mirror? The best way to tell is look among AOL's Favorite Sites. All Favorite Sites are mirrors. Another way is to look for the announcement window pictured in Figure 7-8. At least for the time being, AOL will announce mirrored sites in this way. It's pretty hard to miss the message.

Figure 7-8: The mirrored-site announcement window.

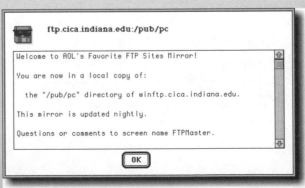

```
ftp.cica.indiana.edu:/pub/pc

Welcome to AOL's Favorite FTP Sites Mirror!

You are now in a local copy of:

   the "/pub/pc" directory of winftp.cica.indiana.edu.

This mirror is updated nightly.

Questions or comments to screen name FTPMaster.

                    OK
```

To access a Favorite Site, all you need to do is scroll to it and double-click.

## Other sites

Everyone has their own favorites; eventually you're going to want to explore sites of your own choosing, and they might not be listed among AOL's favorites. When that time comes, click the Other Site button pictured in Figure 7-2, then fill in the site's address as pictured in Figure 7-3.

### Finding sites

Where do you find a listing of other sites and their contents? This used to be the $64,000 question. Lately a number of books have appeared on the subject (The *Internet Yellow Pages* come to mind—see the Bibliography), but AOL's own FTP Search is your best resource. Are you interested in electronic publishing? Try **ftp.spies.com** and look in the */Library/Article/Publish* directory. Are you a David Letterman fan? A comprehensive library of his top-ten lists are available at **quartz.rutgers.edu** in the */pub/tv+movies/letterman/top-ten* directory.

How do I know this? I found 'em via *FTP Search*. If you hope to successfully break out of AOL's favorites and browse the remaining thousands of anonymous FTP sites on your own, click the Search button in the primary FTP window (review Figure 7-2).

America Online places no restriction on site accessibility. If you spell a site's name correctly, if it's currently available on the Internet, and if anonymous users are allowed access to it, you'll connect soon after you click the Connect button pictured in Figure 7-3.

## Files, directories & symbolic links

Look carefully at the listing window pictured in Figure 7-9. You'll note icons there for files, directories and symbolic links.

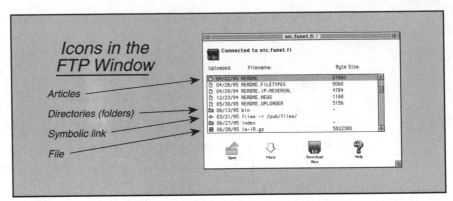

*Files* are represented by tiny icons in the form of a page with turned-down corners (**README**) or a diskette (Is-IR.gz). Most of these are suitable for downloading.

*Directories* are represented by folder icons. Double-clicking a directory icon will produce a listing of that directory.

As do many other sites, **nic.funet.fi** has a *pub* directory (we'll discuss public directories in a few pages). Within the *pub* directory is another directory named *files*. The path you would follow to get to subdirectories such as this is frequently represented with a series of forward slashes: *pub/files*. Contrast this notation to the backslash (\) notation that's common on DOS machines.

## Filename extensions

The realm of Internet servers is dominated by computers—often mini- or mainframe computers—running a variety of operating systems and applications. Many of the files available via FTP are suitable only for programs that run on these machines—they're often not suitable for Macs or PCs.

How can you tell? Generally, look for a *filename extension*. The extension is more familiar to DOS users than Mac users, but it's generally a three-letter unique character sequence (preceded by a period) that's appended to a file's name. The most common extensions are shown in Figure 7-10. If you encounter a file without an extension, or a file with an extension that doesn't appear in Figure 7-10, chances are your computer can't make sense of it.

Figure 7-10: The most common microcomputer-compatible filename extensions used on the Internet.

| Filename Extension | File Type & Required Software |
|---|---|
| .eps | Encapsulated PostScript Files are intended for placement in word-processing or desktop-publishing documents, and for printing on PostScript-compatible printers. |
| .gif | Graphics Interchange Format files are common for online graphics intended for use on microcomputers. Your AOL software can open GIF files. |
| .jpg | These are graphics documents, compressed with the Joint Photographic Experts Group (JPEG) lossy compression method. Your AOL software can open most .jpg files. |
| .ps | PostScript files are intended to be printed on a PostScript-compatible printer. Most word processors and desktop-publishing programs can import PostScript files and print them. |
| .sit | Archives compressed with the StuffIt utility or a similar program. Your Macintosh AOL software can decompress some .sit files; use UnStuff (PC) or StuffIt Lite (Mac) to decompress the others. UnStuff and StuffIt Lite are shareware, available on AOL. |
| .txt | Text file. Your AOL software can open text files up to 32k. Use a word processor for longer text files. |
| .zip | Archives compressed with the PKZIP utility or a similar program. Your AOL software can decompress some .zip files; use PKUNZIP (PC) or UnZip (Mac) to decompress the others. PKUNZIP and UnZip are shareware, available on AOL. |

🔗 Though symbolic links (see the linking icon that appears in Figure 7-9) can represent links to specific files in other directories, or even other sites on the Net, they most often represent shortcuts to nested directories. The *files -> pub/files* link pictured in Figure 7-9, for example, leads directly to the *pub/files* directory, bypassing the */pub* directory and the */files* directory.

### Public (pub) directories

Browsing the Net, it's easy to lose perspective. There's so much material available via FTP that you might assume the Internet is nothing more than a downloader's nirvana.

For a dose of reality, look at the directory listing in Figure 7-11.

Figure 7-11: The FTP directory listing at **ftp.csn.net** offers scores of directories, yet only one is intended for public access.

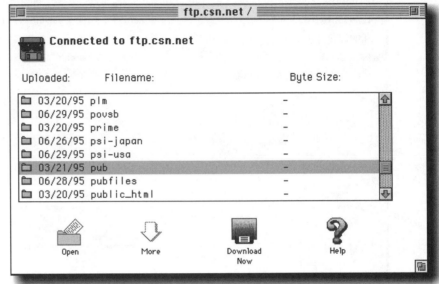

Though the figure doesn't show them all, there are scores of directories available in **ftp.csn.net**'s window. Most of those displayed belong to private concerns: this *plm* directory probably belongs to an individual; the *prime* directory may be a research project; the *psi-japan* directory may contain a database that's not available for download without an authorized password. In fact, probably the only directory in view that's open to the public is the *pub* (public) directory that's highlighted.

Public directories are common on the Net. Most anonymous FTP sites offer one. You should always start your exploration of a specific site by examining its public directory: there's probably a README file there that will tell you where the good stuff is, and you'll avoid hours of trial and error.

**The electronic petri dish**

Public directory or not, don't expect files posted on the Internet to be virus-free. Unlike files posted on AOL, where every uploaded file is subjected to careful scrutiny before it's posted, files posted on the Net can serve as hosts for all kinds of nasty toxemia. Many viruses get their start on the Net, after all, where the progenitor can post anonymously and watch his or her spawn replicate in the most obliging electronic viral environment available today. This applies principally to programs downloaded via FTP, though data files aren't immune.

You should have a good virus-detection program and you should use it on *everything* you download from the Net. A number of good shareware virus-detection programs are posted on AOL. Use the keyword: FileSearch, then search with the criterion: Virus.

## README & INDEX files

Nearly every anonymous FTP site offers a README file; many offer index files as well (see Figure 7-12). A README file is to the FTP browser what *TV Guide* is to the TV viewer: you can get along without it, but you'll probably miss something you wanted to know about.

Figure 7-12:
This listing from
**ftp.cica.indiana.edu**
offers a README file
and an INDEX file.

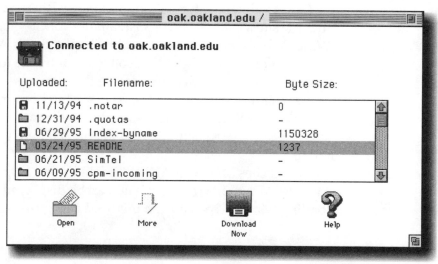

Not all README files are spelled in exactly the same way. Some are capitalized and some are not; some are symbolic links; and some use completely different titles. They share one common attribute, however: they are all titled in such a way as to solicit your attention. A typical README appears below:

Welcome to the Anonymous FTP Site at FTP.ocf.Berkeley.EDU!

Files called .cache, .cap, .names & .Links are scattered throughout the archives. They are used by the OCF gopher server and don't contain anything useful. Please don't waste our time and yours by transferring these files.

The files in this archive are also available via gopher from gopher.ocf.berkeley.edu or via WWW at FTP:// FTP.ocf.berkeley.edu/pub or gopher:// gopher.ocf.berkeley.edu/11/FTP

Files ending in .z or .gz have been compressed with gzip (GNU zip) which is available from a large number of sites on the net, including FTP.uu.net in the systems/gnu/ directory.

If you find any problems, or have any comments about this site, please mail them to: FTP@ocf.Berkeley.EDU.

About ocf.Berkeley.EDU...

This is valuable information. Berkeley's README file indicates that the site's contents are also available via Gopher and the World Wide Web (Gopher is discussed in Chapter 8; the Web is discussed in Chapter 6). The README also tells you where to find public domain software for decompressing the compressed files and archives commonly found on the Net (see the Compress sidebar).

Berkeley's README file also includes the mailing address for the site's operators and an invitation to contact them with your comments.

Not all sites offer a README file that's this helpful, but many are. Most README files are brief and can be displayed without downloading (via the Open button pictured in Figure 7-12).

### Compress

The Internet is rife with compressed files. File compression conserves resources, especially disk space and transmission time—both of which are precious on the Net.

In the DOS environment, we're used to ZIP; in the Mac environment, it's StuffIt. But in the diverse Internet community, you'll see all kinds of compression schemes, with filename extensions that include .z, .Z, .gz, .tgz, .shar, .tar.z and .tar.Z.

We need software that's capable of detecting and decompressing these files—and fortunately it's available.

DOS-based computers are served by a program called *gzip* from Jean-loup Gailly at MIT. It's freeware, and it's available via FTP from **prep.ai.mit.edu** in the */pub/gnu* directory. Read the README files that come with it for usage instructions.

Mac users should explore *Stuffit Expander* in conjunction with *DropStuff*, both of which are from Aladdin Systems, Inc. Files with the extension .z as well as .Z are served by a program called *MacCompress* by Lloyd Chambers. For archives with the .tar extension, you can use *Suntar* by Sauro Speranza. These programs are available on America Online by using the keyword: FileSearch, then searching on the program names. If you would like a comprehensive collection of compression tools, investigate the collection available via FTP at **ftp.aol.com** in the */pub/compress* directory.

Many sites offer text files representing their directory structures as well. These files are often named *INDEX*, though you'll see other names for them as well (including *ls* [and numerous variations thereof], which is the name of the command that's used to display a listing of files on an FTP site).

INDEX files are more than a convenience for sites with complex directory structures and myriad files. If you visit a particular site frequently and that site's directories are a navigational maze, look for an INDEX file, download it and print it. Consult the printout before you visit the site again.

## FlashSessions

Imagine this: a mail program that signs on to the Net, posts all of the mail you've written and receives all of the mail that's been sent to you, then signs back off—all automatically, without you in attendance. Ideally, this should happen in the early morning hours, when system activity is light.

It would be nice to collect all of those files you've marked for download in one place as well, so that you could download them all with a single command. Even better: a command that would sign off after your files have been downloaded, so that you don't have to monitor the operation. You could simply start the download and walk away.

Best yet: combine the two, so that your machine automatically signs on in the early morning, posts and receives your mail, and downloads all of the files you've queued for retrieval. It then signs off—again automatically—and waits for you patiently, with all of your files and mail immediately available on your hard disk.

Pie in the sky? Hardly. The paragraphs above describe FlashSessions and the Download Manager, both of which are described in Chapter 9. Be sure to read it.

## Moving on

There's yet another resource that's awaiting our scrutiny: the Gopher system. Gopher offers menu-driven access to the Net. Gopher is ideally suited for searching as well as browsing. Faster than the Web, easier than FTP, with access to more diverse data than newsgroups, Gopher completes your bag of Internet tricks. Turn the page and read on . . . .

# Chapter 8

# GOPHER & WAIS DATABASES

Growth on the Internet is a stupendous thing. Most everyone agrees that it exceeds 100 percent a year; in the introduction to this book I contend that it's as high as 20 percent *per month*. Regardless of the figure, navigating the Net has become somewhat like navigating the Atlantic Ocean: relatively easy if you have the right tools, but challenging—some might say hazardous—if you don't.

## Gopher

One solution to the dilemma is *Gopher*. Originating at the University of Minnesota (where the school mascot is the Golden Gopher), Gopher is a sort of "table of contents," a system that keeps track of where things are on the Net and presents that information as a series of nested menus (see Figure 8-1). All you have to do is keep choosing menu items until you find what you're after, then Gopher "goes for" (it's kind of a double pun: mascot and "gofer") your material on the Net.

Figure 8-1: Burrowing for census information, I just select menu items and let AOL and Gopher navigate the Internet.

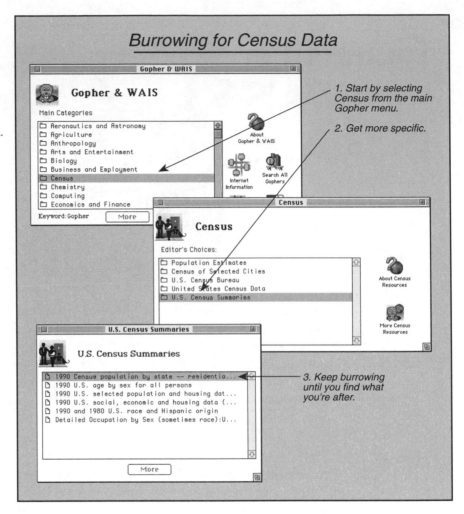

The Gopher system (keyword: Gopher) actually comprises a number of gopher *servers*, located around the world. Don't let the nomenclature throw you. A server is a computer, that's all. It usually runs unattended, handling some menial (but often critical) task. Each of these Gopher servers contains a hierarchical listing (in Gopher's case, the hierarchy is structured as a menu) of Internet information— including other Gopher servers. When you need that information, you access the server, and the server's menu appears on your screen.

**Internet Information**

If you look carefully at the top window in Figure 8-1, you'll note a button labeled "Internet Information." This is a resource worthy of investigation. The WELLGopher—one of the best—is here, as is the Heard on the Net electronic newsletter. All of the FAQs from around the Internet are posted in one place here, a gateway to gophers from the United Kingdom, and the comprehensive InterNIC, from the Network Information Center. If you devour Internet information like popcorn at the movies, click this button.

Though there are a number of Gopher servers, we're rarely aware of them individually: AOL simply groups them all into one massive menu tree that we can peruse as we wish. In a way, that's too bad, because you're usually unaware of the vast distances you're traveling when you access the various Gopher servers on AOL's menus. You might be in Switzerland one moment and Germany the next. That's the nature of the Net: distance has no meaning in cyberspace. (By the way, at AOL efforts are underway to identify the Gopher servers' locations in the future.)

## Browsing Gopherspace

Let's wander through the Internet using America Online's Gopher system. Remember: Gopher is a browsing tool, not a searching tool (for searching you should use *Veronica*, discussed later in this chapter). Your best use of Gopher is for wandering rather than traveling. With Gopher, you randomly stroll through the Internet's meadow of wildflowers, occasionally stopping to sample the rewards so willingly offered.

Use the keyword: Gopher to reach the main Gopher menu (see Figure 8-2).

Figure 8-2: The primary
Gopher menu offers a
few dozen categories.

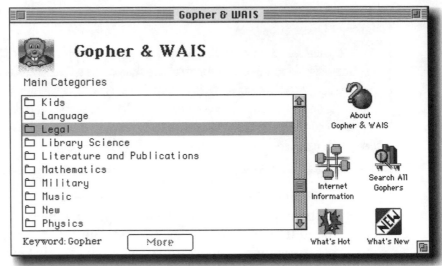

The primary Gopher menu pictured in Figure 8-2 is AOL's construct; this is AOL's Gopher, and it leads to other Gophers all over the world. The categories available from this primary Gopher menu are broad and general, but there are many resources that don't fit nicely into any of these categories, as you will see in a moment.

Let's try Legal. It's one of the richest Gopher menu items AOL offers (Figure 8-3).

Figure 8-3: The Legal
menu offers a diversity
of Internet-related
resources.

**Legal**

Editor's Choices:

- ACLU (American Civil Liberties Union)
- Bureau of Justice Statistics Documents
- Center for Computer-Assisted Legal Instructio...
- Chicago-Kent gopher
- Cleveland State Law Library
- Copyright Information from Library of Congres...
- Cornell Law School
- Disability Information -- Legal
- Electronic Frontier Foundation
- Guides to Law Resouces on the Internet

About Legal

More Legal

**Editor's Choices**

If you look carefully at the list box in the Legal window pictured in Figure 8-3, you'll see the words "Editor's Choices." Each of the selections in the main Gopher and WAIS window leads to the Editor's Choices of resources available for that top menu item. These resources are typically comprehensive, functional and intriguing. (They're not *always* functional, however: Gopher and WAIS are evolving resources and, as such, parts of each are frequently under development. The Information Superhighway is still under construction.)

If you're browsing the Net, always try the Editor's Choices first. This is the best stuff Gopher and WAIS have to offer.

Let's choose the Electronic Frontier Foundation (Figure 8-4).

Figure 8-4: The primary Electronic Frontier Foundation menu is the first menu in this Gopher server's menu tree.

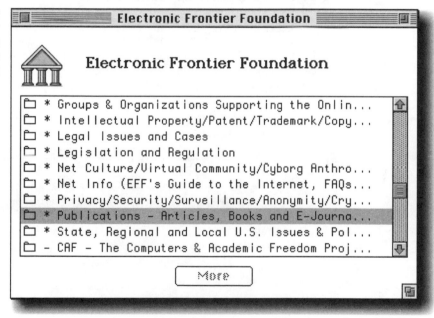

Look again at Figure 8-4. You're seeing the primary menu from the Electronic Frontier Foundation (EFF) Gopher. Figures 8-2 and 8-3 pictured menus from AOL's Gopher; now you're seeing EFF's. In fact, you've just traveled from Vienna, Virginia to San Francisco (home of the EFF) in the wink of an eye. You're traveling up a Gopher menu "tree," following the path Gopher > Legal > EFF. All subsequent commands you issue will go to EFF's Gopher until you move back down the tree.

Choose Publications (Figure 8-5).

Figure 8-5: The Publications menu offers more menus and two WAIS databases.

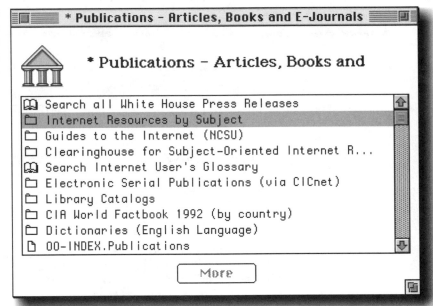

Choose Internet Resources by Subject (Figure 8-6).

Figure 8-6: Note the
More button at the
bottom of the Internet
Resources By Subject
window.

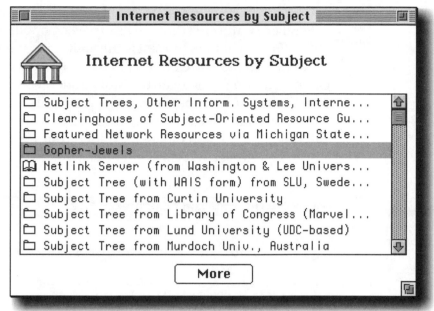

The Internet Resources by Subject list of menus is a lengthy one
(note the More button at the bottom of the window). Again, all this
window offers is a WAIS database (Netlink Server) and more folder
icons—more menus, in other words. Choose Gopher-Jewels (see
Figure 8-7).

Figure 8-7: The
Gopher-Jewels menu
represents another
Gopher server.

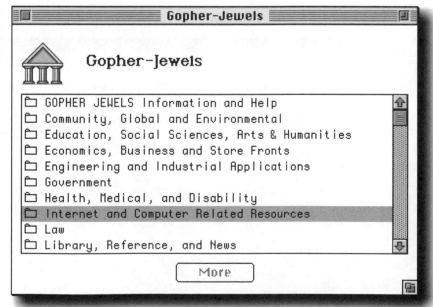

Gopher-Jewels is in fact another Gopher server at the University of Southern California. You've just traveled another 500 miles (south of San Francisco) in your travels through cyberspace.

Notice that the More button in Figure 8-7 is dimmed. America Online will usually activate the More button when more than a certain number of items appear on a list: this list has fewer than that number, so the More button is deactivated. Also notice that we're still looking at a menu of menus: folder icons are all that's available.

Choose Internet and Computer Related Resources (Figure 8-8).

Figure 8-8: The Internet and Computer Related Resources menu offers a Jughead server and a return path to the Gopher-Jewels main menu.

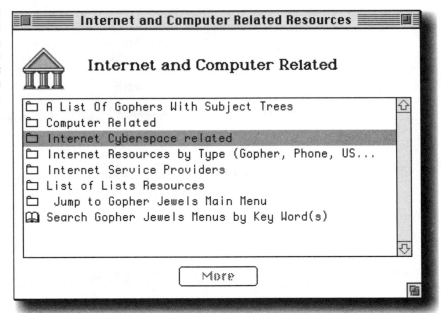

Note the open-book icon at the bottom of the Internet and Computer Related Resources menu in Figure 8-8. This icon represents a Jughead server, which searches the Gopher-Jewels Gopher. (Jugheads are explained later in this chapter in the "Jughead" sidebar).

**Gopher-Jewels**

*Gopher-Jewels* is a catalog of especially interesting Gopher resources on the Net. It originates at the University of Southern California and offers over 2,000 pointers to information organized by category; a Jughead Gopher-searching mechanism; the option to jump to the main Gopher-Jewels menu from any other menu (see Figure 8-8); Gopher tips and archives; and an Internet mailing list for those who want to stay on top of this fertile Gopher resource. If Gophering appeals to you, this Gopher is a great place to begin.

If you want to subscribe to the Gopher-Jewels mailing list, send mail to **listproc@einet.net**. The Subject: field is ignored by the mailing list's server, but you must place **SUBSCRIBE GOPHERJEWELS [firstname] [lastname]** (with your real first name and last name) in the message field.

Back at the Internet and Computer Related Resources menu, choose Internet Cyberspace related (Figure 8-9).

Figure 8-9: The Internet Cyberspace related menu offers over 20 additional Gopher menus.

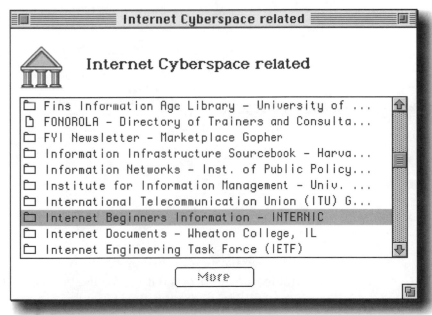

*Whew!* We're—let's see—seven menus deep in our quest for Gopher nuggets, and we still have yet to find anything but more Gopher menus. (Admittedly, I've taken the scenic route to reach this destination. If you become a regular user of the Gopher-Jewels Gopher, you'll discover a more direct path to its menu.) Note that nearly all of the icons in the list box in Figure 8-9 are folders, and folders indicate additional Gopher menus. Choose Internet Beginners Information (INTERNIC) then Introductions to the Internet (Figure 8-10).

Figure 8-10: The Introductions to the Internet window offers a variety of articles to assist newcomers to the Internet.

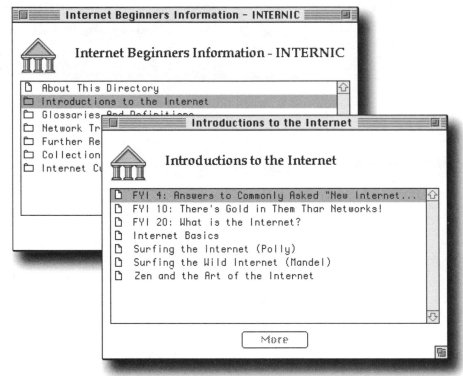

Finally, we happen upon something we can use. Each of the page-with-folded-corner icons within the list box in the Introductions to the Internet window is an article (a textual document). If you're interested in any one, simply double-click on it.

The Internet Beginners Information resource that's pictured in Figure 8-10 is a gold mine of information for all of us who are new to the Internet. The Further Reading, Collection of USENET FAQs (FAQs are discussed in Chapter 4, "Newshounds Anonymous").

**Logging**

The Internet Beginners Information Gopher pictured in Figure 8-10 represents an occasion when logging your explorations might be in order. Choose Logs from the File menu, enter your log file's filename (if you don't want to use the default), and select a location. Every article you display on the screen will be copied to the log, available for review later, when you're offline and the clock's not running.

If you use the logging feature, be sure to close the log before you sign off, then open it by choosing Open from AOL's File menu. If the log is lengthy, your AOL software will cut it up into manageable chunks and number the chunks sequentially.

For our purposes, this Gopher browsing session has run its course (though we could go on indefinitely). In the vernacular, Gopher servers are referred to as Gopher "holes," and holes they are—not unlike the White Rabbit's Hole in *Alice in Wonderland*. They're infinite and full of wonder. Approach them with an Alice attitude and you won't be disappointed.

## Veronica

The original Gopher server at the University of Minnesota was established to bring convenience to the users of that university's system. A number of Internet sites were selected—sites of interest to the University of Minnesota—and included on their Gopher's menus.

This selectivity is typical of Gopher servers all over the world: they point to Internet resources that are deemed to be of interest to that Gopher's users. Each Gopher server reflects the particular interests of its user community. As you might expect, there are scores of Gopher servers now, and *searching the servers* has become a common task.

Enter Veronica, a tool that searches Gopher servers. Veronica is the mother of Gopher servers, containing copies of participating Gopher servers' directories. Participation in the Veronica system is voluntary and not all Gopher site administrators choose to dedicate the human and technical resources required by the system, but it's quite comprehensive nonetheless.

**Jughead**

Before you ask, yes, there is a *Jughead,* and, like Veronica, it is an acronym: Jonzy's Universal Gopher Hierarchy Excavation And Display. Jughead is usually used to search a specific site (Veronica searches all sites). Figure 8-8 shows a Jughead server that searches only the Gopher-Jewels Gopher.

The result of a Veronica search is an automatically generated Gopher menu, customized according to your criteria. Items on this menu are usually drawn from many Gophers; you'll probably never know which Gopher your information was pulled from.

Unlike Gopher, Veronica is intended for searching, not browsing. Veronica users aren't interested in spelunking in a labyrinth of subterranean burrows; they have a destination in mind. Theirs is not an exploratory mission, it's goal-oriented, and Veronica is a quick way of achieving the goal.

To access Veronica, click the Search All Gophers icon in the main Gopher and WAIS window (Figure 8-11).

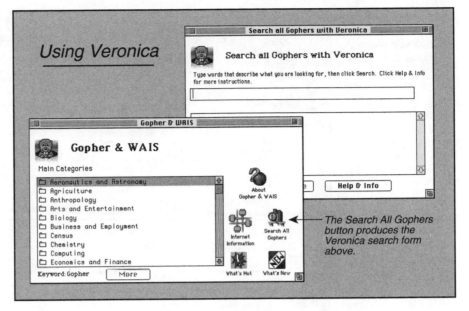

Figure 8-11: The
Search All Gophers
button invokes the
Veronica Gopher-
searching program.

Searching Veronica without a specific goal can sometimes be
enlightening, but normally you'll know what you're after. Using the
previous Gopher adventure as an example, let's search for Veronica
with the criterion: Gopher-Jewels (Figure 8-12).

Figure 8-12:
Searching Veronica
for references to
Gopher-Jewels, we
find 106 diverse
matches, including
(from the top) a
Jughead search form,
a secondary Gopher
menu, an article, a
newsgroup message
and a mailing-list
FAQ sheet.

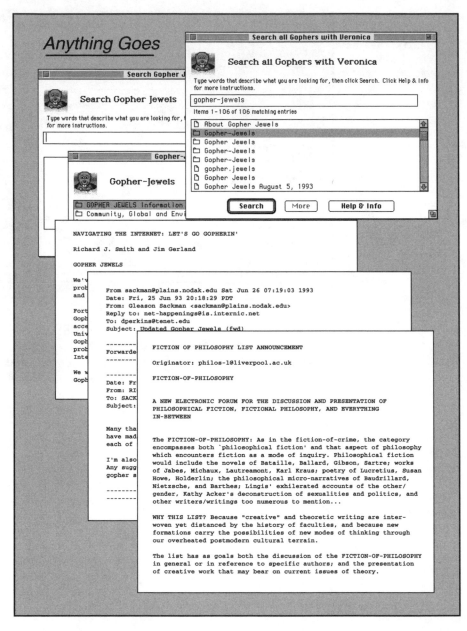

Figure 8-12 identifies an intrinsic component of all Gopher activities: a Veronica search finds everything Gopher has to offer, and Gopher plays no favorites. Mailing lists, newsgroups, databases, files—they're all disclosed during a Gopher session regardless of whether Veronica is involved or not.

It's important to note that Veronica searches are not full-text searches of data at Gopher-server sites; Veronica locates only the names of files and directories at those sites. Don't expect Veronica to find *Sartre*, for example, based on the mailing-list announcement in Figure 8-12, even though the word *Sartre* appears in the body of the message.

### Rodent-Oriented?

Computer programmers are an iconoclastic lot, and many of them relax by reading comic books. The Archie series of comics is big in cyberspace, so the Veronica resource was named for the Veronica comic book character. Typical of computerdom, Veronica is also an acronym: Very Easy Rodent-Oriented Net-wide Index to Computer Archives.

A few other notes regarding Veronica searches and criteria:

- Veronica queries are not case-sensitive. You can search for GOPHER-JEWELS or gopher-jewels and find the same thing.

- Veronica queries may contain the Boolean operators *AND*, *OR* and *NOT*. Always use all-caps for Boolean operators.

- Veronica assumes *AND* if you leave a space between two words.

## WAIS

Gopher, Veronica and Jughead aren't the only methods of searching for data on the Net, WAIS (pronounced "wayz") is another. WAIS (an acronym for Wide Area Information Server) is a searching mechanism that searches keywords drawn from the contents of Internet resources.

Let's be sure this alphabet soup of Internet tools is properly understood.

- *Gopher* is a menu-based system. The menus are established by the people at each Gopher site who administer their niche in the Gopher system. Often, one Gopher menu will point to other Gophers.

- *Veronica* is a system that searches Gophers. Gopher administrators voluntarily elect to participate in the Veronica system, periodically building indexes of their Gophers' contents and storing them at the Gopher site for access by the Veronica system.

- *WAIS* is also a searching mechanism. Unlike Veronica, which searches Gopher sites' menus, WAIS searches keywords describing the contents of the individual resources available on the Net.

Earlier I mentioned that you wouldn't find the Fiction-of-Philosophy mailing list that appears in Figure 8-12 by searching for the word *Sartre*. You probably would if you used WAIS.

### The subtlety of icons

Take a moment to look at Figure 8-13. Note the variety of icons pictured to the left of the menu topics.

Figure 8-13: Each page, folder and book icon on America Online's Gopher menus has a specific meaning.

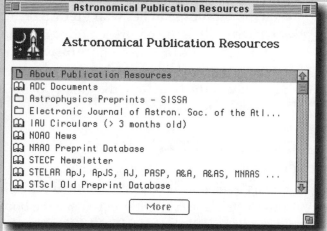

Typical of America Online, the page icon (the one at the top of the list with the turned-down corner) represents an article: a textual document suitable for reading onscreen or for saving or printing.

The folder icon represents another menu. Double-click a folder and you get another menu of choices. All Gopher-based information-searching is based on this nesting system.

The open-book icon is a WAIS database. When you double-click it you will see a criteria entry form (pictured in Figure 8-14). You'll then be able to enter search criteria and conduct the search itself.

WAIS servers allow you to search large volumes of information for very specific items. The WAIS system is composed of searching software and numerous databases of keywords found in the articles to which the databases refer. When you search a WAIS database, these keywords speed the processing of your search. Words that appear often in the file—words such as *the* and *is*—are ignored. As a result, sometimes searches won't return results from "obvious" search terms. If *Sartre* occurs too often in a mailing list announcement (Figure 8-12), a search on *Sartre* would result in no matches. The "keeper" of a WAIS database can modify parameters to improve the quality of the search, so the quality of searches varies from one WAIS server to another.

## Conducting a WAIS search

One of the Internet's finest jewels is its exhaustive collection of "e-texts"—electronic versions of the world's literature. While electronic texts can never entirely replace the bookshelf, with its smell of old bindings and the crackle of stiff pages, the immediacy of e-text retrieval can mean the difference between reading the text or not.

There are so many e-texts now on the Internet that a number of searching mechanisms have emerged, including the ALEX retrieval system pictured in Figure 8-14.

Figure 8-14: Searching the ALEX retrieval system for the electronic text of Lincoln's *Gettysburg Address*.

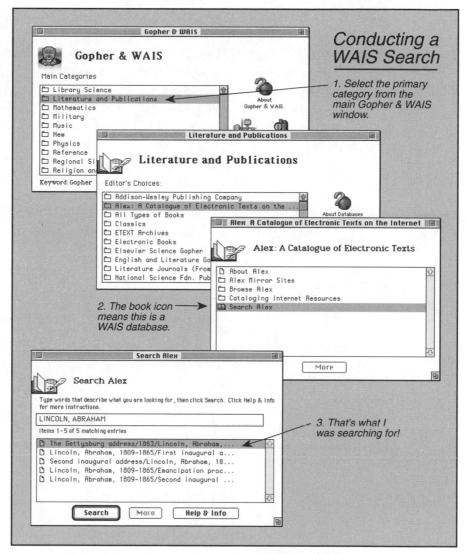

Note that I had to know about ALEX, and I had to know that it's to be found in the Literature and Publishing section of AOL's Gopher. WAIS is for searching the Internet when you know what you're after and you know where to look for it. Your awareness of these things will develop over time. Don't expect to become a WAIS expert in a visit or two. Good things take time.

**False drops**

Remember that Gopher and WAIS produce menus or listings based on information that's kept at the Gopher server or the WAIS database of keywords. Though that information is (usually) quite recent and reflective of the condition of data represented, it's not necessarily up to the minute. In some cases, it may be weeks old (depending on how ambitious the staff is at any particular site).

Thus, "false drops" occur (see Figure 8-15). False drops are occasions when you make a choice from a Gopher or WAIS menu or list and nothing's there.

Figure 8-15: One of many forms of error message that the Internet displays to report a "false drop."

> Internet error: Sorry, we are unable to retrieve this menu at this time
>
> [ OK ]

Don't blame AOL for false drops. The Internet site you're attempting to access may be offline, or the article in question may have been removed an hour ago, or an undergrad at MIT may have been playing with wildcards and the DEL command and . . . .

False drops are endemic in the Internet system. They're part of the price we pay for anarchy.

## Searching tips

Conducting WAIS searches is something of an art. You not only have to know where the databases are and how to get to them, you have to know how to talk to them. The following is by no means a comprehensive monograph on the subject—I know consultants who charge $200 an hour (plus expenses, which can be considerable) for online searching and earn every dime of it—but it may provide a little perspective on the subject.

Let's say I was interested in the performance of the legislature. Specifically, I wanted to see how many health-care bills had actually passed both houses of Congress and, optionally, read a few that had.

I begin with a Veronica search using the criterion: House Bills, and discover six matches (Figure 8-16).

Figure 8-16: A
Veronica search for
House Bills produces
six matching items.
Veronica is available
by clicking on the
Search All Gophers
button in the main
Gopher & WAIS
window.

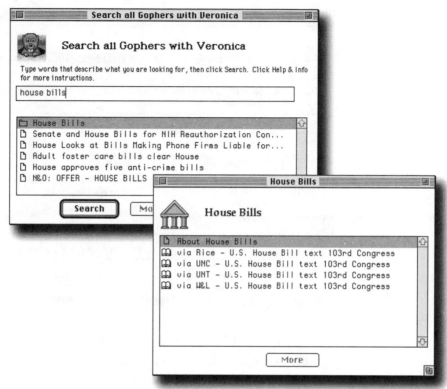

There are many paths to the same destination on the Net. Note that I can access the House Bills WAIS database via a number of Gopher servers. If one's busy (or slow), I'll try another. I chose a Saturday to do my searching, however, so that most of the academics and politicians would be out of their offices. I have the database to myself (relatively speaking), so I'll use Rice University—the first option on the list.

I enter "health care" as my criterion; the WAIS server responds with what appears to be 40 matches (Figure 8-17).

Figure 8-17: It appears
that 40 health-care
bills have been
entertained by the
House during the
103rd Congress.

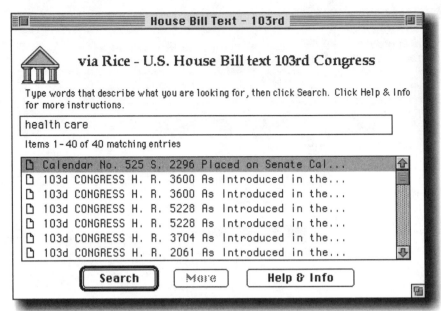

In fact, something's wrong here. Many, many more than 40
health-care bills are before the 103rd Congress. Fortunately, the last
match (of the 40 indicated) of this server's list offers a search report
(see the "Practice session" sidebar), where the search data is more
reliable.

**Practice session**

Because it's a large and fast database, and because it always offers a detailed search
report, the WAIS server at the U.S. Congress is an excellent learning tool for becoming
familiar with WAIS searches. Use Veronica to find it (as indicated in the text), or follow
the path: Government & Politics > Politics from the Whole Earth Gopher > Library of
Congress > US Congress > Federal Legislation > House Bills.

Here's a tip: give the server a nonsense search criterion such as AND NOT. It will
respond with a brief discourse on the proper use of search criteria. Read it carefully and
try the examples cited. Read the search reports at the end of your "hit list." There's lots
to be learned by doing so.

The search report for my "health care" search provides the following information:

Searching USHOUSE—house—bill—text—103rd...

Your query was:

health care

The database contains 19,361,094 words in 9,354 documents.

There are 45,205 different words.

health occurs 66,969 times in 2,114 documents.

care occurs 32,533 times in 1,378 documents.

The search found 2,328 documents. It took about a second.

Hmmm . . . While the number of matches (40) pictured in Figure 8-17 seems small, the number of matches cited above (2,328) seems excessive. That's a lot of bills for a single subject during a single congressional session.

The problem is in the implied operator. The server thought that I wanted to see all of the bills where the word *health* and the word *care* appeared as keywords. For all I know, CARE is an acronym and means something that differs significantly from my interests. The word *health* probably appears as a keyword for bills having to do with the health of the economy and AIDS as well—it appears almost 67,000 times, after all.

Typically, this server assumes the AND operator if you enter more than a single word as a search criterion. I intended for my two words *health care* to serve as a single phrase, not *health AND care*.

The solution is the ADJ operator, meaning adjoin. I want the two words to serve as one: I want to adjoin them. I try the search phrase *health ADJ care* (most WAIS servers require that operators appear in all caps) and the server responds with a more predictable result:

health ADJ care

is equivalent to:

((health) ADJ (care))

...health occurs 66,969 times in 2,114 documents.

care occurs 32,533 times in 1,378 documents.

The search found 813 documents. It took about 2 seconds.

That's more like it. The 103rd Congress has entertained 813 health-care bills.

How many are on their way to the President? For that, I add another clause in my criterion: *(health ADJ care) AND version=enrolled.* (The word *enrolled,* in this context, signifies bills that have passed both houses of Congress.)

The server responds predictably:

Searching USHOUSE—house—bill—text—103rd...

Your query:

(health ADJ care) AND version=enrolled

is equivalent to:

(((health) ADJ (care)) AND ((version) = (enrolled)))

...health occurs 66,969 times in 2,114 documents.

care occurs 32,533 times in 1,378 documents.

enrolled occurs 3,611 times in 639 documents.

The search found 31 documents. It took about 2 seconds.

There's my answer: 31 health-care bills have passed both houses of Congress.

**Watch those parentheses!**

Consider the algebraic statement *x = 5 plus 2 times 7*. What's the value of x: 49 or 19? Do you first add the 5 and the 2, then multiply? Or do you multiply first, then add?

The same goes for WAIS searches. A Congressional WAIS search such as *nafta OR free ADJ trade AND version = enrolled* is ambiguous. Do you want to see all of the bills that (1) address NAFTA or free trade, and (2) have passed both houses? Or do you want to see all of the bills that have passed both houses and address free trade, as well as those that address NAFTA?

Parentheses are the answer, in WAIS searches as they are in algebra. If you want to see all of the bills that address NAFTA or free trade and that have passed both houses, your criteria should be: *(nafta OR free ADJ trade) AND version = enrolled*. The alternative would be: *nafta OR (free ADJ trade AND version = enrolled)*.

Fortunately, the Congressional WAIS server not only responds with the number of matches, it also includes its algebraic interpretation of your criteria. Look at the search reports on these pages and match up the parentheses. It's not only necessary for the validation of the report, it's also a great way to get to know how the machine is thinking.

There are hundreds of WAIS databases available online. Their potential is wondrous. Pick one at random and start exploring. When you're traveling the Internet, there's no reward for caution.

## Moving on

In *Walden*, Henry David Thoreau said, "It is not worth the while to go round the world to count the cats in Zanzibar." Thoreau wasn't wrong about many things, but he didn't have Internet access either. Indeed, traveling around the world, exploring nooks and crannies along the way, may very well be the best way to count the cats in Zanzibar—when you're traveling at the speed of light.

The next time the urge to travel strikes you, use the keyword: Gopher and bounce around the world for a while. There's an abundance of opportunity out there.

# Chapter 9

# FlashSessions & the Download Manager

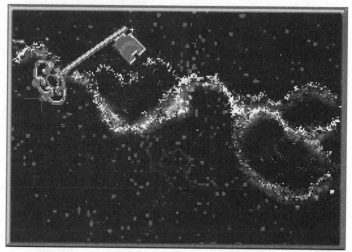

I've been getting a lot of e-mail lately. I've made a number of online friends and we correspond a lot, and I get tons of mail from readers. If I read all this mail online, they would have to deliver my AOL bill with a forklift.

There's an additional challenge to my finances: I'm a downloading zealot. I beta-test a lot of software, all of which has to be downloaded. I collect utilities, fonts and graphics for my desktop publishing ventures. I'm constantly downloading snippets from the Internet via FTP. I probably download three or four hours' worth of material a week. Starting a 59-minute download is one thing; remembering to return to the computer 58 minutes later is another. If I go outside to mow the lawn during a long download, there's a high probability I won't remember the computer when the download is finished. When I do remember it—usually about 20 minutes after the download is finished—I've just paid for 20 minutes of idle connect time. This is not frugal.

Happily, AOL offers solutions to my problems: FlashSessions and the Download Manager.

## What are FlashSessions?

Rather than try to explain FlashSessions, let me tell you about my typical morning. After making coffee, I sit down at my Mac and run AOL. I do not sign on; rather, I choose Read Incoming Mail from the Mail menu. All the mail I've received in the past 24 hours appears there—including my Internet mail. I read it all, forwarding, replying and composing new mail. Then I check the Online Downloads folder subdirectory on my hard disk. A few downloaded files usually appear there—selected the previous day during an FTP session— and I move them elsewhere on my hard drive, to wherever I want them to be. All of this happens offline, at my leisure: there are no clocks running. My Mac, you see, signed on at 6:00 a.m. It sent the mail I had prepared the previous day; retrieved and stored any mail AOL was holding for me, and downloaded the files I had requested from AOL or from the Internet. It did all this while I slept the sleep of innocence, while system activity was light and nobody wanted to use the phone.

On many days, that's all the computing I do. I'm sound asleep when the Mac is online, and my connect time is reduced to the absolute minimum: about a minute a day when I'm not download-ing. This kind of absentee management is called a *FlashSession*.

FlashSessions sign on, send and receive mail, download predesignated files and sign off, all without human participation. You can schedule a FlashSession to occur at a predetermined (and unattended) time, you can invoke a FlashSession manually (whether you're online or off), or you can conclude an online session with a FlashSession. The work is done quickly, efficiently and without complaint. This is what computing is supposed to be.

## Futility revisited

In Chapter 3, you sent yourself a letter. Yes, it was an exercise in futility, but you saw e-mail in action. We're about to repeat the exercise, but this time we'll have the computer do it for us. We'll not only experience futility, we'll experience *automated* futility. This is *not* what computing is supposed to be, but it might prove to be enlightening.

△ Do not sign on. Rather, choose Compose Mail from the Mail menu. As you did in Chapter 3, prepare a short message to yourself. Your Compose Mail window should look something like that pictured in Figure 9-1. (Be sure to put your screen name, *not mine*, in the To: box. You'd be amazed at the amount of mail I receive with "This is a test of FlashSessions" in the message field.)

Figure 9-1: Compose a message to yourself, substituting your screen name in the To: field.

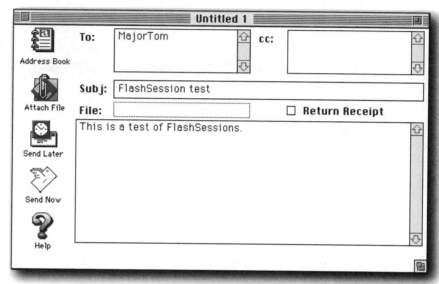

△ Note that the Send button is dimmed. Since you're not online, this command is not available. Instead, click the Send Later button. America Online will reply with the message pictured in Figure 9-2.

Figure 9-2: America Online confirms your request to Send Later.

> Your message has been saved for later delivery.
>
> You have not scheduled a session to send this message.
>
> [ OK ]     [ Set FlashSession ]

⚠ Note that two buttons are available in Figure 9-2. Click the one marked Set FlashSession.

⚠ A FlashSession window will appear (see Figure 9-3), including all of the check marks. If your window isn't displaying all three check marks, double-click any option that isn't checked.

Figure 9-3: Configure FlashSessions in the FlashSessions windows.

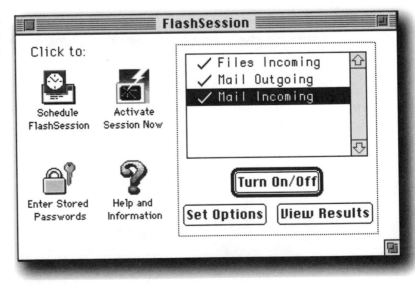

🔺 Now click the button marked Enter Stored Passwords and complete the resulting form as pictured in Figure 9-4. Enter the password you use when you sign on to AOL. Your screen name will appear in place of mine, and the number of characters in your password will probably differ as well. (Notice that your password isn't displayed as you type: asterisks representing each letter in your password appear instead. That's as it should be. You never know who's looking over your shoulder.)

Figure 9-4: Complete the Stored Passwords form.

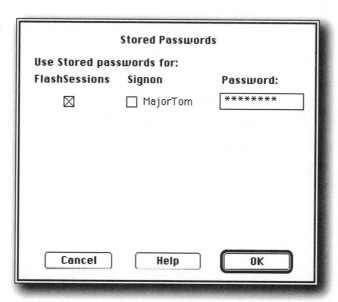

🔺 When you have completed the Stored Passwords form, click the OK button. America Online may respond with an online sermon regarding the advisability of using stored passwords. Read it carefully and understand that by storing a password— even for something as apparently benign as a FlashSession— you're providing access, at least to your mail, to anyone who turns on your machine.

🔺 Back at the FlashSessions window, click the Activate Session Now icon. America Online will respond with the form pictured in Figure 9-5.

Figure 9-5: The
Activate FlashSession
Now form makes more
sense when you have
more than one screen
name.

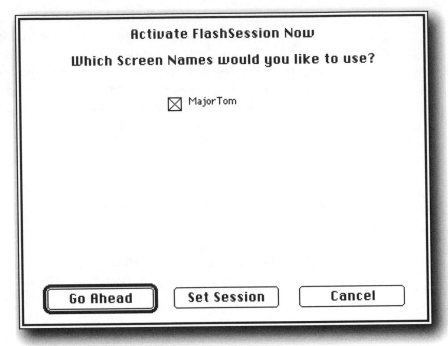

- Understand that many people use more than one screen name. When multiple screen names are used, they all appear on this form. Nevertheless, you must turn on the check box for your screen name, even if you only have one (screen names are discussed in Appendix B, "Making the Connection").

- Click the button marked Go Ahead. America Online takes over (Figure 9-6).

Figure 9-6: The
FlashSession "flashes"
your mail to AOL
Headquarters in
Virginia and back in
seconds.

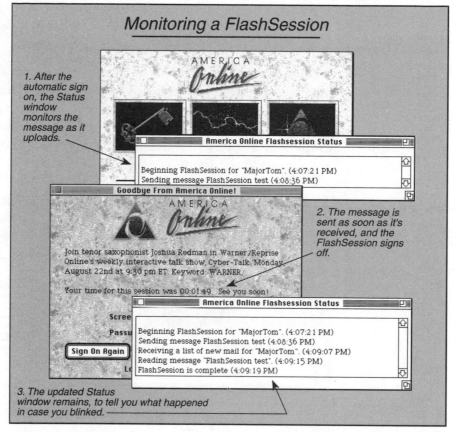

A. Because of AOL's rapid e-mail turnaround, this FlashSession has resulted in both an upload and a download. Not only did you send mail to yourself, you also received it. Whether you noticed it or not, you've got mail and you need to read it. But you're not online. How do you read mail when you're offline?

A. Pull down the Mail menu. Choose the Read Incoming Mail command, which should now be available (see the top portion of Figure 9-7).

A. The Incoming Mail window will appear (see the middle portion of Figure 9-7). Double-click the entry representing your test.

⚠ A second window will open (Figure 9-7, bottom), containing the text of your test. After you've read it, delete it by clicking the Delete button in the lower right corner.

I'm reminded of a big Mercedes sedan I read about the other day. In an irrational effort to remain the technological leader among automobiles, Mercedes equipped the car with . . . *motorized headrests*! Now *that's* technology. Our exercise was a little like that. We threw technology at a task that was no doubt best left undone. At least we're in good company.

Figure 9-7: You can read mail offline when it's convenient for you and the clock's not running.

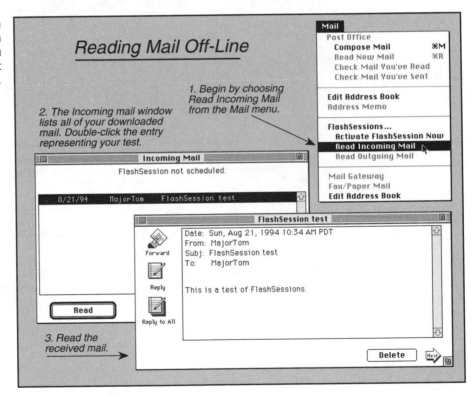

## Scheduling FlashSessions

You can invoke a FlashSession at any time, whether you're online or offline. Alternatively, you can schedule FlashSessions to occur at predetermined intervals: every day, every hour—whenever you please. Before any FlashSession can get under way, however, you have to tell AOL some things it needs to know.

### FlashSession setup

I can hear it now: it's 6:00 am and the AOL voice calls from the other room. "Tom," it says, "come out here and type in your password!" Bleary-eyed, I stumble to my Mac and type my password. I crawl back into bed and start to drift off when the voice calls again. "Tom," it says (is that a smirk in the voice?), "come out here and tell me which screen name to use!" Again, I stumble to the Mac, tripping over the dog, who, rudely awakened, runs yelping into the hall table, knocking over the Waterford crystal vase. I pick up the pieces, hiding those that don't seem to fit together any longer, and Band-Aid the laceration across the dog's nose. I do all this smiling, of course. Always smiling.

Do I make my point? The manual entry of passwords and screen names would defeat the whole purpose of unattended FlashSessions. These things have to be communicated to the Macintosh before the first FlashSession begins. Once communicated, they're stored on disk, eliminating the need for reentry.

### Using multiple screen names

Many AOL members use more than one screen name. Perhaps more than one member of your family uses the service. Maybe you have an alter ego. Perhaps you're shy, or famous, or reclusive, and you don't want anyone to see your real name onscreen. Whatever the reason, if you use more than one screen name, you have to tell your Mac which of these names to use for its FlashSessions, and you'll have to enter a password for each screen name.

### Entering stored passwords

Entering passwords is easy, and once it's done you won't need to do it again unless you want to reconfigure your FlashSessions. Figure 9-8 shows you how to do it.

Figure 9-8: The FlashSession command under the Mail menu takes you to the entry form for stored passwords.

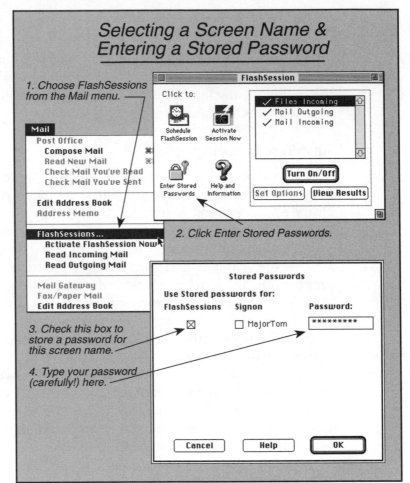

Though Figure 9-8 illustrates the entry of a single password for a single screen name, the Stored Passwords form can accommodate a number of passwords and screen names. Enter as many passwords as you wish for your various screen names—the same passwords you use when you sign on.

**A free pass to Disneyland**

Note that the bottom form pictured in Figure 9-8 allows you to enter stored passwords not only for FlashSessions but also for the attended sign-on sequence as well. Storing your sign-on password is a quick route to calamity. Once your sign-on password is stored, you can sign on to AOL without using your password. While this is convenient, it means that anyone with access to your computer can sign on using your account. This is like a free pass to Disneyland, with one significant exception: it's not free for you. At the end of the month, you're billed for the time, which can be a shocking experience if someone else has been discovering the wonders of AOL on your computer. While entering a stored password for FlashSessions isn't much of a risk (because it can only be used for a FlashSession), entering a sign-on password is. If access to your computer is absolutely secure, you might find this feature to be of convenience. If it isn't, or if you don't mind typing your password once in a while, leave the sign-on password unchecked.

### Declaring the download destination

One more setup task remains before you can start a FlashSession: you must declare a destination for downloaded files. Figure 9-9 illustrates the process and offers a brief glimpse of the Download Manager, a subject we will discuss later in this chapter.

Figure 9-9: The Download Manager lets you specify where you want downloaded files saved. Once this location is set, your Mac will remember this destination indefinitely; so this is a command you won't issue often.

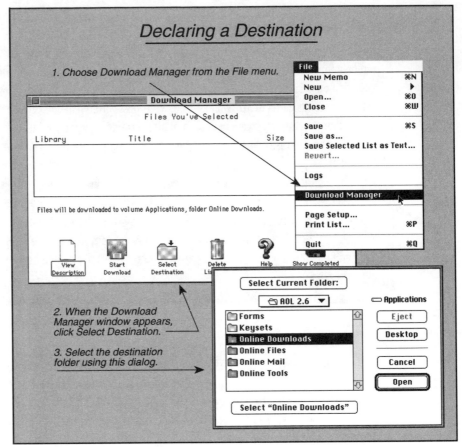

## Attended FlashSessions

Now that you've stored your screen names, passwords and destinations, you're ready to run a FlashSession. The exercise that began this chapter describes an *attended FlashSession*—one that occurs when you issue a FlashSession command. Let's examine attended FlashSessions first.

Many FlashSessions occur when you're about to wrap up an online session. There's something organic about the flow of an online session: after a couple of months online, you'll glide from one task to another with all the fluidity of warm honey. About the last thing you'll want to do is interrupt your progress with a download or the transmission of a piece of mail. Instead, schedule a FlashSession to take care of these things when your session has concluded. More about this in a moment.

Another kind of attended FlashSession occurs when you're offline and want your Mac to sign on, transfer files and sign off. As you saw during the earlier exercise, the advantage here is speed. Flash-Sessions know exactly what they're doing; they waste no time, they waste no money, and you don't have to stick around while they're under way.

### Offline attended FlashSessions

This is exactly what we did during the earlier exercise in this chapter. You begin an offline FlashSession not by signing on but by choosing Activate FlashSession Now from the Mail menu (shown at the top of Figure 9-10). When the Activate Session Now form appears (see the bottom of Figure 9-10), select the screen name you want to use, then click the Go Ahead button.

Normally, this is all you need to do to run an offline attended FlashSession. When you click the Go Ahead button, your Mac signs on, does everything it's been told to do, then signs off. It repeats the process for as many screen names as you've indicated. When the dust settles, a FlashSession Status window remains on your screen to inform you of what happened (Figure 9-11). This is more a necessity than a convenience. Without the FlashSession Status window, you might have to perform some major sleuthing to find out what happened during a FlashSession, especially one that occurred in your absence.

Figure 9-10: Once your
screen name and
password are stored, a
menu selection and a
mouse-click are all it
takes to run an offline
attended FlashSession.

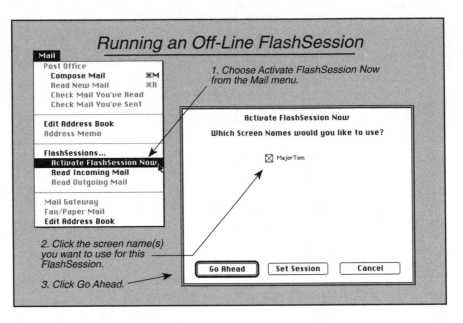

Figure 9-11: The
FlashSession Status
window lets you know
what happened
during a FlashSession,
just in case you
weren't watching.

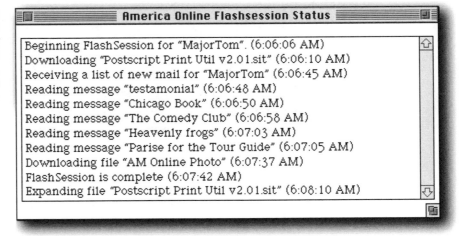

Look again at Figure 9-11. I received five pieces of new mail (one with an attached file) and downloaded a file I'd scheduled for download earlier. The America Online software even extracted (decompressed) my downloaded file for me.

It isn't uncommon for only two entries to appear there, representing the start and finish of a FlashSession, with nothing in between. This isn't as meaningless as it might seem. If a no-activity session occurs in the middle of the night, I would know the next morning that nothing happened during my 6:00 am FlashSession, and I wouldn't waste my time looking for mail or files that were never there. Of additional benefit is notification of errors. If I misaddressed some mail or if the session was interrupted for some reason, I'd read about it here.

### Online attended FlashSessions

Another form of attended FlashSession is the one that occurs at sign-off. During a typical online event, you might visit an FTP site or two, mark some files for downloading, reply to some mail and perhaps compose some new mail. Downloads in particular can be disruptive to the flow of an online session. Sitting at your Mac watching a progress gauge tally your tedium is not the best use of your time. That's why AOL provides sign-off FlashSessions.

When you've finished everything you want to do online, choose Activate FlashSession Now from the Mail menu (rather than selecting Sign Off from the Go To menu—see the top of Figure 9-12), click Sign Off When Done, then click the Go Ahead button (see the bottom of Figure 9-12). This is one alternative to the Sign Off command; the other is the Download Manager, which I'll discuss later in this chapter. Either one will work if activity remains that doesn't require your involvement.

Figure 9-12: Rather than choose Sign Off from the Go To menu, choose Activate FlashSession Now. All of your queued downloads and mail routines will become a part of the sign-off routine.

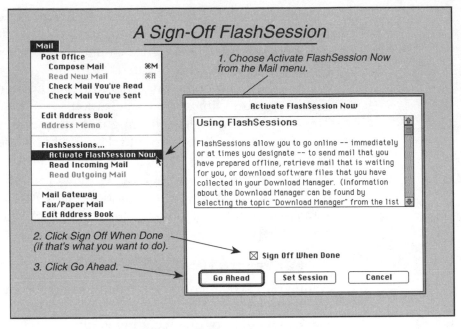

One more thing: if you accidentally choose Sign Off from the Go To menu while mail or files are queued for a FlashSession, AOL reminds you of your oversight (Figure 9-13). One way or another, you always have an opportunity to save queued material.

Figure 9-13: America Online politely reminds of your oversight if you choose Sign Off with material remaining in the FlashSession Queue.

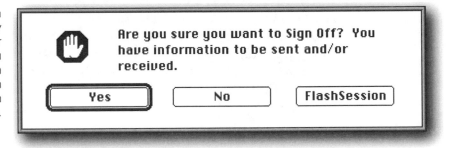

### Delayed FlashSessions

A few months ago I went to the hardware store and purchased one of those timers that turns electrical appliances on and off at preset times. I plugged my Mac into it and set it to come on at 6:00 am. I declared AOL as a start-up application and instructed it to sign on and run my FlashSession soon after the timer turns the Mac on. The key to all this automated profundity is the *delayed FlashSession*, our final FlashSession topic.

I just displayed some old-Mac chauvinism. Old Macs turn on with a switch that stays turned on, not a button on top of the keyboard. Those less fortunate—those of you who have Macs with power-on buttons on top of the keyboard—must either discover alternative methods (see the PowerKey sidebar) or forever suffer old-Mac envy.

---

**PowerKey**

Users of Macintoshes with keyboard-activated power switches will revel in a tool called *PowerKey* from Sophisticated Circuits. It's a hardware device into which you plug your Mac. When you run the provided software, you can program PowerKey to turn on your Mac at a predetermined time and run your AOL software. At that point, a FlashSession can sign on, get your mail, download files you've marked for later downloading and sign off. PowerKey can turn the Mac off a few minutes after that.

PowerKey enables the keyboard power switch for those Macs that don't normally use it (a raw nerve for some Mac owners: if it's there, why doesn't it work?). To learn more, send e-mail to the screen name "SophCir" and ask them to send product literature.

---

### Setting the start-up application

Buying a timer from the hardware store isn't enough. Normally, the Macintosh starts up with the Finder running, and the Finder can't sign on to AOL. Unless you are using the device mentioned in the sidebar, you must declare AOL as your start-up application. That's easy enough, but it has to be done using the Finder, not the AOL software. If you're running System 6.0x, it's a relatively easy process.

▲ If necessary, quit AOL. The Finder should be the only application running on your Macintosh.

🔺 Open all the necessary folders until you reach the one containing the AOL software.

🔺 Click the icon once to select it. Do not double-click.

🔺 Choose Set Startup from the Special menu.

That does it. The next time your Macintosh starts, it will start the AOL software automatically. You are still able to quit AOL and return to the Finder whenever you want to run other programs, and you can always follow the procedure described above to select the Finder as the startup application again. This will return your Mac to the condition in which you found it.

If you're running System 7.x, the process is just as easy:

🔺 First, make an alias of your AOL application by selecting the AOL icon (again, *don't* double-click it) and choosing Make Alias from the Finder's File menu.

🔺 Store the newly made alias in the Startup Items folder, located in your System Folder. This will instruct your Mac to launch AOL once your start-up routine is complete. Everything else about your Mac functions will remain exactly the same, except now, every time you start your Mac, AOL will automatically launch as soon as the Finder appears.

*Note: If you don't want AOL to launch when you start your Mac, hold down the Shift key when you turn on your Mac and keep it held down until the Mac's boot-up operations conclude. This will disable (for that session only) any items stored in your Startup Items folder.*

### Scheduling the date & time

One more task remains before AOL will conduct its FlashSessions unattended: scheduling the time of day and the days of the week that you want AOL to conduct its FlashSessions. Figure 9-14 illustrates the procedure.

Figure 9-14: The
Schedule
FlashSessions
window lets you
declare the days and
times to be used for
unattended
FlashSessions. Be sure
to check the box
indicated in step 2 or
the FlashSession
won't run.

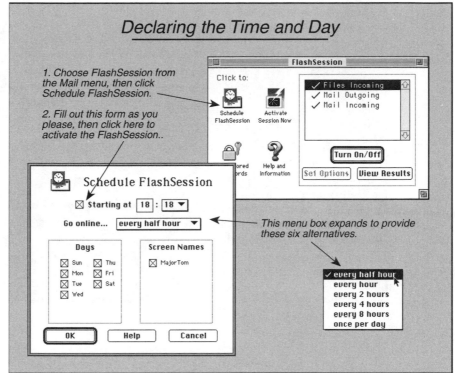

I've assumed here that you've checked all the activities you want
AOL to carry out during a FlashSession using the FlashSessions
window (pictured at the top of Figure 9-14). Usually you'll want to
select all of the activities shown in the illustration.

Look again at Figure 9-14. Note that my FlashSessions are scheduled for 18 minutes after the hour. In fact, I only have two choices: 18
or 48 minutes after the hour. America Online arbitrarily assigned
these times when I joined. Yours will differ from mine, and so will
everyone else's. America Online staggers FlashSession times to
distribute the load on AOL's machines. If given our druthers, most
of us would probably choose to run our FlashSessions on the hour or
the half-hour. But AOL's machines would bog down, answering
thousands of simultaneous phone calls. Offering limited random
times is AOL's way of avoiding FlashSession overload.

**Excepting incoming files**

Just last week, I attempted to send some e-mail to a friend. Attached to the message was a 270k file. Unfortunately, I misspelled his screen name in the To: box of the Compose Mail form. Even more unfortunately, the misspelling resulted in that mail being sent to another legitimate AOL screen name—along with the 270k file. Though I re-sent the mail to the proper person later, the person who was on the receiving end of the misaddressed mail was no doubt quite displeased with me if his FlashSession downloaded my file. My error might have cost him ten minutes or more of connect time.

In other words, to protect yourself from encountering a mistake like the one I inadvertently inflicted on that unsuspecting AOL member, you might want to deactivate the Files Incoming option in the FlashSessions window (see the top window in Figure 9-14). On is the default; you might want to change that. After all, you can always sign back on to download files, but you can't undo the cost of a lengthy unwanted download once it's done.

**Leave it on**

If you follow my lead and elect to use a timer to turn on your Mac, it's probably best that you not instruct the timer to turn the Mac off at a later time. Some hard disks aren't fond of having the rug pulled out from beneath them. Leave the Mac running until you shut it down manually. If you're concerned about power consumption and the environment, turn off the monitor. There's no one to watch it at 6:00 am anyway.

## Reading FlashMail

It only makes sense that AOL lets you read incoming FlashMail. What's interesting is that you can read *outgoing* FlashMail as well. This is especially comforting for those of us who suffer from occasional bouts of second-guessing. Until it's actually sent, mail is ours to edit, append or "wad up and throw away." (Now that I think about it, you can edit, append or wad up and throw away mail even after it's sent—as long as it's not Internet mail and no one has read it. Refer to Chapter 3, "Electronic Mail," if you're not familiar with this feature.)

### Reading incoming mail

Incoming FlashMail is stored in a hidden file that AOL refers to as your "Flashbox." The Read Incoming Mail command under the Mail menu is active whenever a FlashSession has received incoming mail. Typically, this is the first command you'll choose after a Flash-Session is finished. To read incoming mail using this command, follow the steps illustrated in Figure 9-15.

Figure 9-15: Reading incoming mail is easy. Save it if you want, but don't forget to delete it (note the Delete button at the bottom of the illustration) after you read it!

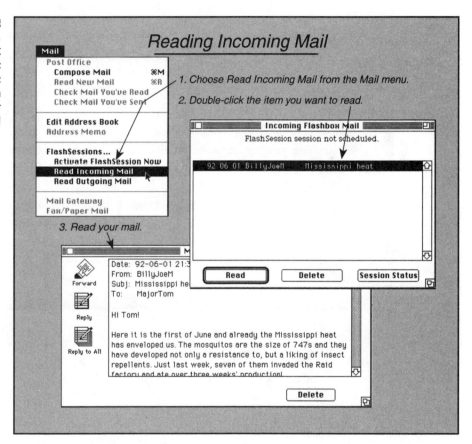

Don't confuse the Read Incoming Mail command with the Check Mail You've Read command, which also appears under the Mail menu. Check Mail You've Read is an online command that allows you to review mail you've already read. The Read Incoming Mail command discussed here is usually issued offline, after a Flash-Session has concluded. (Again, review Chapter 3 for a thorough explanation of e-mail commands.)

**Watch those screen names!**

It's important to note that the only mail appearing in the Read Incoming Mail window is that addressed to the screen name currently appearing in the window that was onscreen when you signed on. If you've used a FlashSession to download mail for more than one screen name, you must change the screen name in the Welcome window (or the Goodbye window, if you've signed on and signed off earlier) to identify incoming mail for each of your screen names. Only then will you find all the mail that came in during the session.

**Avoid clutter**

As I mentioned earlier, incoming FlashMail is stored in your Incoming Mail folder in a file with the same name as your screen name. All incoming FlashMail messages are stored there until they're deleted, even after they have been read. In other words, if you don't delete incoming FlashMail (by using the Delete button pictured at the bottom of Figure 9-15) after you've read it, the Read Incoming Mail command will remain active, and all incoming mail—past and present—will appear in the Incoming FlashMail window. This is confusing, to say the least. Save incoming FlashMail elsewhere on your hard drive if you wish, but always delete it from your Flashbox after you've read it.

## Reading outgoing mail

The Read Outgoing Mail command allows you to read outgoing FlashMail before you send it. It can be invoked either online or off, as long as you've prepared FlashMail for sending but haven't sent it yet.

Again, don't confuse this command with the Check Mail You've Sent command. Check Mail You've Sent is an online command letting you review mail you've sent during the past five days. The Read Outgoing Mail command pertains only to mail you've scheduled for delivery that hasn't been sent yet.

Figure 9-16: The Read
Outgoing Mail
command is available
only when mail has
been scheduled for
delivery but hasn't
been sent.

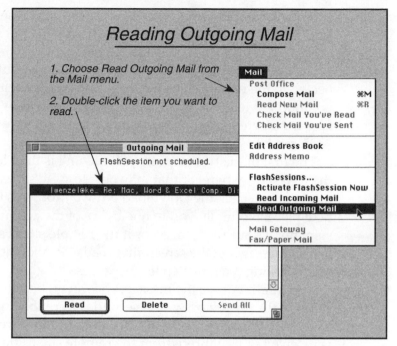

## The Download Manager

Many people use the Internet solely to access files available via
anonymous FTP. Thousands of files reside on the Net—millions,
probably—and many of them can be downloaded to your computer.
Using the Download Manager, you can establish a queue of files
while you're browsing the Net. When your session is almost over,
you can instruct the Download Manager to download the queue and
sign off. Once the process has begun, you can walk away.

Let's watch a typical Download Manager session to see what the
screens look like. We'll schedule a file for downloading; then we'll
instruct the Download Manager to handle the downloading process
and sign off automatically.

### File caching

This is the tricky part. You're going to want to read the next few
paragraphs carefully.

America Online uses a caching system for files selected for downloading via FTP. In this context, the word *cache* refers to a two-step process, similar to that discussed in Chapter 6, "The World Wide Web." As you read on, remember this: your computer is not connected to the remote site; your computer is connected to AOL. AOL is connected to the remote site and thus must act as an intermediary: files transferred via FTP must first be transferred to AOL before AOL can transfer them to you.

The first of the two steps in FTP caching is the file transfer from the FTP site—wherever that may be—to AOL's hard disks. The moment you click the Download Now button, this transfer begins to take place. Normally you're not aware of the activity involved in this step; but if your file is large, or if the remote site is slow, you may see a brief message on the screen that reads "Retrieving Data." If you do, you're seeing the first step in the process.

You might not see the message, however, because AOL starts sending the file to you within seconds after it begins to receive it from the remote site. AOL doesn't wait, in other words, until the file is received in its entirety from the remote site to start sending it to you: the two processes—in one side, out the other—often occur concurrently, separated only by a few seconds. In computerspeak, AOL is *caching* the data on its hard disks for you.

Here's what most folks don't know: data cached on AOL's hard disks this way remains there for a while—not forever, but long enough for you to finish a download later, using a FlashSession, when you sign off. This is where the Download Manager comes in.

## Selecting files for downloading

Now that you understand the caching concept, I can describe the process of selecting then transferring a file via FTP using the Download Manager.

First, you must select a site. One that's particularly significant—at least if you're a newsgroup user—is **rtfm.mit.edu**, where most of the USENET FAQs are filed for FTP retrieval. (USENET, FAQs and newsgroups are discussed in Chapter 5.) The **rtfm** part of this address is the acronym for "Read The Faithful Manual"—something like that—and it's appropriate for this site, which is almost entirely composed of FAQs. The **mit.edu** part is, of course, the Massachusetts Institute of Technology, where the site is located.

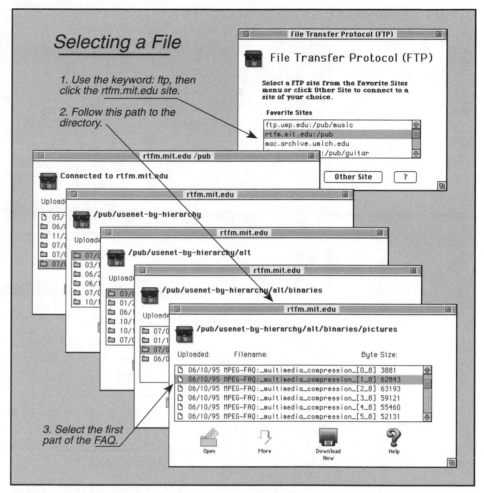

Figure 9-17: The FTP
site **rtfm.mit.edu**
offers the FAQs for
most USENET
newsgroups.

When you arrive at the window shown at the bottom of Figure
9-17, you'll see the filenames of the FAQs available in that directory.
I've chosen the FAQ for MPEG (Motion Picture Experts Group)
viewing. Online multimedia is an emerging medium, and video
technology often frustrates even the best of us. The MPEG FAQ—all
415k of it—is an excellent treatise on the subject.

Figure 9-18 illustrates the beginning of the file-transfer process:
the Download Now button is clicked, the file's name and location
are identified, and the image transfer—the caching process described
earlier—begins.

Figure 9-18: Download
Manager FTP file
transfers are initiated
normally but
interrupted with the
Finish Later button.

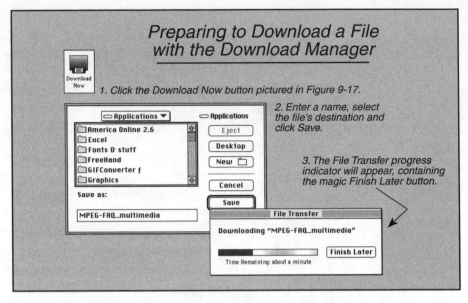

But wait: note the Finish Later button that's available in the lower window of Figure 9-18. It's active, and it's the key to this entire process. When you click this button, AOL stops the transfer of the file to your machine (you may be told that the download was aborted), notes where it left off, and adds the file to the list of files (if any) in your Download Manager. Regardless of your interruption, the file from MIT will be transferred in its entirety to AOL's hard disks—where it will remain for at least a couple of hours—ready to complete its transfer to your machine.

You may queue as many files as you wish in this manner, adding them to your batch of files to be downloaded later via the Download Manager. I queued all eight parts of the MPEG FAQ, which you'll see later.

### Running the Download Manager

Eventually, the time will come to reap the harvest. Rather than sign off, choose Download Manager from the File menu. This is a second alternative to the Sign Off command (the first being Activate FlashSession Now—under the Mail menu—described earlier in this chapter). The Activate FlashSession Now command accommodates both delayed mail and downloading activities, but it doesn't offer the control that the Download Manager does. The Download Manager—under the File menu—doesn't send or receive queued mail but it offers access to all of the options pictured in Figure 9-19. If you have mail to send and files to download when you sign off, choose Activate FlashSession Now (and configure the Download Manager ahead of time). If you have only files to download, choose the Download Manager.

Figure 9-19: The Download Manager window lists all files scheduled for download, including sizes, destinations and the estimated amount of time required to download the entire queue.

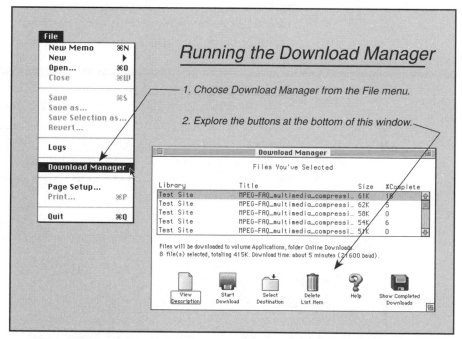

Note the buttons across the bottom of Figure 9-19. This is an impressive array of commands. America Online wants you to have complete control over the downloading process, especially now that it's about to begin.

- *View Description* doesn't apply to files that are to be downloaded via FTP. Only the files selected from AOL's libraries offer descriptions; this button is for those files.

- *Start Download* begins the download process. We'll use it in a moment.

- ▲ *Select Destination* allows you to declare a destination directory other than the Download folder, which is the default. **Note:** All the files in the queue must download to the same folder.

- ▲ *Delete List Item* allows you to remove a file (or two, or three) from the list. Sometimes, enthusiasm exceeds resources.

- ▲ The *Help* button produces the Download Manager help screens. These are offline help screens—they reference the help files that are stored locally on your hard disk—thus they're available whether you're online or offline.

- ▲ *Show Completed Downloads* lets you review your past downloads. The number of downloads available for review is set with the Download Preferences button (which is discussed in Appendix A, "Preferences"). There's no value in downloading the same file twice. Though AOL will warn you if you try to download a file you've already downloaded, you can save yourself the trouble by checking this list first.

---

**Pick up where you left off**

Occasionally, the downloading process is interrupted. Lightning strikes. A power cord gets tripped over. The phone line develops a stutter. These kinds of things don't happen often, but when they do they always seem to occur when you're 80 percent of the way through a 47-minute download. *Poof!* There goes 35 minutes of connect time.

   Don't worry about it. If a file was interrupted during a download, your AOL software makes a note of it and will resume the download queue where you left off the next time you return to the Download Manager.

---

The downloading process commences when the Start Download button is clicked (Figure 9-20).

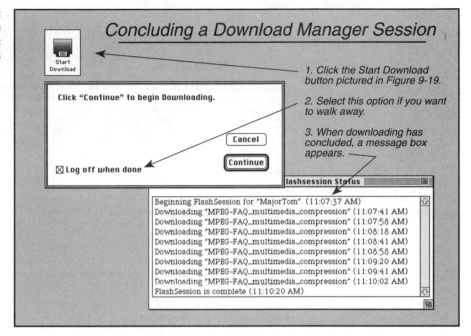

Look again at Figure 9-20. When the Log off when done option is
selected, you can walk away from the computer while all this is
going on, secure in the knowledge that the Download Manager will
sign off when everything has been downloaded satisfactorily.

Figure 9-21: When the transfer is complete, a 415k FAQ on the use of MPEG video is ready for review.

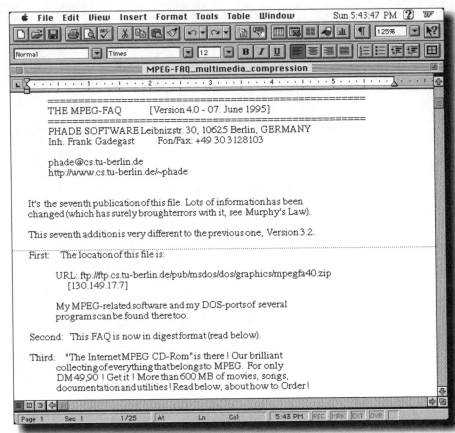

## Moving on

All this time spent talking about FlashSessions and the Download Manager might make you feel like a real yahoo if you don't use them. Don't worry about it: not all AOL members get enough mail or download enough files to make FlashSessions and the Download Manager worthwhile. In other words, you've got plenty of company: the yahoos are the majority.

There's a political statement there, I'm sure; but to explore it would hardly be the way to conclude a chapter. Instead, reward yourself for reading this far by turning the page. The "Roadside Attractions" chapter follows, containing listings of my favorite places to visit on the Net. It's the pot of gold at the end of the rainbow.

# ROADSIDE ATTRACTIONS

The previous chapters have paved the Infobahn with fresh asphalt, ready to speed you on your journey toward discovery. Unfortunately, the path we've made is not only loaded with opportunity; it's also convoluted, under construction—and littered with dead-ends.

To keep you on the right track, what's needed is a list of selected Roadside Attractions: places that have been rewardingly traveled, places that offer the promise of success. This chapter provides such a list—my list of the Internet resources I have found worthwhile.

## Change is assured

Change is an axiom in the vernacular of anarchy. The Attractions in this chapter, while more stable than many Internet resources, are nonetheless subject to change—in names, locations, availability and value. In other words, by the time you read this, some of them may not appear as promised. Should you become interested in a specific resource that's seemingly unavailable, try searching for the general subject, using Veronica (discussed in Chapter 8) or FTP Search (discussed in Chapter 7). Use the Yahoo server (mentioned later in this chapter) to search for information on the Web. Obtain the latest lists of newsgroups and mailing lists from the **news.answers** newsgroup and search through those as well. If you do, you will probably find resources even more interesting than those described on these pages.

This material is a work in progress. Consequently, I'd like to hear about your favorite Internet Attractions. Send me e-mail (MajorTom) and tell me about your favorites. Perhaps they'll appear on these pages in subsequent editions.

## Anonymous

1 The *anon.penet.fi* anonymous server allows you to post to newsgroups and send e-mail anonymously. When you send your first message to the server, it automatically allocates an ID for you. You may then use this ID in all your subsequent anonymous

posts or mailings; any mail sent to your anonymous address gets redirected to your real address.

In the anonymization process all headers indicating the true originator are removed, and an attempt is made to remove any signatures as well.

---

**If there's no one home . . .**

Johan Helsingius runs the **anon.penet.fi** server from Finland with the following disclaimer: "…remember this is a service that some people (in groups such as **alt.sexual.abuse.recovery**) need. Please don't do anything stupid that would force me to close down the service. As I am running my own company, there is very little political pressure anyone can put on me, but if somebody starts using the system for criminal activities, the authorities might be able to order me to shut down the service." In other words, this is a voluntary service, administered by a lone person in a faraway land. Keep that in mind if no one answers when you send your sign-up message.

---

To find out more, send e-mail to **anon.penet.fi** and put the word **help** in the message field.

## CERFnet

The **California Education and Research Federation Network (CERFnet)**, is a regional network operating throughout California. CERFnet was established in 1989 to advance science and education by "… assisting the interchange of information among research and educational institutions through high-speed data communications techniques."

That's the official description of the resource. In spite of its proclaimed academic exclusivity, however, CERFnet offers a significant Internet presence, especially for those with FTP access. Use Veronica to search all Gophers using the criterion: CERFnet. Well over a hundred resources are offered.

CERFnet offers a public service (**ftp.cerf.net**) that's especially rich in content, including an extensive repository of Internet information in the *internet/readings* and *internet/resources* directories. The *pub/infomagic—cd* directory reveals a gold mine of Internet data, including the Hitchiker's Guide to the Internet. Download the directory listing (don't even try to examine it online—it's almost 100 letter-size pages long), which you'll find in the root directory of the service.

CERFnet's Web site (**http://www.cerf.net/**) doesn't offer the wealth of resources its FTP site does.

## Computer stuff

The interest in computer issues on the Net is almost inordinate, but computers are what we all have in common, after all, so our collective interest in them shouldn't come as a surprise. An entire primary hierarchy of newsgroups (**comp.**) is devoted to the subject, comprising over 500 newsgroups ranging from **comp.ai.fuzzy** to **comp.virus**, and who knows how many FTP sites offer computer-related files for downloading. Though we'll spotlight a few newsgroups here, you should obtain a recent listing of USENET newsgroups (see "List of Active Newsgroups" later in this chapter) and search it for groups of interest to you; or use the Search All Newsgroups button in the AOL Newsgroups area.

### Newsgroups

**3** The newsgroup **alt.folklore.computers** is a busy group about computer nostalgia. They've discussed almost everything at one time or another, so be sure to read this group for a while before you contribute.

**4** The two announcement newsgroups, **comp.os.ms-windows.announce** and **comp.sys.mac.announce,** offer important news and announcements about their respective platforms. Moderators keep the noise down, and the information is relevant.

**5** The **comp.risks** newsgroup offers several long digests per month about risks to the public from computers and computer users. The Clipper encryption chip proposal may be the premier topic of conversation at net.weenie cocktail parties, but it receives an intellectual analysis in this newsgroup. Until this issue is settled, this newsgroup is a must. The newsgroup is fully moderated; on the average, its digests are released weekly.

**The Clipper chip**

The Clipper chip is a proposed security device that would allow law enforcement agencies to decipher encrypted communications between computer users who use the Clipper encryption format.

Proposed by the National Security Agency, the Clipper chip would be mandatory equipment in all computers purchased by the U.S. government. The government's purchasing power could then be used to force U.S. manufacturers to build Clipper products or risk losing government business. This could make Clipper a de facto standard if the costs associated with alternatives are too high. To the industry, the costs of ignoring Clipper come in the form of lost government market share, costly support for multiple versions of incompatible products, and nonexportability of non-Clipper products.

The Clipper flap died down for a while, but after the Oklahoma City bombing, its potential once again became part of the industry's current affairs.

In a recent **comp.risks** newsgroup digest, a National Security Agency official was quoted as saying, "The American Public has no problem with relying on us to provide the technology that prevents the unauthorized launch of nuclear weapons. If you trust us to protect against that, you can trust us to protect private records."

Ponder that last paragraph one more time before you read on.

6 Telephony is probably the most fluid and consequential technology of our time, and the **comp.dcom.telecom** moderated newsgroup is a vital source of relevant information.

## Web sites

The World Wide Web is quickly becoming the primary Internet repository for computer stuff, especially software.

7 **The CSUSM (California State University at San Marcos) Windows Shareware Archive** is remarkably comprehensive and now includes a searching mechanism. You'll find it at **http:// coyote.csusm.edu/cwis/winworld/**.

8 Macintosh users should try the **Mac Software Catalog** at the University of Nottingham in the UK. The address is **http:// pubweb.nexor.co.uk/public/mac/archive/welcome.html**. This site carries most of the files offered by the University of Michigan Mac

archives, which are better accessed via FTP. The FTP address is mentioned below.

9 The **Used Software Exchange** at **http://www.hyperion.com/usx/** is not only what its name promises it to be; its searching page is also an excellent example of a form-driven Web page.

10 The **USENET list of FAQs** is available at **http://www.cis. ohiostate.edu:80/hypertext/faq/usenet/**, though you might consider acquiring the same data via FTP. Read on.

## FTP sites

11 The mother lode of all Mac, DOS and Windows computer resources is the **garbo.uwasa.fi** FTP site at the University of Vaasa, in Finland. The site is resplendent with games, fonts, utilities, graphics, icons, multimedia files—enough stuff to make even Garbo blush with abundance.

### Brando & Garbo

How did a computer in Finland come to have the name "Garbo?" In his article "A Brief History of Garbo Program Library at the University of Vaasa," Professor Timo Salmi explains: "— Users have sometimes wished to know how the name garbo came about. Well, Palosaari (the section of Vaasa where the server is located) is Brando in Swedish. The main computer acquired for Information Technology teaching at Palosaari was naturally called brando. Garbo just continued the same tradition of stardom."

Unfortunately, the Garbo server is overseas for most of us, and overseas lines are notoriously overloaded. You might consider e-mailing for a copy of the server's help file. Address your mail to **mailserv@garbo.uwasa.fi**, and place the words **garbo-request** in the subject field, and the words **send help** in the message field. Once you receive the help file, utilize the **wuarchive.wustl.edu** server, which "mirrors" the garbo server in the */mirrors/garbo/uwasa.fi* directory.

12 The **winftp.cica.indiana.edu** FTP site at Indiana University in Bloomington houses a wealth of Windows applications, utilities, graphics and sound files. It's mirrored at AOL.

13 The **Info-Mac Archive** at **sumex-aim.stanford.edu** is also mirrored at AOL. Be sure to read the README file.

14 The **Macintosh Archive** at **mac.archive.umich.edu** is as comprehensive as that at Stanford. Mac users should become familiar with both. Frankly, this is a better avenue to the University of Michigan Mac archives than the Mac Software catalog mentioned in the Web section a few pages back: the FTP site is mirrored on AOL's machines—not a Web site in the UK—and is thus much faster.

15 The FTP site **rtfm.mit.edu** offers the FAQs for most USENET newsgroups and it's mirrored at AOL. This is the easiest and fastest way to access the FAQs.

## Mailing lists

A couple of lists of computer resources on the Net are available.

16 The **List of Moderators of Anonymous FTP Sites**, prepared by Professor Timo Salmi at the University of Vaasa in Finland, is available via FTP at **garbo.uwasa.fi** in the */pc/pd2* directory. The file name is *moder15.zip*. Look at the other files in this directory as well.

17 Tom Czarnik's even more comprehensive list is available via FTP at **garbo.uwasa.fi** in the */pc/doc-net* directory under the file name *ftpsites.lst*. This list is also posted periodically in the **news.answers** newsgroup. Czarnik's list doesn't offer as much detail as Salmi's, but it includes more sites.

## Commerce

With the advent of the World Wide Web, the Internet's tacit opposition to commercial activity is beginning to crumble. Commercial sites are appearing by the hundreds every day, thus it's best if we confine our mention of commerce on the Net to those few sites maintaining listings of the others, allowing you to search out your own.

18 **CommerceNet** at **http://www.commerce.net/** is a not-for-profit mutual benefit corporation which is conducting the first large-scale market trial of technologies and business processes to support electronic commerce via the Internet. There's a bit of

everything here, and it's required reading if you intend to participate commercially on the Internet.

19 **NetSearch** is a searching mechanism (see "Searching," also
in this chapter) that allows you to locate companies and
other commercial resources on the Web. You'll find them at
**http://www.ais.net/netsearch/**.

20 **BizWeb** at **http://www.bizweb.com/** organizes its extensive
listings of online business in a hierarchical fashion, similar to
a Gopher menu.

21 Finally, **Open Market's Commercial Sites** Index at **http://
www.directory.net/** offers either a search engine or an extensive alphabetical listing of commercial sites and services on the Web.

## CyberCash

Some would say that the Internet's most fertile potential for riches
lies in purse strings. Credit-card numbers can't be exchanged with
adequate security on the Net, and you can't very well send cash.
New tender is required: legal, convenient and secure. Indirectly,
Microsoft made a play for this market with its attempted buyout of
Intuit, makers of the Quicken personal finance package. That
Microsoft fought so valiantly for what seems like a small market
niche should be indication enough that there was more than just a
personal finance product at stake. What was at stake was an oppor-
tunity to set the rules for the online banking industry, and if
Microsoft wanted to play in that game, the stakes must be high.

Enter *CyberCash*—online "currency" that offers security not only
for the consumer but for the vendor as well. This is significant, as
none of the "Card Not Present" risks that plague vendors are poten-
tials here. It all works with software installed in your machine. A
CyberCash "Pay" button appears on Web pages when you're offered
a product; you click the button and a statement appears on the
screen; you supply your debit or credit card number; the data is
encrypted and sent to the CyberCash system. CyberCash picks up a
small fee "equal to the cost of a postage stamp" for its service. The
significance of 20 or 30 cents per online transaction is yours to
ponder, but the software is free if you choose to download it from
**http://www.cybercash.com**.

## CyberCud

Sometimes there's something to be said for a recess: a time to chew our electronic cud and ponder matters of no significant consequence whatsoever. The Internet offers plenty of recesses. Too many, in fact. You'll spend years trying to digest the potential unless you limit yourself to the morsels we've culled below.

22 The newsgroups **alt.barney.dinosaur.die.die.die** and **alt.swedish.chef.bork.bork.bork** offer a surfeit of lunacy. Flames abound and everyone takes profound interest in frivolous controversy.

### Rules of the road

America Online's codified guidelines for USENET participation are now available. You can read the Newsgroups Terms of Service by using the keyword: USENET, then double-clicking Newsgroups Terms of Service. It has also been posted in several Internet Connection Message Boards and in the **aol.newsgroups.help, aol.motd** and **alt.online-service.america-online** newsgroups.

23 If you promise not to worry about it, subscribe to **alt.angst**, an appropriate home for all the anxiety-ridden people on the planet. It's soul food for the paranoid appetite, as long as they don't take it away . . . .

24 For the fun of it, see if AOL's newsreader will subscribe to **alt.this.group.has.the.longest.name.of.any.alt.group.there.is. just.to.mess.up.your.newsreader**. AOL is gonna love me for making this suggestion.

25 Tread lightly in the **alt.folklore.urban** newsgroup: newbies are baited regularly. The traps are benign and the humor is gentle. This newsgroup's volume, however, is prodigious. As cud goes, **alt.folklore.urban** is a substantial wad, but it's worth the chew.

26 The **rec.humor.funny** and **alt.humor.best-of-usenet** newsgroups are both moderated and thus much more palatable than their unmoderated brethren.

**27** Wackos and rational people alike are drawn to **alt.conspiracy**. Some of them may be right . . . .

**28** Elvis died 15 years before the Web was introduced, yet thousands of people have seen him there, at **http://sunsite.unc.edu/elvis/elvishom.html**.

**29** Both **Mirsky's Worst of the Web** at **http://turnpike.net/metro/mirsky/Worst.html** and **The Useless WWW Pages** at **http://www.primus.com/staff/paulp/useless.html** pride themselves on being the most fatuous offerings available on the Web, but it's not true. They're actually great resources for HTML programmers and wannabes, who can learn from (bad) examples. See how it's *not* done here.

## Electronic fortune cookies

**30** There are many thought/quote/meditation-for-the-day ("fortune-cookie") services. One is an e-mail "bounce-back" service that responds only when you ask it to. To receive a fortune cookie on demand, send e-mail to **almanac@oes.orst.edu** with the words **send quote** in the message field. You'll receive return mail within a few hours.

**31** If you prefer your fortune cookies unbidden, subscribe to the **Thought for the Day** mailing list from Texas A&M University. They'll send an adage every night, which will be waiting in your e-mailbox each morning. Subscribe by sending e-mail to **listserv@tamvm1.tamu.edu**, including the words **sub tftd-l [full name]** (substitute your full name) in the message field (the server ignores the Subject: field: put anything you want there). As is the case with many LISTSERV procesors, your full name must be at least two words.

**32** You might also try the **On-this-day** mailing list. Subscribers receive a daily listing of interesting birthdays, events, religious holidays, and astronomical events. To subscribe, contact **geiser@pictel.com** (Wayne Geiser).

**33** You'll find the **A Word A Day Home Page** at **http://www.wordsmith.org/awad/home.html**. I prefer to get my daily words via e-mail, however. You can do the same by sending e-mail to **wsmith@wordsmith.org**. Put **Subscribe [your first name your last name]** in the Subject: field. The message field is ignored.

## Electronic Frontier Foundation

34 The **Electronic Frontier Foundation (EFF)** was started in 1990 by Mitchell Kapor (founder of Lotus Corporation and designer of the 1-2-3 spreadsheet program) and John Perry Barlow (lyricist for the Grateful Dead). From this unlikely union emerged EFF, a public-interest group originally devoted to defending the civil liberties of computer hackers. Since then, EFF's interests have broadened to include universal online access, diversity and innovation. This is the place from which to view the cutting edge of the societal and legal implications of telecommunications.

As you might expect, EFF has a large presence online in the form of their FTP site **ftp.eff.org**. Services range from the EFFector online magazine (see "Zines," elsewhere in this chapter) to an eccentric counterculture graphics library.

The Foundation's Web site is fully integrated into AOL's online presentation. Use the keyword: EFF to get there.

EFF charges $40 per year for membership. Though the resources mentioned here are free, membership provides many more. For additional information about membership, contact the Foundation via e-mail at **membership@eff.org**.

## Environmental resources

35 This isn't the only mention of the WELL (Whole Earth 'Lectronic Link) in this chapter (see the following "Great Gophers" section for more). In addition to extensive services for its members (the WELL is in Sausalito and only offers local access numbers, so most members are in the Bay area), the WELL offers a particularly rewarding Gopher server (the *WELLgopher*), which AOL has distributed among its primary Gopher menu items. To access the environmental options on the WELLgopher, follow the path Environment > Environmental Issues WELLgopher.

Among other things, the WELLgopher provides access to the catalogs provided by Natural Literacy, a mail order bookseller with an uncompromised list of environmental titles. Look for the WELL on the Web also, at **http://www.well.com/**.

**36** The **EnviroLink Network** is the largest online environmental information service on the planet, reaching well over 450,000 people in 95 countries. The Network offers mailing lists (for sending U.S. Mail, not the Internet variety—send an e-mail message to **listproc@envirolink.org** with the words **help** and **list** in the message field on separate lines). Also available is a World Wide Web interface (at **http://envirolink.org/**), and anonymous FTP at **envirolink.org**. Among all of these things, the Network's "EnviroGopher" offers a legislative scorecard that tracks the environmental performance of the nation's legislators.

**37** The **Consortium for International Earth Science Information Network (CIESIN, pronounced "season")** was created to address environmental data management issues raised by the United States Congress and the Administration.

CIESIN provides Web access to the NASA Earth Observation System Data and Information System, including the Environmental Internet Catalog. Topics include health, history, humanities, law, molecular biology, nutrition, oceanography, politics, weather and meteorology. The URL is **http://www.ciesin.org/**.

**38** The Environmental Protection Agency also offers an online service, **EPA Futures**, available through WAIS (Wide Area Information Servers). The name of the WAIS database is **epafutures.src**. Use Veronica if you don't want to wade through Gopher menus.

Perhaps most interesting is the EPA's Megatrends Project—a collaborative effort between the EPA and the World Resources Institute. This study addresses the question: "What major forces, trends, events, uncertainties, and/or surprises will have significant impacts—positive or negative—on the quality of the global environment, or on our ability to protect the environment, over the next 30 years?" Available are findings concerning water, urbanization, innovative technologies, energy and the environment, biodiversity and synthesis.

39 The newsgroups **sci.environment** and **talk.environment** are both high-quality and low-noise discussion forums for environmental issues and events. As is the case with all newsgroups with this level of formality, read the messages in these groups for at least a couple of weeks (and obtain the FAQs) before you participate.

## Erotica

The Internet is deservedly renowned for its terabytes of violations of copyrighted visuals in the form of binary newsgroups. Few of the offerings on these newsgroups, however, qualify as erotica, and we'll mercifully omit them from this discussion.

40 The newsgroup **rec.arts.erotica** is a moderated forum of prose and poetry, complete with a 1-to-10 ratings system. The moderator keeps the content on a respectable level and noise to a minimum. Submissions range from 17-syllable haiku to 17-installment series.

41 John Cleland's 1749 erotic masterpiece *Fanny Hill* returns to the literary frontier in the form of a hypertext offering by John Noring. Appearing in the Windows Help format, the file is fully searchable, bookmarks facilitate your return to favorite sections, and jump lines abound. It's available via FTP at **ftp.netcom.com** in the /*pub/noring/books* directory.

42 The Web is infamous for erotic sites that appear and disappear with the alacrity of fireflies, but one that seems to endure is *Erotic City* at **http://www.euro.net/5thworld/erotic/erotic.html**. This is a commercial site requiring CyberCash, but its links to other sites are free.

## Great Gophers

43 **Gopher Jewels** is a catalog of especially interesting Gopher resources on the Net. It originates at the University of Southern California and offers over 2,000 pointers to information by category, a Jughead Gopher-searching mechanism, the option to jump to the main Gopher Jewels menu from any other menu, Gopher tips and archives, and an Internet mailing list for those who want to stay on top of this fertile Gopher resource. If Gopher-

searching appeals to you, this Gopher is a great place to begin. Perform a Veronica search using the criterion: Gopher Jewels.

If you want to subscribe to the Gopher-Jewels mailing list (an ongoing list of the best Gophers discovered on the Net), send mail to **listproc@einet.net**. The Subject: field is ignored by the mailing list's server, but you must place **SUBSCRIBE GOPHERJEWELS [first name] [last name]** (with your real first name and your real last name) in the message field.

44 **GopherJewels-Talk** is a similar list, though without a moderator it became particularly noisy in late 1994. The solution was an on-again, off-again moderator, providing a mix that's more offbeat than Gopher Jewels and occasionally more enlightening.

If you wish to join, send a message to **listproc@einet.net**. Place anything you want in the Subject: field, and place the message **SUBSCRIBE GOPHERJEWELS-TALK [first name last name]** in the Subject field. (Note the capitalization and substitute your real first name and your real last name where indicated.)

45 **The Library of Congress Machine-Assisted Realization of the Virtual Electronic Library (LCMARVEL)** is an especially rewarding Gopher that combines a vast collection of information available about the Library with access to diverse electronic resources around the Net. MARVEL's menu subjects include U.S. Congress information, the Global Electronic Library, and an extensive collection of Internet resources.

Though MARVEL fragments appear on many of AOL's Gopher menus, if you want to start at the top, follow the Gopher path Government and Politics > List of U.S. Government Gophers > Library of Congress MARVEL.

46 The **WELLgopher** is another Gopher that's fragmented on AOL's Gopher menus, but it's worth exploring from the top by following the Gopher trail Regional Sites > The Whole Earth (WELL) Gopher.

The WELLgopher is more of a publishing experiment than a true Gopher. Like a magazine, the WELLgopher features editors, editorial control and comments, and a clear point of view. All articles are signed; content and form are paramount. This individualistic philosophy is somewhat unique among Gophers, but it may be a harbinger of what Gophers are to become. And it's always interesting reading.

## Internet learning tools

The Internet Network Information Center (InterNIC) is your home base for Internet information. Founded in 1992, the InterNIC offers three primary services: Information Services, Directory and Database Services, and Registration Services. The first two are of interest to cyberjockeys; the last one is for network administrators.

47 **InterNIC Information Services** offers information about how to get connected to the Internet, pointers to network tools and resources, and seminars on varied topics held in locations around the country. Be sure to investigate the InfoSource: a unified collection of Internet information. There are sections for getting started and for general information of interest to everyone. Also included is information on all the services offered by InterNIC Information Services. Click the Internet Information button in the main Gopher window (keyword: Gopher), then look for the InterNIC Directory and Database Services folder.

InterNIC Information Services also offers an announcements-only mailing list for anyone interested in Internet information. To subscribe, send e-mail to: **listserv@is.internic.net**. In the body of the message, type **SUBSCRIBE ANNOUNCE [your name]** and substitute your real first and last names. Place anything you want in the Subject: field.

48 **The InterNIC Directory and Database Services Directory of Directories** enable users to obtain references to information resources, products and services associated with the Internet. It includes pointers to such resources as computing centers, network providers, information servers, white and yellow pages directories, library catalogs, data and software archives, training services and the like. This is one of the richest and most rewarding collections of information available on the Net. Use the URL **http://www. internic.net/** to get there.

49 **The Big Dummy's Guide to the Internet**, by Adam Gaffin, used to be *the* free categorical guide to the Internet. In February of 1995, the *Big Dummy's Guide* was updated and its title changed to *EFF's (Extended) Guide to the Internet*. You'll find it at keyword: EFF.

50 **Zen and the Art of the Internet: A Beginner's Guide**, by Brendan Kehoe, was the primary Internet learning tool during the early 1990s. The first edition is one of the Resources available in the main Internet Connection window. There's a version available via Gopher: follow the path Computing > Computer Info from Around the Net > Networks and Networked Information Tools. It's a relatively short document (30 pages) that's certainly worth the read in spite of its age and UNIX-centric perspective. The second edition joins the thousands of Internet books (including this one) now overwhelming your local bookstore. It's from Prentice-Hall, ISBN 0-13-010778-6.

51 The **Hitchhiker's Guide to the Internet** is more technical and offers greater depth than the others mentioned here, but it will fill in many gaps once you've read *Big Dummy's* and *Zen*. Follow the Gopher trail Computing > Computer Info from Around the Net > Networks and Networked Information Tools for this resource.

52 **The Internet Services List** (also known as "The Yanoff List" after Scott Yanoff, who compiles it) is an indispensable weekly list of network resources available using telnet and FTP. It includes a few Online Public Access Catalogs, chat lines, weather servers, Campus Wide Information Systems, and reference resources. Search for it in Gopherspace using Veronica. You'll also find it via FTP at **ftp.csd.uwm.edu** in the */pub* directory. There you can download the HTML version of the list (be sure to download all three parts!) and open it with AOL's browser—that's the best way to use Scott's list.

53 **The New User's Guide to Unique and Interesting Resources on the Internet** is available from the New York State Education and Research Network. Measuring over 145 pages, it lists some 50 databases, information resources and more. Search Veronica with the criterion: User's Guide for a mother lode of guides, including this one. The latest version (called "netguide.eff") is also available via FTP at **nysernet.org** in the directory */pub/resources/guides*. There are a number of other good resources in this directory as well, including Jean Armour Polly's excellent Surfing the Internet.

54 **NorthWestNet** offers a 300-page guide to the Internet, covering electronic mail, file transfer, remote login, discussion groups, online library catalogs, and supercomputer access. NorthWestNet User Services Internet Mail Guide is available via anonymous FTP at **ftphost.nwnet.net** in the directory */user-docs/ netguides.* This is an excellent site for Internet learning and training materials. Download its directory and look it over.

55 **Network News** is an irreverent compendium of tidbits, resources, and net factoids that is a must for true Internet surfers. To subscribe, send an e-mail message to **listserv@vm1. nodak.edu**. Put anything you want in the Subject: field, but in the message field place **SUBSCRIBE NNEWS [first name]    [last name]** (with your real first and last names).

56 **Starting Points for Internet Exploration** is an often overlooked but rewarding Web site, rich with links to some of the Web's most popular attractions. Look for it at **http://www.ncsa.uiuc. edu/SDG/Software/Mosaic/StartingPoints/NetworkStartingPoints**.

## The Internet Wiretap

Not as prominent (or as politically active) as the Electronic Frontier Foundation, the **Internet Wiretap** is nonetheless a government watchdog worthy of your investigation. It offers complete texts of all White House Press Releases and in-depth current features. As I write this, the Wiretap is spotlighting the NAFTA agreement, the Patent Office Final Report, and President Clinton's Economic Plan. Other directories offer literary classics in e-text form, including Ambrose Bierce, Booker T. Washington, Charles Darwin, Edgar Allan Poe, Francis Bacon, and much more. Use the Web to get there. The URL is **http://www.spies.com/**.

## Libraries

57 The **Colorado Alliance of Research Libraries (CARL)** may be the most extensive resource for library access and research. CARL offers access to academic and public library online

catalogs, current article indexes such as UnCover and Magazine Index, databases such as the Academic American Encyclopedia and Internet Resource Guide, and is a gateway to scores of other library systems. Send e-mail to **help@carl.org**, and include the word **help** in the message field. If you prefer to use the Web, CARL's URL is **http://www.carl.org/**.

**58** The **Library of Congress** serves our nation's leaders with what may be the most extensive collection of resource materials available at any single resource. Its MARVEL Gopher is what your Congressperson probably uses. For more information, look under the heading "Great Gophers" earlier in this chapter.

**59** The mother lode of all online library references, gratefully offered by the University of Wisconsin's Madison Electronic Library, is at **http://www.library.wisc.edu/libraries/Libraries.html**. Well over 100 links are available here, including links to other listings of library references.

**60** The Davidson Library at the University of California in Santa Barbara offers **InfoSurf!**, an online resource of significant merit. Among other things, InfoSurf! offers access to MELVYL (the University of California's extensive online catalog), the Reference Shelf (online dictionary, thesaurus and more); and the Arts, Law, Engineering, Social Science and Humanities Libraries. It's displayed on AOL's main Health Gopher menu as UCSB Virtual Library. You'll find MELVYL on the Web at **http://dla.ucop.edu/.**

**61** Hundreds—perhaps thousands—of libraries publish their indexes on the Net. Most university and county libraries offer this information to the public without charge. All you have to know is the phone number; all you have to have is telecommunications software (probably included with your modem). The **comp.internet.library** newsgroup is your best resource for locating leads to appropriate libraries.

### List of active newsgroups

62 The list of currently available newsgroups (actually, there are several of them) is posted periodically in a number of newsgroups, including **news.lists, news.groups, news.announce. newusers, news.announce.newgroups** and **news.answers**. The best place to get it, however, is via FTP at **rtfm.mit.edu/pub**, which is listed as a Favorite Site (and therefore locally mirrored) at keyword: FTP.

### List of mailing lists

63 A comprehensive **List of Internet Mailing Lists** is periodically made available by anonymous FTP at **rtfm.mit.edu** in the */pub/usenet/news.answers/mail/mailing-lists* directory. It is also posted in the **news.answers** newsgroup whenever it's updated. The list includes nearly every mailing list that's generally available on the Internet, along with subscription information and descriptions of list activity. Measuring well over 300 letter-size pages when printed, this document is best kept as a word-processor file, where it's available for searching when a topic of interest strikes you.

### Movies, TV & videos

Everybody likes to talk about the movies. Movies are our culture, and now they're available on videotape after they've played in the theaters.

The Internet reflects that obsession, with over 50 newsgroups and mailing lists on the subject of movies and video. This is especially true with regard to popular television programs: the **alt.tv.xxx** series (fill in the name of your favorite show for the xxx's) is as volatile as the medium itself.

64 If you want to limit yourself to one or two resources, consider the newsgroup **rec.arts.movies.reviews**. This group is moderated, so its volume is manageable and the noise is minimal. The unmoderated equivalent is **rec.arts.movies**.

For a narrower focus, subscribe to **rec.arts.sf.movies, alt.cult-movies, alt.cult-movies.rocky-horror, alt.movies.monster** or **alt.sex.movies** (unmoderated).

65 Television viewers will find scores of newsgroups dedicated to the subject, including one for nearly every popular television show that's currently airing. Of the bunch, **rec.arts.tv** is the granddaddy, but there's also **rec.video.cable-tv**, **comp.ivideodisc**, **alt.video.laserdisc**, **rec.video.releases** and **rec.video.satellite**. For the others, download the list of mailing lists mentioned earlier and investigate the **alt.tv** listings.

66 The **Internet Movie Database** (incorrectly but frequently called the **Cardiff Movie Database**) is an extensive resource, complete with an effective search engine. You'll find it at **http://www.msstate.edu/Movies/**.

67 It's a little goofy, but the **TV Picture of the Day** does offer a new screen shot each day, along with some interesting links. You'll find it at **http://ocf.berkeley.edu/~milesm/tvpict.html**.

68 If you shop at Ralph's Pretty Good Grocery, subscribe to **rec.arts.wobegon** to discover the latest bargains.

## Outer space

69 Who knows how many NASA satellites are venturing through space at any point in time, and what they're seeing? Actually, that information is in the public domain and available from NASA via the World Wide Web. You'll find NASA's "jukebox" of over 80 CD-ROMs of interstellar graphics taken by the Magellan, Viking and Voyager satellites at the Ames Research Center, and thousands of images of earth (perhaps your home town!) at the Lyndon B. Johnson Space Center.

NASA offers a map of their locations at **http://www.gsfc.nasa.gov/NASA_homepage.html**. All you have to do is click on the one that interests you.

70 **International Student Space Simulations (ISSS)** is a teaching method that challenges students to design, construct and live in a self-contained habitat for an extended period of time. The mailing list is sent to sponsors and participants only, but it's fascinating reading.

To subscribe, send your request to the moderator— Chris Rowan: **chris@tenet.edu**—with your name, institution, grade level (if applicable) and reason why you would like to be added to the list. Please indicate whether you are a current ISSS member.

71 **Space Digest** is probably the most active and comprehensive of the dozens of space-related mailing lists. To subscribe, send e-mail to **space-request@isu.isunet.edu**. Place anything you want in the Subject: field; in the message field place the message **SUBSCRIBE SPACE DIGEST [first name]      [last name]** (substitute your real first and last names).

## Personal ideologies

72 **Belief-L** exists as a free-form conference for the discussion, debate and discourse on beliefs—specifically, those held on a personal level. This is a broad definition, but it describes the content of the list: expansive, diverse and always a little provocative. Belief-L is not intended to be a forum for the proselytization of a particular religion and/or its dogma: this is a forum for personal expression on a variety of topics. Lightly moderated by AOL's own Internet Feedback/Response/Information Team Manager, David B. O'Donnell.

To join Belief-L, follow the instructions in the AOL Mailing List database (keyword: MAILING LISTS). Belief-L is also available via e-mail and USENET. Several related texts are available: send e-mail to **atropos@aol.net** with the subject **HELP BELIEF-L** for directions, or write to **OWNER-BELIEF-L@BROWNVM.BROWN.EDU**.

## Project Gutenberg

73 **Project Gutenberg** was established to encourage the creation and distribution of electronic text. The charter is ambitious: they hope to have a *trillion* e-texts in distribution by the end of 2001.

To reach the project, follow the Gopher path Books and Literature > ETEXT Archives > Gutenberg. **TIP:** Read the Indexes; the file names won't make much sense unless you do.

## Searching

With its explosive growth, the Web could be just another incomprehensible resource, laden with mystery and frustration. Fortunately, the Internet community had matured by the time the Web was introduced, so, among other things, the Web has always offered a number of effective searching mechanisms.

74 Everyone knows of **Yahoo**, but few know that it's really an acronym for "Yet Another Hierarchical Officious Oracle." Operated by Stanford University, Yahoo is probably the Web's most-visited site, and with good reason: tens of thousands of links are offered here, in an effective, hierarchical format. If your Favorite Places list only contains one entry, make it **http://www.yahoo.com/**.

75 *WebCrawler* has emerged as one of the Web's favored devices for searching, so much so that AOL recently bought it. It's still available to anyone on the Web at **http://webcrawler.cs. washington.edu/WebCrawler/WebQuery.html**.

76 For those really tough searches, consult **SavvySearch** at **http:/ /www.cs.colostate.edu/~dreiling/smartform.html**. SavvySearch actually feeds your search criteria to multiple other search engines (including Yahoo and WebCrawler, mentioned above) and reports the results back to you. It's a remarkable facility, as comprehensive as a Web-searching tool can be.

## Testing

So many people send messages to newsgroups and mailing lists to see if they work that a number of test-only newsgroups and mailing lists have been established for just this purpose. Don't test anywhere but here. For newsgroup testing, join **alt.test** and **aol.test**. For mailing list testing, subscribe to **bit.listserv.test**. None of these resources makes very good reading.

## The USENET Oracle

**77** Mentioned in Chapter 5, the **USENET Oracle** follows the ancient tradition of oracular consultation and reply. Hercules consulted the Delphic Oracle; King Cepheus consulted the Oracle of Ammon (who told him to chain his daughter Andromeda to the rocks of Joppa: some oracles are more malevolent than others).

There's a twist, however: as atonement for a reply, the USENET Oracle often asks a question in return. Your e-mailed reply is reviewed by the Oracle "priesthood," and, if it's worthy, it becomes an "Oracle" posting itself. Befitting of the Internet anarchy, the Oracle is actually members of the list, asking and answering questions of one another. The priesthood maintains the quality and character of the Oracularities, but the members are the source.

The Oracle is available either as a mailing list or as a newsgroup. If you want to learn about the mailing list, send e-mail to **oracle-request@cs.indiana.edu**; place the word **help** in the subject line. To participate in the newsgroup, subscribe to **rec.humor.oracle**.

## Weather

If there's one thing the Internet has plenty of, it's weather. Few media are better suited to weather data: the Internet is almost immediate, it's convenient, and it's capable of posting graphics—satellite images in particular—in formats that can be downloaded and displayed by any Macintosh or Windows-compatible machine.

Frankly, one of the best weather resources around is AOL's own, accessible via the keyword: Weather. It's not an Internet resource, but it offers many of the images posted on the Net, all properly organized and available for quick downloading, even if you don't have FTP access.

**78** For inveterate Internet surfers, you can FTP to **earlybird.think.com** and look in the directory */pub/weather/ maps/*. Most of the images there are in GIF format.

**79** A number of interesting NOAA (National Oceanographic and Atmospheric Administration) images are available via FTP to **photo1.si.edu**. Look in the directory **/More.Smithsonian.Stuff/**

**nasm.planetarium/**. Some of these images are rather large. Be sure you investigate their file size before downloading them, especially during periods of high network activity.

80 A map of the U.S. overlaid with the current (usually within the hour) satellite weather image is always available at **http:// rs560.cl.msu.edu/weather/uscmp.gif**. **TIP:** Click the Reload button in the browser's window if the broswer retrieves an old image from your cache.

81 You can download radar and infrared "movies" of thunderstorms and cloud formations before they're broadcast on the 6 o'clock news, by connecting to **http://rs560.cl.msu.edu/weather/**.

82 A final, comprehensive weather-map resource is **The Daily Planet**, available at **http://www.atmos.uiuc.edu/**.

83 This is by no means a complete listing of all weather-related sites on the Internet. The **Sources of Meteorological Data FAQ** lists hundreds of other meteorological sources and is available via anonymous FTP from **rtfm.mit.edu**. Look for the file *weather/ data/part1* in the directory */pub/usenet/news.answers*. The FAQ is also posted every two weeks in the **sci.geo.meteorology**, **news.answers** and **sci.answers** newsgroups. These sources are constantly changing and new sources appear as unique weather conditions warrant.

## Women

The Internet is rich with resources for women, a welcome fact for Internet women who—according to most sources—comprise less than 10 percent of Internet users.

84 The **Women's Wire Gopher** serves the information and networking needs of women, offering a central source for women's legislation, health issues, movie reviews and calendars. To get there, follow the AOL Gopher path Other Gophers > Women's Wire Gopher.

85 **Women's Web** contains news, Internet resources, and a forum for the discussion of women's issues. You'll find it at **http://cyber.sfgate.com/examiner/womensweb.html**.

86    For an extensive listing of most of the women's resources available on the Net, search Veronica with the criterion: Women. Women doing so will never feel in the Net minority again.

## Zines

The Internet is the premier home for *zines* (pronounced zeens): the alternative magazines of the electronic age. Zines take many forms, though the electronically formatted ones posted directly to the Net are the most effective use of the medium—and perhaps most indicative of what will be offered in the future.

87    The ultimate reference to zines both electronic and conventional is the newsgroup **alt.zines**. Here you'll find everything from subscription offers for traditional (mailed paper) zines, Internet mailing-list zines, zines in Windows Help format, zines in PostScript format, and zines in Macintosh TeachText format. You'll also find the zine-scene invertebrate life-forms here (often the best): the text-only zines, which are often posted directly to the newsgroup.

88    **Computer Underground Digest (CuD)** is a moderated weekly electronic journal/newsletter dedicated to the sharing of information and to the presentation and debate of diverse views. The quality of this publication is praiseworthy: the topics are contemporary, the prose is sensible and it's free.

To subscribe to CuD, send a one-line message: **SUB CUDIGEST [your name]** (substitute your real name) to **listserv@vmd.cso.uiuc.edu**.

Past issues of CuD can also be found in the USENET **comp.society.cu-digest**. You can review archives of CuD via FTP at **etext.archive.umich.edu in** */pub/CuD/*.

89    **EFFector Online** is the online publication of the Electronic Frontier Foundation. Like CuD, EFFector Online serves as a watchdog over cyberspace, including privacy, freedom, and first amendment rights. Join EFF to be added to their mailing list; discover more by using the keyword: EFF.

90 Tables of Contents for over 200 top printed magazines available around the country are available at **http://www.mag-browse.com/.**

91 The **World Wide Web Virtual Library** offers, among other things, an exhaustive listing of electronic journals and, of course, every item on the list is a link. Check it out at **http://www.w3.org/hypertext/DataSources/bySubject/Electronic_Journals.html.**

92 **WIRED Magazine**—the penultimate zine—is available at most newsstands around the country. The subject is electronic telecommunications, though it's approached from a very nontechnical perspective.

Being a journal of electronic communications, however, WIRED is also available electronically at **http://www.wired.com/.** Typical of the magazine, this site is not only a salient information resource, it's also an artistic journey through avant-garde design.

The newsgroup **alt.wired**, while not sanctioned by the magazine, is a lively forum of discussion without the potential for editorial interference. The magazine's editors compare the newsgroup to "a fire-hydrant of commentary and passionate opinions," and it's indeed that.

For the most convenient WIRED access, use the keyword: WIRED and explore AOL's ultra-fast search mechanism to access past issues of WIRED.

93 In fact, *America Online* is becoming quite aggressive with scores of newsstand magazines in electronic format, ranging from *Car & Driver* to *The New Republic*. Most of these magazine "forums" are maintained by independent producers, and their quality varies significantly. Notably, *Smithsonian*, *National Geographic* and *Omni* offer both textual and graphical "outtake" material that may not appear in the magazines' paper counterparts. Sign on and use the keyword: Newsstand.

# Appendix A
# PREFERENCES

The Internet means many things to many people. America Online recognizes the wide variety of ways members use its resources. With these differences in mind, AOL offers the opportunity to customize the software to your needs. You may wish to change the type size of your mail so that Internet e-mail is easier to read. Or you may wish to have your Internet mail saved as text for easier reference. You may even prefer to change the colors of your Web browser.

These are all just a matter of preference—Member Preferences, that is. You can set your own particular preferences for most functions by choosing Set Preferences from the Members menu or using the keyboard shortcut Command+=. Web preferences can be set by selecting Configure from the Edit menu while in the Browser or by pressing Command+Option+C. Preferences can be set online or off, so you're best advised to set them offline while the meter isn't running. Seven categories of preferences are available under Set Preferences, listed on the left side of your screen (see Figure A-1). To select a preference category, click it once. Then you can double-click any item from the preference list on the right side of the screen to turn it on or off. A preference that's turned on is indicated by a check mark next to it.

Figure A-1: The
Preferences dialog
box.

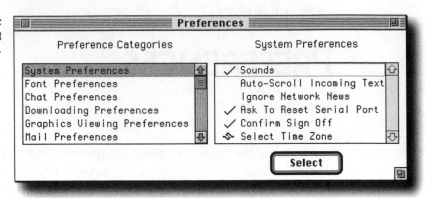

There are many functions you can change with the preferences in
America Online, but we'll concentrate on those which are relevant to
the Internet. Here they are:

## System Preferences

This dialog box is where you control the basics of your AOL software (see Figure A-1 again).

- *Sounds* allows you to disable (or enable) the basic sounds
  within the AOL software, such as "Welcome," "Good-bye,"
  and "File's done." Other sounds are controlled from within
  their own preference category, including chat sounds and the
  "You've got mail" notification. If you download files via FTP
  often, you might prefer to turn your sounds off to avoid
  waking up your neighbors. (The default setting is On.)

- *Auto-Scroll Incoming Text* scrolls the text of articles when they
  are opened online or off. At 9600 baud or faster, you can't read
  this fast, so scrolling incoming text is of no particular value. It
  makes the screen a busy place to watch, and, in some cases,
  may actually slow down the transmission speed of text transfers. That's why the default is Off. It's always better to log
  incoming text and read your logged text after you sign off.
  However, if for some reason you prefer to have articles scroll
  as they are received, turn this preference on.

🔊 *Ignore Network News* will turn off the occasional informational bulletin that AOL sends to members. These consist primarily of announcements about when AOL is going down for maintenance, so you are advised to keep these on. You don't need to do anything to receive them—they automatically appear at the top of your screen, and they don't interrupt what you're doing. If you would prefer not to see these messages while you're online, leave the "Ignore Network News" feature turned off (which is the default). **Note:** If you are using the Web browser, you will not see these messages unless you return to the AOL program.

🔊 *Confirm Sign-Off* allows you to disable the "Are you sure you want to sign off?" dialog box that appears when you select Sign Off from the Go To menu. While this may seem annoying, it is a good idea to leave this one turned on in case you accidentally hit Command+Q (for Quit) which signs you off before it quits. Left on (which is the default), this command interrupts that potential accident.

🔊 *Select Time Zone* will change the date stamp which appears in your incoming e-mail. If you don't live in the Eastern time zone (the default), you may consider changing this.

## Font Preferences

America Online allows you to declare your preference for the font and size of the typeface you see in online text, articles, in chat and conference rooms, and in your mail (see Figure A-2). For example, if you receive a lot of Internet mail, you might prefer to change the size of your mail font to 9, which will accommodate the fixed line length of Internet mail. You can select any font and size that you have installed on your Macintosh system. The font you select as your mail font will be seen when you compose and receive mail, *but the formatting will not be seen by the recipient if you sent the mail over the Internet.*

Figure A-2: The Fonts
Preferences provide
control over text seen
online.

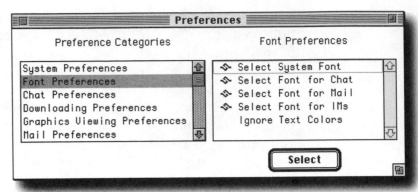

**Tip**
Many areas of the Internet use a "tabular" arrangement for information (that is, text
and numbers in columns and rows). If you receive or send a lot of mail in this format,
or if you frequently access information received in this way, you might prefer to use a
monospaced font, such as Monaco or Courier.

## Chat Preferences

Here you can opt to have incoming text in chat rooms (such as the
Internet chat room) appear on your screen double-spaced. Also, you
can turn off sounds that other members might send you in chat
areas.

Figure A-3: Chat
Preferences allow you
to customize chat and
conference rooms.

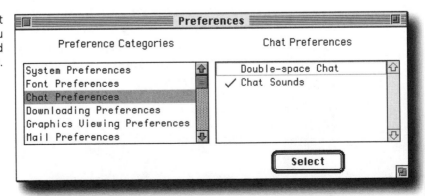

## Downloading Preferences

Your AOL software contains two decompression utilities: StuffIt and UnZIP (the decompression technology used by most DOS and Windows computers). You will find that many files are "stuffed" or "zipped"—that is, they've been compressed so they take up less space. The advantage to this is that they take less time to download, which saves you time and money. Your software also contains the routines necessary to expand most self-extracting archives (SEA files). Before you use these files, however, they must be expanded using the decompression utilities that come with your AOL software. Use these preferences to customize downloading to suit your needs (see Figure A-4).

Figure A-4: The Downloading Preferences provide control over your downloading configuration.

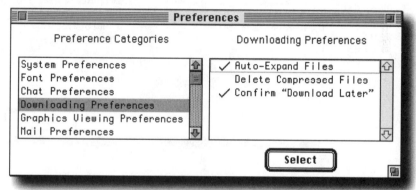

    *Auto Expand Files* decompresses any files you've downloaded when you sign off. If you prefer that these files not be expanded, you can turn off this preference. You'll want to do this if you download to floppies, which might not be capable of holding both the downloaded archive and the files it creates when it's expanded. (The default is On.)

    *Delete Compressed Files* will automatically delete any compressed file that was expanded when you signed off. This will save space on your hard drive. On the other hand, the compressed file is a form of insurance, and you might want to save it on a floppy for archival purposes. You be the judge. (The default is Off.)

⚠ *Confirm "Download Later"* will ask you to verify that you really want to download a file later when you click a "Download Later" button. This preference turns the message off if you wish. (The default is On.)

## Graphics Viewing Preferences

These preferences pertain to the onscreen viewing of graphics as they're received in the AOL software (see Figure A-5), such as an image you might find in a newsgroup.

Figure A-5: The Graphics Viewing Preferences allow you to control how and when graphics are viewed.

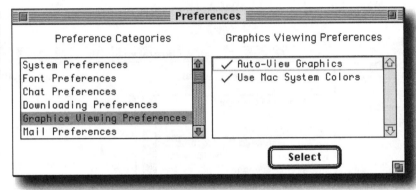

⚠ *Auto-View Graphics* allows you to view most graphics as they're received. Viewing them allows you to abort the download if you don't like (or need) what you see. It's best to leave this preference on unless your Mac is very low on memory, or very slow. (The default is On.)

⚠ *Use Mac System Colors* will speed the display of graphics a bit. Some graphics arrive with their own "palette," and while this may make them look better, it means the Mac has to consult the palette for every pixel in the graphic. Using the Mac's system colors eliminates the need for this consultation and speeds things up a bit. Leave this on (the default) if you want speed; turn it off if you want the most faithful colors in your graphics.

## Mail Preferences

Electronic mail is an important part of the Internet (e-mail is discussed in Chapter 3). Here are the preferences that apply to your e-mail.

Figure A-6: The Mail Preferences offer control over mail sent and received.

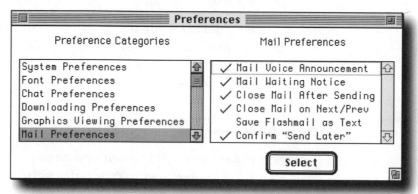

    *Mail Voice Announcement* will play the "You've Got Mail!" when you first sign on, or if you receive a piece of mail in your empty mailbox while you're online. If you prefer not to be interrupted by the announcement, or don't want to disturb those around you, turn off the Mail Voice Announcement. (The default is On.)

    *Mail Waiting Notice* flashes a little mailbox icon on your menu bar when you have mail. If you don't like this notice, you can turn it off. (The default is On.)

    *Close Mail After Sending* will close an e-mail window after you've sent it to the recipient. If you would like to keep a document you've already sent open on your screen, turn this preference off. (The default is On.)

    *Close Mail on Next/Previous* will automatically close a mail window after you've finished reading it and clicked on either the "Next" or "Previous" arrow (located at the bottom of the mail window). This prevents leaving a "bread crumb" trail of open windows across your screen. If you want these windows to stay open, turn this preference off. (The default is On.)

▲ *Save FlashMail as Text* allows you to save incoming Flashmail as a text-only document, rather than the proprietary format it will use otherwise. This is useful if you want to review your Flashmail with other software, such as a word processor. If you do, however, you'll not have access to automated replies and forwards—a major inconvenience. (The default is Off.)

▲ *Confirm "Send Later"* displays a message that confirms your intention to send mail later when you compose mail offline and click the "Send Later" button. If you would rather not encounter that message, turn this option off. (The default is On.)

## WWW Preferences

In addition to the preferences discussed already, the Web Browser has its own set of preferences to customize your Web walking tours. These preferences are found within the Browser—select Configure... under the Edit menu and click the Web icon (see Figure A-7). Keep in mind that these preferences should be set *before* you enter the Web and that the Configure window must be closed for any changes to take effect.

Figure A-7: The World Wide Web Preferences provide a number of configuration options.

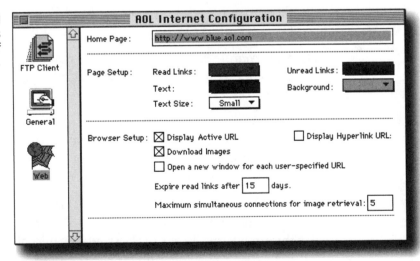

🔺 *Home Page* allows you to designate the page you'd like to start at when you first enter the Web. Change this to another URL if you'd like to begin at that page instead. (The default setting is the address for AOL's own Web site.)

🔺 *Page Setup* provides control over the colors and text sizes used in the Browser. The colors for the read and unread links (red and blue, respectively) are the standard for Web browsers in general, so you are advised to keep these colors unchanged. You may find it easier to view pages with a white background as opposed to gray (the default). If you are using a mono-chrome monitor, you will want the background white and everything else black. Change the text size if you find the default hard to read.

## Browser Setup

🔺 *Display Active URL* gives you the URL (address) at the top of the window for the Web page you are on. This is useful if you want to double-check that you are where you meant to be, but it isn't necessary. You may disable this option if you'd prefer more room in your browser window. (The default setting is On.)

🔺 *Display Hyperlink URL* will show the URL for a link when your cursor moves over the word/phrase (hypertext) or button (hypergraphic) that leads to it. The destination address appears directly below the active URL. This serves as an added cue that there is another link available from a Web page, as well as clueing you in to where the link will go. (The default setting is Off.)

🔺 *Download Images* will download graphic files when you click on their respective hyperlinks in a page. This can be a surprise if you weren't expecting a file download, and you can turn this option off if you prefer. (The default is On.)

🔺 *Open a new window for each user-specified URL* will place a new Web page in its own window when you either manually type in a URL address or double-click an item in a Hot List. This is useful if you want to keep a page, such as your home page, always visible while you move about the Web. Be careful though—with this preference enabled you can collect many windows and use more memory than necessary. (The default is Off.)

🔺 *Expire read links after XX days* allows you to set the amount of time that a link you've already visited will appear as such in a page. Remember, links you've read appear in a different color than unread links. In general, it is useful to know if you've visited a page in the past, but the choice is yours. (The default is 15 days.)

🔺 *Maximum simultaneous connections for image retrieval* provides a safeguard when you've opened a number of pages at the same time. This option is set to a low number for your own protection—if you have many connections, it could take hours for a large number of graphic-intensive pages to download. (The default is 5.)

In addition to the Web options, there are more browser preferences you can access by clicking the appropriate icon in the browser window. In general, these default to the options most people will prefer. If you are an advanced user, investigate these and experiment with them to find out what best suits your needs.

Be sure to explore all of the preferences described in this appendix. Alter every one of them and live with the changes for a week. You may discover something you didn't know about yourself!

# Appendix B
# MAKING THE
# CONNECTION

If you have never used America Online—if you have never even installed the software—this appendix is for you. It's written for novices—those who hold disks in their sweaty palms and wonder if they are stalwart enough to connect their Macs to the outside world.

Most of us think of computers as machines—functional, autonomous and independent. We've come to accept computing as an isolated activity, and our dialogs with the computer as closed circuits. The only external device we've ever encountered is a printer. Oh, we might personify our Macs. We might give them names and even voices, and we might think of their error messages and dialog boxes as communication, but we know better.

Computers don't think. Computers don't respond with imagination or indignation or intelligence. They react—to comply with our wishes—only as they have been preprogrammed to do. There are no threats to us here.

Connecting to AOL and the Internet puts human intelligence at the other end of the line. That's because America Online isn't just a computer complex in Virginia; it's people, and people online expect a dialog. People respond, with innovation and humor.

This is not the familiar, predictable universe we're accustomed to. So why mess with it?

Because there's more to life, that's why. Think of your first car, your first love, your first child—experiences resplendent with reward but not without their share of anxiety. We're talking about discovery here, and while AOL and the Internet may not rank with love and birth, they do offer other rewarding opportunities.

Before you read any further, I want you to understand that this appendix describes the process of installing the AOL software and making the first connection with AOL itself. If you already have an established AOL account, then you probably won't need to read all of this information. Feel free to skim it and take what you need.

## Things you'll need

Let's take inventory here. There are a few things you need before you can connect with America Online. You may already have them, but let's be sure.

### The computer

You need a Mac, of course. Almost any Macintosh will do—a Mac Plus or better running System 6.0.5 or higher. That's one of the benefits of telecommunications: nearly any computer is adequate. I bought my first Macintosh in 1984. It's a bandaged relic, but I still use it to sign on to AOL, and for that purpose it has power to spare.

You will need at least 4 megabytes of random access memory (RAM) and a hard disk with 3.5mb of free space. (If you plan to install the Web browser, make that 5.5mb.) You will also need a CD-ROM drive if your AOL membership kit came with the software installed on a CD.

### To cache or not to cache

The minimum disk-space requirement mentioned above is for the installation of the software only. America Online offers a disk-based cache feature for use with the World Wide Web that speeds the presentation of Web pages. The speed gain is so significant that anyone planning to use the Web should also plan to use the cache.

If you do plan to use the cache, be sure to read Chapter 6 of this book. Among other things, the cache's disk-space requirements are discussed there.

Finally, a monitor capable of displaying 256 colors or more is recommended. Your AOL software works with 16-color and black-and-white systems, but the presentation of the service is optimized for 256 colors.

I digressed. Essentially, just about any Macintosh will do. If yours isn't the latest model—if it doesn't have 435 horsepower and fuel injection and a 5-speed transmission—don't worry.

### The telephone line

You need access to a telephone line. Your standard residential phone line is fine. A multiline business telephone might be more of a challenge. What's really important is that your telephone plug into a modular telephone jack (called an *RJ-11* jack, if you care about that sort of thing). It's the one with the square hole measuring about a quarter of an inch.

Whenever you're online, your telephone is out of commission for normal usage. If you try to make a voice call, it's as if you picked up your phone and someone else was using the line on another extension—except that you'll *never* want to eavesdrop on an AOL session; the screeching sound that modems make when communicating with each other is about as pleasant as fingernails on a blackboard—and about as intelligible.

### The membership kit

America Online membership kits come in a number of forms, but they all have two things in common: they include the software, a registration number and a registration password. The software may come on a single floppy disk, two floppy disks or a CD. Find the software, the registration number and the password, and set them by your Mac. Keep this appendix nearby as well.

If your kit came with floppy disks, it is a good idea to make copies of them right now. Standard Macintosh disk-copying routines work just fine. Your Macintosh manual contains the necessary instructions for copying a floppy, if you don't already know how. Once you've copied the software, put the original AOL disk(s) away somewhere safe. You never know when you might need them again.

### The modem

A modem (short for *modulator/demodulator*) is a device that converts computer data into audible tones that the telephone system can transmit. Modems are required at both ends of the line: AOL has a number of them at their end as well.

Modems are rated according to their data-transmission speed. If you're shopping for a modem, get one rated at 28,800 baud if you can. Modems rated at 28,800 baud are fast and are capable of extracting every bit of performance AOL has to offer. (If AOL doesn't offer 28,800 baud capability in your area when you read this, be patient. It's in the works.) On the other hand, high-speed modems really only strut their stuff when you're downloading files (discussed in Chapter 9, "FlashSessions & the Download Manager"), and unless you do a lot of downloading you may never miss the higher speed. In other words, a 2400 baud modem might satisfy your needs if you don't plan on a lot of downloading. A 2400 baud modem, however, should be considered the minimum.

I prefer modems with speakers and lights. A speaker lets you hear the phone being dialed and the modem at the other end answering—very reassuring stuff. At that point—when the connection is established—most modem speakers become silent so you don't have to listen to the screeching sound of two computers talking to each other.

As I said earlier, lights are nice. My modem has nine of them. I don't understand most of them, but they look important, and the one marked "RD" (receiving data) is worth watching when you are transferring a file (I discuss file transfers via ftp in Chapter 7). It should stay on almost continuously. If, during a file transfer, your RD light is off more often than it's on, you've got a noisy phone line or the system is extremely busy. Whatever the cause, it's best to halt the file transfer (AOL always leaves a Cancel or Finish Later button on the screen for that purpose) and resume it another time. That's why I advise buying a modem with lights: if you don't have them, how can you tell what's going on?

A number of Macs now offer internal modems: modems inside the Mac itself. If you have an internal modem, you won't tie up the modem connection on the back of your Mac (leaving it available for some other purpose) but you won't have any lights to watch either. Life is full of compromises.

If your modem is the external variety, it will need power of some kind. Some external modems use batteries, but most use AC power and plug into the wall. Be sure an outlet is available.

### Baud Rates

The term *baud rate* refers to the signaling rate, or the number of times per second the signal changes. You might hear this term confused with bits per second (bps), which isn't entirely accurate. By using modern electronic wizardry, today's modems can transmit two, three or four bits with each change of signal, increasing the speed of data transfer considerably. Since it takes eight bits to make a byte, a rate of 9600 bps means that anywhere between 1200 and 4800 bytes per second can be transferred. A byte is the amount of data required to describe a single character of text. In other words, a baud rate of 9600 should transmit at least 1200 characters—about 15 lines of text per second.

Alas, the world is an imperfect place—especially the world of phone lines. If static or interference of any kind occurs on the line, data transmission is garbled. And even one misplaced bit can destroy the integrity of an entire file. To address the problem, AOL validates the integrity of received data. In plain English, this means that AOL sends a packet of information (a couple of seconds' worth) to your Mac, then waits for the Mac to say, I got that! before it sends the next packet. Validation like this means things run a little slower than they would without validation, but it's necessary. We're probably down to a minimum of 1,000 characters per second once we factor in the time it takes to accommodate data validation.

Then there's noise. You've heard it: static on the line. If you think it interferes with voice communication, it's murder on data. Often your Mac says, That packet was no good—send it again, and AOL complies. The reliability of any particular telephone connection is capricious. Some are better than others. Noise, however, is a definite factor, and packets have to be re-sent once in a while. Now we're probably down to a minimum of 900 characters per second on a good telephone line on a good day—a little over 11 lines of text per second at 9600 bps.

In other words, a 28,800 bps modem isn't sixteen times faster than a 2400 bps model, and a 9600 bps modem isn't four times as fast as one rated at 2400 bps. On the other hand, a 9600 bps modem doesn't cost four times as much as a 2400 bps model, and a 28,800 bps screamer doesn't cost twice as much as a 14,400 bps model. What I'm trying to say is in terms of baud per buck, 28,800 is your best buy.

Most important, be sure you have the proper cables. For an external modem, you need two: one to connect the modem to the Mac and another to connect the modem to the phone jack. The modem-to-phone-jack cable bundled with many modems rarely exceeds six feet. If the distance between your modem and your phone jack exceeds that distance, you can buy an extension cable at a phone, electronics or hardware store. Extension cables are standard equipment and are inexpensive.

Few external modems include a Mac-to-modem cable. You will probably have to purchase one if you're buying an external modem. Check your modem's manual to see if your modem requires a hardware-handshaking cable. If it does, it's essential that you use one, as it will provide for a more reliable connection at high speed.

You will also need to make some provision for using your phone on the same line. It's less complicated if the modem has a jack for your phone. In that case, you can plug the modem into the phone jack, then plug the phone into the modem. The jacks on the back of the modem should be marked for this.

If your modem is internal, or if your external modem only has a single jack and you want to continue using your phone as well as your modem, you might also want to invest in a modular splitter, which plugs into the phone jack on your wall, making two jacks out of one. You plug your phone into one of the splitter's jacks and your modem into the other. Plugging both devices into the same jack won't interfere with everyday telephone communications; incoming calls will continue to go to your phone, just as they did before. You should be able to find a splitter at a phone, electronics or hardware store for less than $3.

If all this sounds like a lot of wires to keep track of and you have trouble plugging in a toaster, don't worry. Most modems come with good instructions, and the components are such that you can't connect anything backwards. Just follow the instructions and you'll be all right.

## The money

Before you sign on to AOL for the first time, there's something else you'll need: money. America Online wants to know how you plan to pay the balance on your account each month. Cash won't do. Instead, you can provide a credit-card number: VISA, MasterCard, American Express or the Discover card are all acceptable. So are selected bank debit cards. Or have your checkbook handy: AOL can have your bank automatically transfer the funds each month if you provide it with the necessary numbers.

## The screen name

We're almost ready, but right now I want you to get all other thoughts out of your mind and decide what you want to call yourself. Every AOL member has a unique screen name. Screen names are how AOL tells us apart from each other. You must have one and it has to be different from anybody else's.

A screen name must consist of from three to ten characters— letters, or letters and numbers. Millions of people use AOL, and they all have screen names of ten or fewer characters. Chances are, the screen name you want most is taken, so have a number of alternates ready ahead of time, and prepare yourself for disappointment. Hardly anyone ever gets his or her first choice.

Though screen names aren't case-sensitive—you can address mail to majortom or MajorTom or MAJORTOM and it will still get to me—they always appear onscreen the way they were first entered. I first entered my screen name, for example, as MajorTom. If you send mail to majortom, I will see MajorTom on the To: line of my incoming mail. I'm MajorTom in chat rooms and instant messages as well. Keep this in mind as you enter your screen name for the first time.

There's no going back, by the way. Once AOL accepts your initial screen name, it's yours as long as you remain a member. Though your account can have as many as five screen names (to accommodate other people in your family or your alter egos), your initial screen name is the one AOL uses to establish your identity. For this reason, your initial screen name can't be changed. Be prepared with a zinger (and a half-dozen alternates), or AOL will assign you something like TomLi5437, and you'll forever be known by that name. People have a hard time relating to a name like that.

**MajorTom**

I worked my way through college as a traffic reporter for an Oregon radio station. I was both reporter and pilot. It was a great job: perfect hours for a student, easy work and unlimited access to a flashy plane. It didn't pay much, but somehow that wasn't important—not in the halcyon days of bachelorhood.

I hate to date myself, but David Bowie was an ascending force on the music scene in those days. Impertinent, perhaps—a little too androgynous and scandalous for the conservative element of the Nixon era—but definitely a hit-maker. Our station played Bowie. On my first day, the morning-show disk jockey switched on his microphone and hailed "Ground Control to Major Tom"—a line from Bowie's Space Oddity—to get my attention. The name stuck. I was known as Major Tom from then on.

When the time came for me to pick my screen name years ago, AOL suggested TomLi5437 and I balked. How about just plain Tom? I asked. It's in use, AOL replied. I tried four others and AOL continued to remind me of my lack of imagination. In desperation I tried MajorTom, and AOL accepted it. Once an initial screen name is accepted, there's no going back. I'm MajorTom on AOL now, and I will be forever more.

## The password

Oh yes, you need a password. Without a password, anyone knowing your screen name can log on using your name and have a heyday on your nickel. Passwords must be from four to eight characters in length, and any combination of letters or numbers is acceptable. You will enter your password every time you sign on, so choose something easy for you to remember—something that's not a finger-twister to type. It should be different from your screen name, phone number, Social Security number, address or real name—something no one else would ever guess, even if they know you well.

**A case for elaborate passwords**

In his book *The Cuckoo's Egg*, Cliff Stoll describes computer hackers' methods for breaking passwords. Since most computers already have a dictionary on disk—all spelling checkers use dictionaries—the hackers simply program their computers to try every word in the dictionary as a password. It sounds laborious, but computers don't mind.

Read this carefully: *No one from AOL will ever ask you for your password.* This is another hacker's ruse: lurking in AOL's dark corners, hackers troll for new members. When they spot someone they think is new, they'll send e-mail or an Instant Message (a real-time message that pops onto your screen) masquerading as an AOL employee. They'll say they're verifying billing records or something like that, and ask for your password. *Don't reply!* Instead, make a note of the perpetrator's screen name, then use the keyword: TOS (it's free) to determine what you should do next.

In other words, I'm making a case for elaborate passwords here. Don't make it personal, don't use your Social Security number, don't write it down, select something that's not in a dictionary and never ever give out your password to anyone. This is important.

## Installing the software

Finally, we're ready to get our hands dirty. Unlike some folks who have to access the Internet with terminal emulator programs and fuss with *stop bits* and *parity*, we've got it easy. Installing the AOL software is a straightforward process, since an installation program does all the work for you.

Again, be sure you have at least 3.5mb of space available on your hard disk. Use the Finder (your Mac manual will tell you how) to find out how much free disk space you have.

If your kit came with disks, insert the first (or single) copy of the AOL disk into your floppy disk drive. (The original AOL disk works just as well, but making—and using—a copy is just standard paranoid procedure.) If your kit came with a CD, insert the CD into your CD-ROM drive.

Connect your modem to your Mac and turn it on. Refer to your modem's instruction manual if you're not sure how to connect it.

When you double-click the Install icon, a greeting screen appears, identifying the Installer program (see Figure B-1).

Installation options are disclosed via the Custom button pictured in Figure B-1. Few installations require the use of these options.

Figure B-1: The Installer greeting screen appears as soon as the program is running.

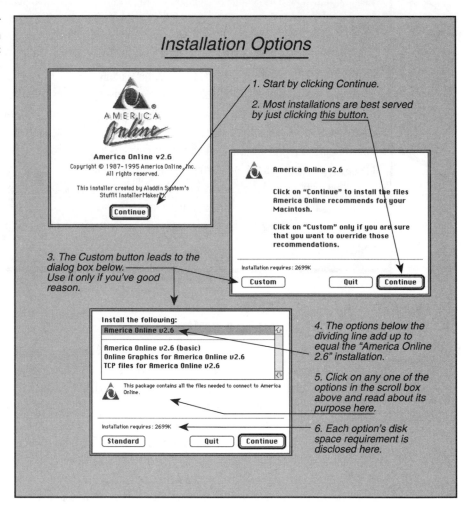

The Installer then displays the window pictured in Figure B-2. It asks you where you want to place AOL's folder.

Figure B-2: The Installer
wants to know which
disk will be used to
install America Online.
Be sure you don't try
to install the program
on a floppy disk!

**Select disk to install onto:**

IBM

[ Eject Disk ]   [[ Install ]]

[ Switch Disk ]   [ Cancel ]

---

**IBM**

Readers with eagle eyes will note that the hard disk on my Macintosh is named "IBM." There's a good reason for this: my hard disk *is* an IBM. When I first received my Mac and popped open the case (not a recommended method for getting to know a Mac, but often educational), the striped-blue "IBM" logo was the first thing I saw. (It's hard to miss in that context.)

As it turns out, IBM makes hard disks and Apple doesn't. IBM is on Apple's list of suppliers and Apple buys hard disks from any supplier who offers the right price at the right time. Apparently, IBM's price was right when my Mac was constructed and it has been a mixed-breed computer ever since. It's kind of embarrassing, but it's mine and I'm not about to hide it.

The moral of the story: open the case only if you're prepared for the consequences.

---

Remember that you're about to install a folder, not a file. You needn't have a folder already prepared for AOL: it makes its own.

Once you click the Install button, the Installer does its work. This takes a couple of minutes. As it's working, a progress gauge keeps you abreast of the program's progress (see the upper window in Figure B-3). If your membership kit contained two disks, you will be asked to insert the second disk. The installer concludes with an announcement of its success (see the bottom window of Figure B-3).

Figure B-3: The installation process is automatic: all you have to do is watch.

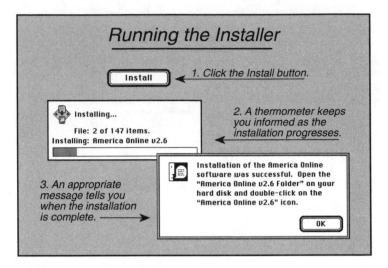

After you click the OK button pictured in Figure B-3, take a moment to explore your hard disk. The Installer has created a new folder where you told it to, containing the AOL application and its associated folders (see Figure B-4). Note that the folder and its contents equal nearly 3mb even though the floppy disk from which it came holds much less than that. The secret is file compression. Using a product called StuffIt, the AOL folder's contents were compressed (stuffed) before they were placed on the floppy disk; the compressed files were copied to your hard disk; then the Installer unstuffed them. It's all logical, I suppose, but it's still magic to me.

Figure B-4: The Installer places a folder on your hard disk containing the America Online software and all of the necessary folders.

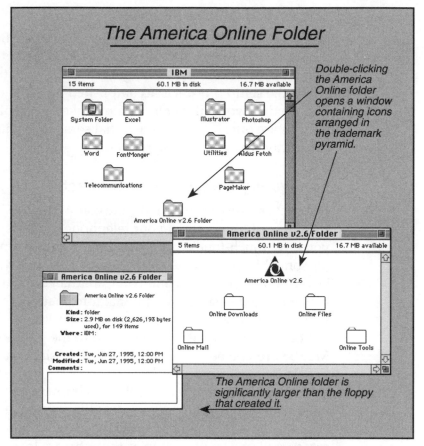

## The pyramid

Look again at the America Online window pictured in Figure B-4. Note how the icons are arranged. Since the AOL logo is a pyramid, the programmers arranged the folder icons in a pyramid shape as well. Little details like this crop up everywhere at AOL; some are functional, some are fanciful like the pyramid. They're part of the fun, but they're also an indication of the care and vigilance that go into the product. In the end, we the members are beneficiaries.

There, you've done it. You've installed the software and you're ready to sign on. Eject the disk, put it in a safe place and let's get on with it.

### The initial online session

The initial online session takes about 15 minutes. Be sure you have the time and uninterrupted access to the phone before you begin. You needn't worry about money: although you'll be online for a while, the setup process is accomplished on AOL's dime, not yours. You needn't worry if you make a mistake either; plenty of Cancel buttons are offered during the initial session. If you get cold feet, you can always hang up and start over.

### Configuring the telephone connection

Before it can successfully make the connection, AOL needs to know a number of things about your telephone. It needs to know whether you have touch-tone or rotary dialing, whether it needs to dial a 9 (or something else) to reach an outside line, and whether a 1 should be dialed before the 800 number. Canadian and international members will need to supply additional information. Don't let me scare you. Most of this stuff happens automatically.

Your modem should be connected to the phone line and to your Mac before you begin the initial online session, and everything should be turned on.

You can resize and relocate the program group's window for a neater desktop if you wish—it's just like any other window. Double-click the America Online icon to launch the AOL software. A welcome screen will greet you as soon as the software loads (see Figure B-5).

Figure B-5: This welcome screen greets you when you first run the America Online software.

**Welcome to America Online!**

We will now take you through a quick and easy set-up and registration process. Before you begin, make sure your modem is turned on and that it is connected to your Macintosh and your phone line.

If you are a new America Online member and have just installed the software for the first time, click the 'Continue' button.

If you are an existing America Online member and have an earlier version of the software installed on your hard drive, click the 'Upgrade' button.

If you are an existing America Online member and have deleted and reinstalled the software, click the 'Continue' button.

[ Cancel ]   [ Upgrade ]   [ Continue ]

**Upgrading**

If you're already an AOL member and you've been using an earlier version of AOL's software on your machine, you should now click the Upgrade button shown in Figure B-5. The Installer will ask you for the location of your old AOL application and use information it finds there—access numbers, address books, preferences, screen names, and mail files—to customize the new edition. The remainder of the installation process described here will be skipped.

A second screen greets you when you click the Continue button shown in Figure B-5. (This screen is shown in Figure B-6.) Carefully read the list of assumptions presented here. If they describe your situation accurately, click the Continue button. If they don't, click the Special Setup button. Special Setup accommodates dial phones, modem connections to the Macintosh printer port, and members calling from Canadian exchanges.

Figure B-6: If the
assumptions aren't
correct, click the
Special Setup button.

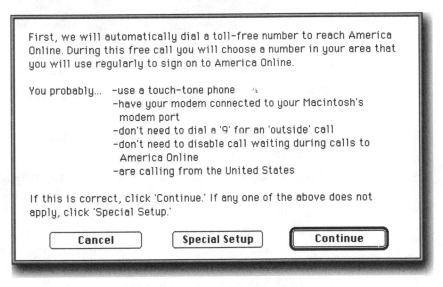

First, we will automatically dial a toll-free number to reach America Online. During this free call you will choose a number in your area that you will use regularly to sign on to America Online.

You probably...  -use a touch-tone phone
                -have your modem connected to your Macintosh's
                 modem port
                -don't need to dial a '9' for an 'outside' call
                -don't need to disable call waiting during calls to
                 America Online
                -are calling from the United States

If this is correct, click 'Continue.' If any one of the above does not apply, click 'Special Setup.'

| Cancel | Special Setup | Continue |

When you click Figure B-6's Continue button, the Installer checks your modem's speed and port, then asks you one more time if you're ready to sign on. Be sure no one is using your phone line, that you have your registration certificate (with its temporary registration number and password), and that your credit card or checking account number is nearby; then click Continue.

Now the Installer dials an 800 number to temporarily connect to AOL and find a local access number for you. You will be able to monitor the call's progress by watching the window pictured at the bottom of Figure B-7. Once you see the message that says "Connected at XXXX baud" (the baud rate is determined by the speed of your modem) you can be sure your Mac and modem are communicating properly. You can be sure that your modem and the telephone system are connected as well. If the AOL software found anything amiss prior to this point, it would have notified you and suggested solutions.

Figure B-7: This window appears as America Online dials its toll-free number during the initial connection.

## Isolating connection errors

Though they rarely do, things can go wrong during the connect process. The problem could be at your end (e.g., the modem or the phone lines), or it could be at AOL's end. You can be sure the problem is at your end if you don't hear a dial tone (assuming your modem has a speaker) before your modem begins dialing. If you hear the dial tone, the dialing sequence and the screeching sound that modems make when they connect, you'll know everything is okay all the way to the common carrier (long-distance service) you're using. If your connection fails during the initial connect process, don't panic. Wait a few minutes and try again. If it fails a second time, call AOL Technical Support at 800-827-3338.

## Selecting your local access numbers

Now you're connected and AOL's anxious to say hello. Its initial greeting is friendly, if a bit laconic (see the top window in Figure B-8). Its singular interest right now is to find some local access numbers for you. To do that, it needs to know where you are. It finds that out by requesting your local area code.

Figure B-8: Using your area code, America Online attempts to select two local numbers for access to the service.

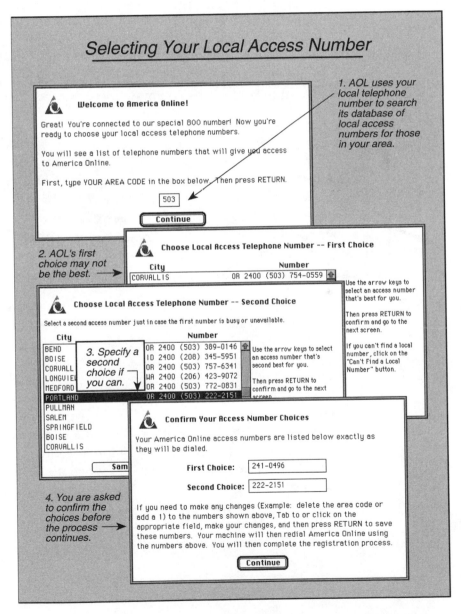

Using your area code, AOL consults its database of local access numbers and produces a list of those nearest you (see the second window in Figure B-8). Look over the list carefully. The phone number at the top of the list isn't necessarily the one closest to you. Also, note the baud rates listed in the third column. Be sure the number you pick represents the baud rate you intend to use.

If there isn't a local number listed for your area, you might have to pay long-distance charges to your telephone company in order to connect to AOL. (You'll know this is true if you have to dial a 1 before your access number in order to complete the call). Once the initial sign-on process concludes and you're online, choose Member Services from the Members menu and investigate AOL's database of access numbers again. You may find a number there after all.

**The 800 number**

In order to serve members who live in remote communities, AOL has established a special 800 number for access from anywhere in the contiguous United States. While this number isn't exactly toll-free, the charge for its use is considerably less than most long-distance tariffs. If you must dial 1 to reach AOL, sign on and investigate the 800 number at keyword: 800.

It's a good idea to have a secondary number as well. A secondary number (if available) is just that: a second number (the proper term is *node*—see the glossary in the back of this book) for your modem to call if the first one is busy (which happens rarely) or bogged down with a lot of traffic (which happens more frequently). Interestingly, dozens of modems can use the same node at the same time by splitting the time available on that node into tiny packets. This is all very perplexing to those of us who think of phone numbers as being capable of handling one conversation at a time, but it's nonetheless true. There is a limit, however, and when it's reached, AOL tries the second number. The third window in Figure B-8 illustrates the screen used to select this alternate.

Finally, AOL presents the screen confirming your selections pictured at the bottom of Figure B-8.

## The temporary registration number & password

Assuming you've clicked on the Continue button shown in Figure 8, your Mac will disconnect from the 800 number and dial your primary local access number. Once the connection is reestablished, AOL presents the screen shown in Figure B-9. This is where you must enter the registration certificate number and password you received with your startup kit. These are the temporary equivalents of the permanent screen name and password you'll soon establish. Enter the words and numbers carefully; they're usually nonsensical and difficult to type without error.

Figure B-9: Enter your registration certificate number and password here. Be sure to type them exactly as they appear on your certificate or label.

**Welcome to America Online!**

**New Members:**

Please locate the Registration Certificate that was included in your software kit and, in the space below, type the certificate number and certificate password as they appear on the printed certificate.

**Existing Members:**

If you already have an America Online account and are simply installing a new version of the software, type your existing Screen Name in the first field and Password in the second. This will update your account information automatically.

Note: Use the "tab" key to move from one field to another.

**Certificate Number (or Screen Name):**

**Certificate Password (or Password) :**

[ Cancel ]  [ Continue ]

## Your name & address

When you click the Continue button shown in Figure B-9, AOL provides directions for using an online form like the one shown in Figure B-10. If you're not familiar with the Mac, you'll want to read the directions carefully. If you've used Macintosh software before—even a little bit—you already know this stuff. It's traditional Mac protocol. **Hint:** Use the Tab key to move from field to field.

Once you've read the form-usage instructions, click the Continue button and AOL will ask you for some personal information (see Figure B-10).

**Please be sure to enter ALL of the following information accurately:**

First Name: | Last Name:

Address:

City: | State:

Zip Code: | Daytime Phone:

Country: UNITED STATES ... ▼ | Evening Phone:

Note: Please enter phone numbers area code first, for example, 703-555-1212, and enter state with no periods, for example, VA for Virginia.

Cancel | Continue

America Online uses this information to communicate with you offline. Though AOL never bills members directly (we'll discuss money in a moment), and though this information is not available online to other members, AOL does, occasionally, need to contact you offline, and they use this information to do so. They might want to send you a disk containing an upgrade to the software, or perhaps you've ordered something from them (this book, for example) that needs to be mailed. That's what this information is for.

**Your phone number**

Your phone number becomes an important part of your record at America Online, not because anyone at AOL intends to call you, but because AOL's Customer Service Department uses this number to identify you whenever you call. Should you ever find the need to call, the first question Customer Service will ask is, What's your phone number? It's unique, after all, so Customer Service uses it to look up your records. It's an efficient method, but only if you provide the number accurately during your initial sign-on.

## Providing your billing information

Let's be up-front about it: America Online is a business run for profit. In other words, AOL needs to be paid for the service it provides. It offers a number of ways to accomplish this. VISA, MasterCard, or American Express are the preferred methods of payment. The Discover card is also acceptable. Certain bank debit cards are acceptable as well, though you will have to confirm their acceptability with your financial institution. If none of these work for you, America Online can also arrange to automatically debit your checking account. (There's a fee for this—more than a credit card costs you—so you might want this to be your last option.)

When you click the Continue button shown in Figure B-10, another screen appears, identifying AOL's connect-time rates. Read it carefully (you need to know what you're buying and what it's costing you, after all), then move on (see Figure B-11).

Figure B-11: All major credit cards are welcome, and the More Billing Options button leads to information on using the Discover card or debiting your checking account.

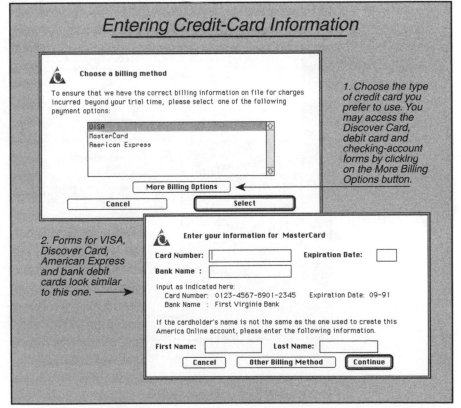

Figure B-11 is an example of the billing information screen for the MasterCard form, but the forms for VISA and Discover are about the same.

## Choosing a screen name & password

When you click the Continue button shown in Figure B-11, AOL provides a series of screens informing you of the significance of screen names, concluding with the screen name input form, pictured at the top of Figure B-12. AOL does not choose a screen name for you. This is an incentive to have your own choices at hand.

Figure B-12: Conclude the registration process by entering your screen name and password.

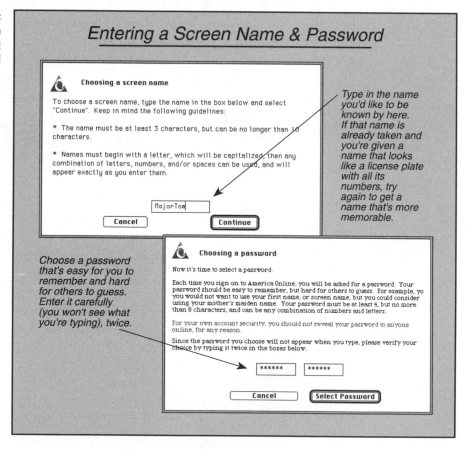

Note that your password doesn't appear on your screen as you type it. Substituting asterisks for the letters of your password is a standard security precaution—you never know who's looking over your shoulder. America Online asks you to enter your password twice, to be sure you didn't mistype it the first time.

### A letter from the president

Now that you've successfully finished setting up and signing on, you enter the AOL service itself. No doubt the first thing that will happen is you'll receive an announcement that you have mail. To read the letter, click on the You Have Mail icon on the Spotlight window, choose Read New Mail from the Mail menu, or press Command+R (see top of Figure B-13). The New Mail window appears, with mail from AOL President Steve Case selected. Click the Read button and read what he has to say (see bottom of Figure B-13).

Figure B-13: Your first activity online is to read a letter of welcome from AOL President Steve Case. How many times have you heard directly from the president of a company when you became a customer? How many times have you been invited to respond?

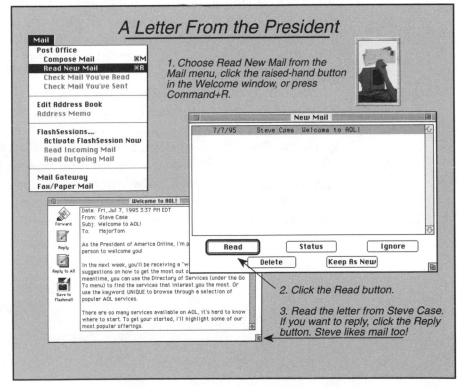

## Upgrading

Like all good things, the America Online software is continually improving. You can always download the latest copy of the software online at keyword: Upgrade. In fact, you may want to stop in there to verify that you have the latest version of software (you can check to see what version you are running by selecting About America Online from the Apple menu).

Chances are good you have the latest version already if you received a membership kit with two floppy disks or a CD. If you used a kit with one floppy disk, you may have an older version of the software, or a streamlined version without some of the bells and whistles. Directions on how to install an upgrade are given in the description of the download—follow these carefully.

## Where to go from here

Once you're online, you have the entire AOL universe to explore. The thought is both enticing and overwhelming. Here's what I suggest: spend a half hour wandering around right after you read Steve's letter. You have quite a bit of free connect time coming, so you don't have to worry about money. You will find all of the online departments' buttons in the Main Menu screen along with a button marked Discover AOL (see Figure B-14). Click that button, then explore a few of the areas offered in the Discover America Online window. The America Online Highlights are always interesting; the Best of America Online may turn up some areas to which you'll return; and What's Hot This Month is always topical. Find an Internet feature that interests you, then, without any particular agenda, explore that feature and perhaps one other.

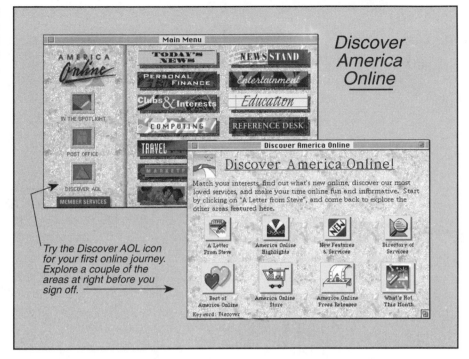

Figure B-14: The Discover America Online feature is an excellent way to begin your online journey.

*Try the Discover AOL icon for your first online journey. Explore a couple of the areas at right before you sign off.*

During this initial session, don't try to absorb the entire contents of AOL or the Net. Rather, wander aimlessly, getting a feeling for the nature of the online universe. Note how Mac-like it is. Everything is predictable and familiar—at least to a Macintosh user.

After a half hour or so, you might want to sign off. Choose Sign Off from the Go To menu. Once the dust settles, turn to the chapter in this book that describes the Internet feature you just visited. Read that chapter, then sign back on and explore that department again. See if you can find the things I described in the chapter. Spend another half hour at this.

Now you're on your own. Explore another department if you wish, or turn to Chapter 3, "Electronic Mail," and learn how to send mail to somebody. You'll probably get a response in a few days. People at AOL are very friendly. It really *is* a community.

# GLOSSARY

*This glossary is an abridgment of the Internet User's Glossary prepared by the User Glossary Working Group of the User Services Area of the Internet Engineering Task Force (IETF). The primary authors are Gary Scott Malkin (gmalkin@xylogics.com) and Tracy LaQuey Parker (tracy@utexas.edu). My thanks to Gary and Tracy for their permission to use the glossary here, and for this commendable Internet resource.*

*The glossary is available online in a searchable format. Click the Internet Information button in the primary Internet Connection window.*

### 10BaseT

A variant of Ethernet which allows stations to be attached via twisted pair cable. *See also:* Ethernet, twisted pair.

### :-)

This odd symbol is one of the ways a person can portray "mood" in the very flat medium of computers—by using "smiley faces." This is "metacommunication," and there are literally hundreds of such symbols, from the obvious to the obscure. This particular example expresses "happiness." Don't see it? Tilt your head to the left 90 degrees. Smiles are also used to denote sarcasm. [Source: ZEN]

### address

There are three types of addresses in common use within the Internet. They are email address; IP, internet or Internet address; and hardware or MAC address. *See also:* email address, IP address, internet address, MAC address.

### Advanced Research Projects Agency Network (ARPANET)

A pioneering longhaul network funded by ARPA (now DARPA). It served as the basis for early networking research, as well as a central backbone during the development of the Internet. The ARPANET consisted of individual packet switching computers interconnected by leased lines. *See also:* Defense Advanced Research Projects Agency. [Source: FYI4]

### alias

A name, usually short and easy to remember, that is translated into another name, usually long and difficult to remember.

### American National Standards Institute (ANSI)

This organization is responsible for approving U.S. standards in many areas, including computers and communications. Standards approved by this organization are often called ANSI standards (e.g., ANSI C is the version of the C language approved by ANSI). ANSI is a member of ISO. *See also:* International Organization for Standardization. [Source: NNSC]

### American Standard Code for Information Interchange (ASCII)

A standard character-to-number encoding widely used in the computer industry. *See also:* EBCDIC.

### anonymous FTP

Anonymous FTP allows a user to retrieve documents, files, programs, and other archived data from anywhere in the Internet without having to establish a userid and password. By using the special userid of "anonymous" the network user will bypass local security checks and will have access to publicly accessible files on the remote system. *See also:* archive site, File Transfer Protocol.

### ANSI

*See:* American National Standards Institute

### application

A program that performs a function directly for a user. FTP, mail and Telnet clients are examples of network applications.

### Application Program Interface (API)

A set of calling conventions which define how a service is invoked through a software package. [Source: RFC1208]

### archie

A system to automatically gather, index and serve information on the Internet. The initial implementation of archie provided an indexed directory of filenames from all anonymous FTP archives on the Internet. Later versions provide other collections of information. *See also:* archive site, Gopher, Prospero, Wide Area Information Servers.

### archive site

A machine that provides access to a collection of files across the Internet. An "anonymous FTP archive site," for example, provides access to this material via the FTP protocol. *See also:* anonymous FTP, archie, Gopher, Prospero, Wide Area Information Servers.

### ARPA

*See:* Defense Advanced Research Projects Agency

### ARPANET

*See:* Advanced Research Projects Agency Network

### ASCII

*See:* American Standard Code for Information Interchange

### Asynchronous Transfer Mode (ATM)

A method for the dynamic allocation of bandwidth using a fixed-size packet (called a cell). ATM is also known as "fast packet."

### ATM

*See:* Asynchronous Transfer Mode

### backbone

The top level in a hierarchical network. Stub and transit networks which connect to the same backbone are guaranteed to be interconnected. *See also:* stub network, transit network.

### bandwidth

Technically, the difference, in Hertz (Hz), between the highest and lowest frequencies of a transmission channel. However, as typically used, the amount of data that can be sent through a given communications circuit.

### bang path

A series of machine names used to direct electronic mail from one user to another, typically by specifying an explicit UUCP path through which the mail is to be routed. *See also:* email address, mail path, UNIX-to-UNIX CoPy.

### BBS

*See:* Bulletin Board System

### BCNU

Be Seein' You

### Berkeley Software Distribution (BSD)

Implementation of the UNIX operating system and its utilities developed and distributed by the University of California at Berkeley. "BSD" is usually preceded by the version number of the distribution, e.g., "4.3 BSD" is version 4.3 of the Berkeley UNIX distribution. Many Internet hosts run BSD software, and it is the ancestor of many commercial UNIX implementations. [Source: NNSC]

### Birds Of a Feather (BOF)

A Birds Of a Feather (flocking together) is an informal discussion group. It is formed, often ad hoc, to consider a specific issue and, therefore, has a narrow focus.

### BITNET

An academic computer network that provides interactive electronic mail and file transfer services, using a store-and-forward protocol, based on IBM Network Job Entry protocols. Bitnet-II encapsulates the Bitnet protocol within IP packets and depends on the Internet to route them.

### BOF

*See:* Birds Of a Feather

### bridge

A device which forwards traffic between network segments based on datalink layer information. These segments would have a common network layer address. *See also:* gateway, router.

### broadband

A transmission medium capable of supporting a wide range of frequencies. It can carry multiple signals by dividing the total capacity of the medium into multiple, independent bandwidth channels, where each channel operates only on a specific range of frequencies. *See also:* baseband.

### BTW

By The Way

### Bulletin Board System (BBS)

A computer, and associated software, which typically provides electronic messaging services, archives of files, and any other services or activities of interest to the bulletin board system's operator. Although BBS's have traditionally been the domain of hobbyists, an increasing number of BBS's are connected directly to the Internet, and many BBS's are currently operated by government, educational, and research institutions. *See also:* Electronic Mail, Internet, Usenet. [Source: NWNET]

### Campus Wide Information System (CWIS)

A CWIS makes information and services publicly available on campus via kiosks, and makes interactive computing available via kiosks, interactive computing systems and campus networks. Services routinely include directory information, calendars, bulletin boards, databases.

### CCITT

*See:* Comité Consultatif International de Telegraphique et Telephonique

### CERT

*See:* Computer Emergency Response Team

### checksum

A computed value which is dependent upon the contents of a packet. This value is sent along with the packet when it is transmitted. The receiving system computes a new checksum based upon the received data and compares this value with the one sent with the packet. If the two values are the same, the receiver has a high degree of confidence that the data was received correctly. [Source: NNSC]

### circuit switching

A communications paradigm in which a dedicated communication path is established between two hosts, and on which all packets travel. The telephone system is an example of a circuit switched network. *See also:* connection-oriented, connectionless, packet switching.

### client

A computer system or process that requests a service of another computer system or process. A workstation requesting the contents of a file from a file server is a client of the file server. *See also:* client-server model, server. [Source: NNSC]

### client-server model

A common way to describe the paradigm of many network protocols. Examples include the name-server/name-resolver relationship in DNS and the file-server/file-client relationship in NFS. *See also:* client, server, Domain Name System, Network File System.

### CNI

*See:* Coalition for Networked Information

### Coalition for Networked Information (CNI)

A consortium formed by American Research Libraries, CAUSE, and EDUCOM to promote the creation of, and access to, information resources in networked environments in order to enrich scholarship and enhance intellectual productivity.

### Comité Consultatif International de Telegraphique et Telephonique (CCITT)

This organization is part of the United National International Tele-communications Union (ITU) and is responsible for making technical recommendations about telephone and data communications systems. Every four years CCITT holds plenary sessions where they adopt new standards; the most recent was in 1992. [Source: NNSC]

### Computer Emergency Response Team (CERT)

The CERT was formed by DARPA in November 1988 in response to the needs exhibited during the Internet worm incident. The CERT charter is to work with the Internet community to facilitate its response to computer security events involving Internet hosts, to take proactive steps to raise the community's awareness of computer security issues, and to conduct research targeted at improving the security of existing systems. CERT products and services include 24-hour technical assistance for responding to computer security incidents, product vulnerability assistance, technical documents, and tutorials. In addition, the team maintains a number of mailing lists (including one for CERT Advisories), and provides an anonymous FTP server, at "cert.org," where security-related documents and tools are archived. The CERT may be reached by email at "cert@cert.org" and by telephone at +1-412-268-7090 (24-hour hotline). *See also:* Defense Advanced Research Projects Agency, worm.

### cracker

A cracker is an individual who attempts to access computer systems without authorization. These individuals are often malicious, as opposed to hackers, and have many means at their disposal for breaking into a system. *See also:* hacker, Computer Emergency Response Team, Trojan Horse, virus, worm.

### CRC

*See:* cyclic redundancy check

### CWIS

*See:* Campus Wide Information system

### Cyberspace

A term coined by William Gibson in his fantasy novel *Neuromancer* to describe the "world" of computers, and the society that gathers around them. [Source: ZEN]

### Cyclic Redundancy Check (CRC)

A number derived from a set of data that will be transmitted. By recalculating the CRC at the remote end and comparing it to the value originally transmitted, the receiving node can detect some types of transmission errors. [Source: MALAMUD]

### DARPA

*See:* Defense Advanced Research Projects Agency

### Data Encryption Key (DEK)

Used for the encryption of message text and for the computation of message integrity checks (signatures). *See also:* encryption.

### Data Encryption Standard (DES)

A popular, standard encryption scheme. *See also:* encryption.

### Defense Advanced Research Projects Agency (DARPA)

An agency of the U.S. Department of Defense responsible for the development of new technology for use by the military. DARPA (formerly known as ARPA) was responsible for funding much of the development of the Internet we know today, including the Berkeley version of Unix and TCP/IP. [Source: NNSC]

### Defense Data Network (DDN)

A global communications network serving the U.S. Department of Defense composed of MILNET, other portions of the Internet, and classified networks which are not part of the Internet.

### Defense Data Network  Network Information Center (DDN NIC)

Often called "The NIC," the DDN NIC's primary responsibility is the assignment of Internet network addresses and Autonomous System numbers, the administration of the root domain, and providing information and support services to the DDN. It is also a primary repository for RFCs. *See also:* Autonomous System, network address, Internet Registry, Network Information Center, Request For Comments.

### Defense Information Systems Agency (DISA)

Formerly called the Defense Communications Agency (DCA), this is the government agency responsible for managing the DDN portion of the Internet, including the MILNET. Currently, DISA administers the DDN, and supports the user assistance services of the DDN NIC. *See also:* Defense Data Network.

### DEK

*See:* Data Encryption Key

### DES

*See:* Data Encryption Standard

### dialup

A temporary, as opposed to dedicated, connection between machines established over a standard phone line.

### Distributed Computing Environment (DCE)

An architecture of standard programming interfaces, conventions, and server functionalities (e.g., naming, distributed file system, remote procedure call) for distributing applications transparently across networks of heterogeneous computers. Promoted and controlled by the Open Software Foundation (OSF), a consortium led by Digital, IBM and Hewlett Packard. [Source: RFC1208]

### distributed database

A collection of several different data repositories that looks like a single database to the user. A prime example in the Internet is the Domain Name System.

### DNS

*See:* Domain Name System

### domain

"Domain" is a heavily overused term in the Internet. It can be used in the Administrative Domain context, or the Domain Name context. *See also:* Administrative Domain, Domain Name System.

### Domain Name System (DNS)

The DNS is a general purpose distributed, replicated, data query service. The principal use is the lookup of host IP addresses based on host names. The style of host names now used in the Internet is called "domain name," because they are the style of names used to look up anything in the DNS. Some important domains are: .COM (commercial), .EDU (educational), .NET (network operations), .GOV (U.S. government), and .MIL (U.S. military). Most countries also have a domain. For example, .US (United States), .UK (United Kingdom), .AU (Australia). It is defined in STD 13, RFCs 1034 and 1035. *See also:* Fully Qualified Domain Name.

### dot address (dotted decimal notation)

Dot address refers to the common notation for IP addresses of the form A.B.C.D; where each letter represents, in decimal, one byte of a four byte IP address. *See also:* IP address. [Source: FYI4]

### EFF

*See:* Electronic Frontier Foundation

### Electronic Frontier Foundation (EFF)

A foundation established to address social and legal issues arising from the impact on society of the increasingly pervasive use of computers as a means of communication and information distribution.

### Electronic Mail (email)

A system whereby a computer user can exchange messages with other computer users (or groups of users) via a communications network. Electronic mail is one of the most popular uses of the Internet. [Source: NNSC]

### email (e-mail)

*See:* Electronic mail

### email (e-mail) address

The domain-based or UUCP address that is used to send electronic mail to a specified destination. For example an editor's address is "gmalkin@xylogics.com." *See also:* bang path, mail path, UNIX-to-UNIX CoPy. [Source: ZEN]

### encapsulation

The technique used by layered protocols in which a layer adds header information to the protocol data unit (PDU) from the layer above. As an example, in Internet terminology, a packet would contain a header from the physical layer, followed by a header from the network layer (IP), followed by a header from the transport layer (TCP), followed by the application protocol data. [Source: RFC1208]

### encryption

Encryption is the manipulation of a packet's data in order to prevent any but the intended recipient from reading that data. There are many types of data encryption, and they are the basis of network security. *See also:* Data Encryption Standard.

### Ethernet

A 10-Mb/s standard for LANs, initially developed by Xerox, and later refined by Digital, Intel and Xerox (DIX). All hosts are connected to a coaxial cable where they contend for network access using a Carrier Sense Multiple Access with Collision Detection (CSMA/CD) paradigm. *See also:* 802.x, Local Area Network, token ring.

### FAQ

Frequently Asked Question

### file transfer

The copying of a file from one computer to another over a computer network. *See also:* File Transfer Protocol, Kermit.

### File Transfer Protocol (FTP)

A protocol which allows a user on one host to access, and transfer files to and from, another host over a network. Also, FTP is usually the name of the program the user invokes to execute the protocol. It is defined in STD 9, RFC 959. *See also:* anonymous FTP.

### finger

A program that displays information about a particular user, or all users, logged on the local system or on a remote system. It typically shows full name, last login time, idle time, terminal line, and terminal location (where applicable). It may also display plan and project files left by the user.

### flame

A strong opinion and/or criticism of something, usually as a frank inflammatory statement, in an electronic mail message. It is common to precede a flame with an indication of pending fire (i.e., FLAME ON!). Flame Wars occur when people start flaming other people for flaming when they shouldn't have. *See also:* Electronic Mail

### For Your Information (FYI)

A subseries of RFCs that are not technical standards or descriptions of protocols. FYIs convey general information about topics related to TCP/IP or the Internet. *See also:* Request For Comments, STD.

### FQDN

*See:* Fully Qualified Domain Name

### fragmentation

The IP process in which a packet is broken into smaller pieces to fit the requirements of a physical network over which the packet must pass. *See also:* reassembly.

### freenet

Community-based bulletin board system with email, information services, interactive communications, and conferencing. Freenets are funded and operated by individuals and volunteers — in one sense, like public television. They are part of the National Public Telecomputing Network (NPTN), an organization based in Cleveland, Ohio, devoted to making computer telecommunication and networking services as freely available as public libraries. [Source: LAQUEY]

### FTP

*See:* File Transfer Protocol

### Fully Qualified Domain Name (FQDN)

The FQDN is the full name of a system, rather than just its hostname. For example, "venera" is a hostname and "venera.isi.edu" is an FQDN. *See also:* hostname, Domain Name System.

### FYI

*See:* For Your Information

### gateway

The term "router" is now used in place of the original definition of "gateway". Currently, a gateway is a communications device/program which passes data between networks having similar functions but dissimilar implementations. This should not be confused with a protocol converter. By this definition, a router is a layer 3 (network layer) gateway, and a mail gateway is a layer 7 (application layer) gateway. *See also:* mail gateway, router, protocol converter.

### Gopher

A distributed information service that makes available hierarchical collections of information across the Internet. Gopher uses a simple protocol that allows a single Gopher client to access information from any accessible Gopher server, providing the user with a single "Gopher space" of information. Public domain versions of the client and server are available. *See also:* archie, archive site, Prospero, Wide Area Information Servers.

### hacker

A person who delights in having an intimate understanding of the internal workings of a system, computers and computer networks in particular. The term is often misused in a pejorative context, where "cracker" would be the correct term. *See also:* cracker.

### header

The portion of a packet, preceding the actual data, containing source and destination addresses, and error checking and other fields. A header is also the part of an electronic mail message that precedes the body of a message and contains, among other things, the message originator, date and time. *See also:* Electronic Mail, packet.

### host

A computer that allows users to communicate with other host computers on a network. Individual users communicate by using application programs, such as electronic mail, Telnet and FTP. [Source: NNSC]

### host address

*See:* internet address

### hostname

The name given to a machine. *See also:* Fully Qualified Domain

### host number

*See:* host address

### hub

A device connected to several other devices. In ARCnet, a hub is used to connect several computers together. In a message handling service, a hub is used for the transfer of messages across the network. [Source: MALAMUD]

### IEEE

Institute of Electrical and Electronics Engineers

### IMHO

In My Humble Opinion

### Integrated Services Digital Network (ISDN)

An emerging technology which is beginning to be offered by the telephone carriers of the world. ISDN combines voice and digital network services in a single medium, making it possible to offer customers digital data services as well as voice connections through a single "wire." The standards that define ISDN are specified by CCITT. *See also:* CCITT. [Source: RFC1208]

### International Organization for Standardization (ISO)

A voluntary, nontreaty organization founded in 1946 which is responsible for creating international standards in many areas, including computers and communications. Its members are the national standards organizations of the 89 member countries, including ANSI for the U.S. *See also:* American National Standards Institute, Open Systems Interconnection. [Source: TAN]

### internet

While an internet is a network, the term "internet" is usually used to refer to a collection of networks interconnected with routers. *See also:* network.

### Internet (note the capital "I")

The Internet is the largest internet in the world. It's a three level hierarchy composed of backbone networks (e.g., NSFNET, MILNET), mid-level networks, and stub networks. The Internet is a multiprotocol internet. *See also:* backbone, mid-level network, stub network, transit network, Internet Protocol, Corporation for Research and Educational Networks, National Science Foundation.

### internet address

An IP address that uniquely identifies a node on an internet. An Internet address (capital "I"), uniquely identifies a node on the Internet. *See also:* internet, Internet, IP address.

### Internet Architecture Board (IAB)

The technical body that oversees the development of the Internet suite of protocols. It has two task forces: the IETF and the IRTF. "IAB" previously stood for Internet Activities Board. *See also:* Internet Engineering Task Force, Internet Research Task Force.

### Internet Assigned Numbers Authority (IANA)

The central registry for various Internet protocol parameters, such as port, protocol and enterprise numbers, and options, codes and types. The currently assigned values are listed in the "Assigned Numbers" document [STD2]. To request a number assignment, contact the IANA at "iana@isi.edu." *See also:* assigned numbers, STD.

### Internet Control Message Protocol (ICMP)

ICMP is an extension to the Internet Protocol. It allows for the generation of error messages, test packets and informational messages related to IP. It is defined in STD 5, RFC 792. [Source: FYI4]

### internet number

*See:* internet address

### Internet Protocol (IP)

The Internet Protocol, defined in STD 5, RFC 791, is the network layer for the TCP/IP Protocol Suite. It is a connectionless, best-effort packet switching protocol. *See also:* packet switching, Request For Comments, TCP/IP Protocol Suite.

### Internet Registry (IR)

The IANA has the discretionary authority to delegate portions of its responsibility and, with respect to network address and Autonomous System identifiers, has lodged this responsibility with an IR. The IR function is performed by the DDN NIC. *See also:* Autonomous System, network address, Defense Data Network..., Internet Assigned Numbers Authority.

### Internet Relay Chat (IRC)

A world-wide "party line" protocol that allows one to converse with others in real time. IRC is structured as a network of servers, each of which accepts connections from client programs, one per user. *See also:* talk. [Source: HACKER]

### Internet Society (ISOC)

The Internet Society is a non-profit, professional membership organization which facilitates and supports the technical evolution of the Internet, stimulates interest in and educates the scientific and academic communities, industry and the public about the technology, uses and applications of the Internet, and promotes the development of new applications for the system. The Society provides a forum for discussion and collaboration in the operation and use of the global Internet infrastructure. The Internet Society publishes a quarterly newsletter, the Internet Society News, and holds an annual conference, INET. The development of Internet technical standards takes place under the auspices of the Internet Society with substantial support from the Corporation for National Research Initiatives under a cooperative agreement with the US Federal Government. [Source: V. Cerf]

### interoperability

The ability of software and hardware on multiple machines from multiple vendors to communicate meaningfully.

### IP

*See:* Internet Protocol

### IP address

The 32-bit address defined by the Internet Protocol in STD 5, RFC 791. It is usually represented in dotted decimal notation. *See also:* dot address, internet address, Internet Protocol, network address, subnet address, host address.

### IRC

*See:* Internet Relay Chat

### ISDN

*See:* Integrated Services Digital Network

### ISO

*See:* International Organization for Standardization

### ISOC

*See:* Internet Society

### ISODE

*See:* ISO Development Environment

### Kermit

A popular file transfer protocol developed by Columbia University. Because Kermit runs in most operating environments, it provides an easy method of file transfer. Kermit is NOT the same as FTP. *See also:* File Transfer Protocol [Source: MALAMUD]

### Knowbot

An experimental directory service. *See also:* white pages, WHOIS, X.500.

### LAN

*See:* Local Area Network

### layer

Communication networks for computers may be organized as a set of more or less independent protocols, each in a different layer (also called level). The lowest layer governs direct host-to-host communication between the hardware at different hosts; the highest consists of user applications. Each layer builds on the layer beneath it. For each layer, programs at different hosts use protocols appropriate to the layer to communicate with each other. TCP/IP has five layers of protocols; OSI has seven. The advantages of different layers of protocols is that the methods of passing information from one layer to another are specified clearly as part of the protocol suite, and changes within a protocol layer are prevented from affecting the other layers. This greatly simplifies the task of designing and maintaining communication programs. *See also:* Open Systems Interconnection, TCP/IP Protocol Suite.

### listserv

An automated mailing list distribution system originally designed for the Bitnet/EARN network. *See also:* Bitnet, European Academic Research Network, mailing list.

### Local Area Network (LAN)

A data network intended to serve an area of only a few square kilometers or less. Because the network is known to cover only a small area, optimizations can be made in the network signal protocols that permit data rates up to 100Mb/s. *See also:* Ethernet, Fiber Distributed Data Interface, token ring, Wide Area Network. [Source: NNSC]

### Lurking

No active participation on the part of a subscriber to an mailing list or USENET newsgroup. A person who is lurking is just listening to the discussion. Lurking is encouraged for beginners who need to get up to speed on the history of the group. *See also:* Electronic Mail, mailing list, Usenet. [Source: LAQUEY]

### mail gateway

A machine that connects two or more electronic mail systems (including dissimilar mail systems) and transfers messages between them. Sometimes the mapping and translation can be quite complex, and it generally requires a store-and-forward scheme whereby the message is received from one system completely before it is transmitted to the next system, after suitable translations. *See also:* Electronic Mail. [Source: RFC1208]

### mail path

A series of machine names used to direct electronic mail from one user to another. This system of email addressing has been used primarily in UUCP networks which are trying to eliminate its use altogether. *See also:* bang path, email address, UNIX-to-UNIX CoPy.

### mail server

A software program that distributes files or information in response to requests sent via email. Internet examples include Almanac and netlib. Mail servers have also been used in Bitnet to provide FTP-like services. *See also:* Bitnet, Electronic Mail, FTP. [Source: NWNET]

### mailing list

A list of email addresses, used by a mail exploder, to forward messages to groups of people. Generally, a mailing list is used to discuss a certain set of topics, and different mailing lists discuss different topics. A mailing list may be moderated. This means that messages sent to the list are actually sent to a moderator who determines whether or not to send the messages on to everyone else. Requests to subscribe to, or leave, a mailing list should ALWAYS be sent to the list's "-request" address (e.g., ietf-request@cnri.reston.va.us for the IETF mailing list). *See also:* Electronic Mail, mail exploder.

### Martian

A humorous term applied to packets that turn up unexpectedly on the wrong network because of bogus routing entries. Also used as a name for a packet which has an altogether bogus (non-registered or ill-formed) internet address. [Source: RFC1208]

### MIME

*See:* Multipurpose Internet Mail Extensions

### moderator

A person, or small group of people, who manage moderated mailing lists and newsgroups. Moderators are responsible for determining which email submissions are passed on to list. *See also:* Electronic Mail, mailing list, Usenet.

### Multipurpose Internet Mail Extensions (MIME)

An extension to Internet email which provides the ability to transfer non-textual data, such as graphics, audio and fax. It is defined in RFC 1341. *See also:* Electronic Mail

### Multi-User Dungeon (MUD)

Adventure, role playing games, or simulations played on the Internet. Devotees call them "text-based virtual reality adventures." The games can feature fantasy combat, booby traps and magic. Players interact in real time and can change the "world" in the game as they play it. Most MUDs are based on the Telnet protocol. *See also:* Telnet. [Source: LAQUEY]

### National Science Foundation (NSF)

A U.S. government agency whose purpose is to promote the advancement of science. NSF funds science researchers, scientific projects, and infrastructure to improve the quality of scientific research. The NSFNET, funded by NSF, is an essential part of academic and research communications. It is a highspeed "network of networks" which is hierarchical in nature. At the highest level, it is a backbone network currently comprising 16 nodes connected to a 45Mb/s facility which spans the continental United States. Attached to that are mid-level networks and attached to the mid-levels are campus and local networks. NSFNET also has connections out of the

U.S. to Canada, Mexico, Europe, and the Pacific Rim. The NSFNET is part of the Internet.

### netiquette

A pun on "etiquette" referring to proper behavior on a network.

### Netnews

*See:* Usenet

### network

A computer network is a data communications system which interconnects computer systems at various different sites. A network may be composed of any combination of LANs, MANs or WANs.

### network address

The network portion of an IP address. For a class A network, the network address is the first byte of the IP address. For a class B network, the network address is the first two bytes of the IP address. For a class C network, the network address is the first three bytes of the IP address. In each case, the remainder is the host address. In the Internet, assigned network addresses are globally unique. *See also:* Internet, IP address, subnet address, host address, Internet Registry.

### Network File System (NFS)

A protocol developed by Sun Microsystems, and defined in RFC 1094, which allows a computer system to access files over a network as if they were on its local disks. This protocol has been incorporated in products by more than two hundred companies, and is now a de facto Internet standard. [Source: NNSC]

### Network Information Center (NIC)

A NIC provides information, assistance and services to network users. *See also:* Network Operations Center.

### Network Information Services (NIS)

A set of services, generally provided by a NIC, to assist users in using the network. *See also:* Network Information Center.

### Network News Transfer Protocol (NNTP)

A protocol, defined in RFC 977, for the distribution, inquiry, retrieval, and posting of news articles. *See also:* Usenet.

### Network Operations Center (NOC)

A location from which the operation of a network or internet is monitored. Additionally, this center usually serves as a clearinghouse for connectivity problems and efforts to resolve those problems. *See also:* Network Information Center. [Source: NNSC]

### Network Time Protocol (NTP)

A protocol that assures accurate local timekeeping with reference to radio and atomic clocks located on the Internet. This protocol is capable of synchronizing distributed clocks within milliseconds over long time periods. It is defined in STD 12, RFC 1119. *See also:* Internet. [Source: NNSC]

### NFS

*See:* Network File System

### NIC

*See:* Network Information Center

### NIC.DDN.MIL

This is the domain name of the DDN NIC. *See also:* Defense Data Network..., Domain Name System, Network Information Center.

### NIS

*See:* Network Information Services

### NNTP

*See:* Network News Transfer Protocol

### NOC

*See:* Network Operations Center

### NSF

*See:* National Science Foundation

### octet

An octet is 8 bits. This term is used in networking, rather than byte, because some systems have bytes that are not 8 bits long.

### Online Computer Library Catalog

OCLC is a nonprofit membership organization offering computer-based services to libraries, educational organizations, and their users. The OCLC library information network connects more than 10,000 libraries worldwide. Libraries use the OCLC System for cataloging, interlibrary loan, collection development, bibliographic verification, and reference searching. [Source: OCLC]

### Open Systems Interconnection (OSI)

A suite of protocols, designed by ISO committees, to be the international standard computer network architecture. *See also:* International Organization for Standardization.

### OSI

*See:* Open Systems Interconnection

### OSI Reference Model

A seven-layer structure designed to describe computer network architectures and the way that data passes through them. This model was developed by the ISO in 1978 to clearly define the interfaces in multivendor networks, and to provide users of those networks with conceptual guidelines in the construction of such networks. *See also:* International Organization for Standardization. [Source: NNSC]

### packet

The unit of data sent across a network. "Packet" is a generic term used to describe unit of data at all levels of the protocol stack, but it is most correctly used to describe application data units. *See also:* datagram, frame.

### Packet InterNet Groper (PING)

A program used to test reachability of destinations by sending them an ICMP echo request and waiting for a reply. The term is used as a verb: "Ping host X to see if it is up!" *See also:* Internet Control Message Protocol. [Source: RFC1208]

**Packet Switch Node (PSN)**

A dedicated computer whose purpose is to accept, route and forward packets in a packet switched network. *See also:* packet switching, router. [Source: NNSC]

**packet switching**

A communications paradigm in which packets (messages) are individually routed between hosts, with no previously established communication path. *See also:* circuit switching, connection-oriented, connectionless.

**PING**

*See:* Packet INternet Groper

**Point-to-Point Protocol (PPP)**

The Point-to-Point Protocol, defined in RFC 1171, provides a method for transmitting packets over serial point-to-point links. *See also:* Serial Line IP. [Source: FYI4]

**POP**

*See:* Post Office Protocol and Point Of Presence

**port**

A port is a transport layer demultiplexing value. Each application has a unique port number associated with it. *See also:* Transmission Control Protocol, User Datagram Protocol.

**Post Office Protocol (POP)**

A protocol designed to allow single user hosts to read mail from a server. There are three versions: POP, POP2, and POP3. Latter versions are NOT compatible with earlier versions. *See also:* Electronic Mail.

**postmaster**

The person responsible for taking care of electronic mail problems, answering queries about users, and other related work at a site. *See also:* Electronic Mail. [Source: ZEN]

### PPP

*See:* Point-to-Point Protocol

### Prospero

A distributed filesystem which provides the user with the ability to create multiple views of a single collection of files distributed across the Internet. Prospero provides a file naming system, and file access is provided by existing access methods (e.g., anonymous FTP and NFS). The Prospero protocol is also used for communication between clients and servers in the archie system. *See also:* anonymous FTP, archie, archive site, Gopher, Network File System, Wide Area Information Servers.

### protocol

A formal description of message formats and the rules two computers must follow to exchange those messages. Protocols can describe low-level details of machine-to-machine interfaces (e.g., the order in which bits and bytes are sent across a wire) or high-level exchanges between allocation programs (e.g., the way in which two programs transfer a file across the Internet). [Source: MALAMUD]

### Read the [Frigging] Manual (RTFM)

This acronym is often used when someone asks a simple or common question.

### remote login

Operating on a remote computer, using a protocol over a computer network, as though locally attached. *See also:* Telnet.

### Request For Comments (RFC)

The document series, begun in 1969, which describes the Internet suite of protocols and related experiments. Not all (in fact very few) RFCs describe Internet standards, but all Internet standards are written up as RFCs. The RFC series of documents is unusual in that the proposed protocols are forwarded by the Internet research and development community, acting on their own behalf, as opposed to the formally reviewed and standardized protocols that are promoted by organizations such as CCITT and ANSI. *See also:* For Your Information, STD.

### RFC

*See:* Request For Comments

### RFC 822

The Internet standard format for electronic mail message headers. Mail experts often refer to "822 messages". The name comes from "RFC 822", which contains the specification (STD 11, RFC 822). 822 format was previously known as 733 format. *See also:* Electronic Mail. [Source: COMER]

### route

The path that network traffic takes from its source to its destination. Also, a possible path from a given host to another host or destination.

### router

A device which forwards traffic between networks. The forwarding decision is based on network layer information and routing tables, often constructed by routing protocols. *See also:* bridge, gateway, Exterior Gateway Protocol, Interior Gateway Protocol.

### routing

The process of selecting the correct interface and next hop for a packet being forwarded. *See also:* hop, router, Exterior Gateway Protocol, Interior Gateway Protocol.

### routing domain

A set of routers exchanging routing information within an administrative domain. *See also:* Administrative Domain, router.

### RTFM

*See:* Read the [Frigging] Manual

### Serial Line IP (SLIP)

A protocol used to run IP over serial lines, such as telephone circuits or RS-232 cables, interconnecting two systems. SLIP is defined in RFC 1055. *See also:* Point-to-Point Protocol.

### server

A provider of resources (e.g., file servers and name servers). *See also:* client, Domain Name System, Network File System.

### SIG

Special Interest Group

### signature

The three or four line message at the bottom of a piece of email or a Usenet article which identifies the sender. Large signatures (over five lines) are generally frowned upon. *See also:* Electronic Mail, Usenet.

### Simple Mail Transfer Protocol (SMTP)

A protocol, defined in STD 10, RFC 821, used to transfer electronic mail between computers. It is a server to server protocol, so other protocols are used to access the messages. *See also:* Electronic Mail, Post Office Protocol, RFC 822.

### Simple Network Management Protocol (SNMP)

The Internet standard protocol, defined in STD 15, RFC 1157, developed to manage nodes on an IP network. It is currently possible to manage wiring hubs, toasters, jukeboxes, etc. *See also:* Management Information Base.

### SLIP

*See:* Serial Line IP

### SMTP

*See:* Simple Mail Transfer Protocol

### snail mail

A pejorative term referring to the U.S. postal service.

### SNMP

*See:* Simple Network Management Protocol

### Systems Network Architecture (SNA)

A proprietary networking architecture used by IBM and IBM-compatible mainframe computers. [Source: NNSC]

### T1

An AT&T term for a digital carrier facility used to transmit a DS-1 formatted digital signal at 1.544 megabits per second.

### T3

A term for a digital carrier facility used to transmit a DS-3 formatted digital signal at 44.746 megabits per second. [Source: FYI4]

### talk

A protocol which allows two people on remote computers to communicate in a real-time fashion. *See also:* Internet Relay Chat.

### TCP

*See:* Transmission Control Protocol

### TCP/IP

Protocol Suite Transmission Control Protocol over Internet Protocol. This is a common shorthand which refers to the suite of transport and application protocols which runs over IP. *See also:* IP, ICMP, TCP, UDP, FTP, Telnet, SMTP, SNMP.

### TELENET

A public packet switched network using the CCITT X.25 protocols. It should not be confused with Telnet.

### Telnet

Telnet is the Internet standard protocol for remote terminal connection service. It is defined in STD 8, RFC 854 and extended with options by many other RFCs.

### terminal emulator

A program that allows a computer to emulate a terminal. The workstation thus appears as a terminal to the remote host. [Source: MALAMUD]

### Three Letter Acronym (TLA)

A tribute to the use of acronyms in the computer field. *See also:* Extended Four Letter Acronym.

### token ring

A token ring is a type of LAN with nodes wired into a ring. Each node constantly passes a control message (token) on to the next; whichever node has the token can send a message. Often, "Token Ring" is used to refer to the IEEE 802.5 token ring standard, which is the most common type of token ring. *See also:* 802.x, Local Area Network.

### topology

A network topology shows the computers and the links between them. A network layer must stay abreast of the current network topology to be able to route packets to their final destination. [Source: MALAMUD]

### transceiver

Transmitter-receiver. The physical device that connects a host interface to a local area network, such as Ethernet. Ethernet transceivers contain electronics that apply signals to the cable and sense collisions. [Source: RFC1208]

### Transmission Control Protocol (TCP)

An Internet Standard transport layer protocol defined in STD 7, RFC 793. It is connection-oriented and stream-oriented, as opposed to UDP. *See also:* connection-oriented, stream-oriented, User Datagram Protocol.

### Trojan Horse

A computer program which carries within itself a means to allow the creator of the program access to the system using it. *See also:* virus, worm. See RFC 1135.

### TTFN

Ta-Ta For Now

### twisted pair

A type of cable in which pairs of conductors are twisted together to produce certain electrical properties.

### Universal Time Coordinated (UTC)

This is Greenwich Mean Time. [Source: MALAMUD]

### UNIX-to-UNIX CoPy (UUCP)

This was initially a program run under the UNIX operating system that allowed one UNIX system to send files to another UNIX system via dial-up phone lines. Today, the term is more commonly used to describe the large international network which uses the UUCP protocol to pass news and electronic mail. *See also:* Electronic Mail, Usenet.

### urban legend

A story, which may have started with a grain of truth, that has been embroidered and retold until it has passed into the realm of myth. It is an interesting phenomenon that these stories get spread so far, so fast and so often. Urban legends never die, they just end up on the Internet! Some legends that periodically make their rounds include "The Infamous Modem Tax," "Craig Shergold/Brain Tumor/Get Well Cards," and "The $250 Cookie Recipe". [Source: LAQUEY]

### Usenet

A collection of thousands of topically named newsgroups, the computers which run the protocols, and the people who read and submit Usenet news. Not all Internet hosts subscribe to Usenet and not all Usenet hosts are on the Internet. *See also:* Network News Transfer Protocol, UNIX-to-UNIX CoPy. [Source: NWNET]

### UTC

*See:* Universal Time Coordinated

### UUCP

*See:* UNIX-to-UNIX CoPy

### virus

A program which replicates itself on computer systems by incorporating itself into other programs which are shared among computer systems. *See also:* Trojan Horse, worm.

### W3

*See:* World Wide Web

### WAIS

*See:* Wide Area Information Servers

### WAN

*See:* Wide Area Network

### white pages

The Internet supports several databases that contain basic information about users, such as email addresses, telephone numbers, and postal addresses. These databases can be searched to get information about particular individuals. Because they serve a function akin to the telephone book, these databases are often referred to as "white pages. *See also:* Knowbot, WHOIS, X.500.

### WHOIS

An Internet program which allows users to query a database of people and other Internet entities, such as domains, networks, and hosts, kept at the DDN NIC. The information for people shows a person's company name, address, phone number and email address. *See also:* Defense Data Network Network ..., white pages, Knowbot, X.500. [Source: FYI4]

### Wide Area Information Servers (WAIS)

A distributed information service which offers simple natural language input, indexed searching for fast retrieval, and a "relevance feedback" mechanism which allows the results of initial searches to influence future searches. Public domain implementations are available. *See also:* archie, Gopher, Prospero.

### Wide Area Network (WAN)

A network, usually constructed with serial lines, which covers a large geographic area. *See also:* Local Area Network, Metropolitan Area Network.

### World Wide Web (WWW or W3)

A hypertext-based, distributed information system created by researchers at CERN in Switzerland. Users may create, edit or browse hypertext documents. The clients and servers are freely available.

### worm

A computer program which replicates itself and is self-propagating. Worms, as opposed to viruses, are meant to spawn in network environments. Network worms were first defined by Shoch & Hupp of Xerox in ACM Communications (March 1982). The Internet worm of November 1988 is perhaps the most famous; it successfully propagated itself on over 6,000 systems across the Internet. *See also:* Trojan Horse, virus.

### WRT

With Respect To

### WWW

*See:* World Wide Web

### WYSIWYG

What You See is What You Get

### Yellow Pages (YP)

A service used by UNIX administrators to manage databases distributed across a network.

### YP

*See:* Yellow Pages

# BIBLIOGRAPHY

!%@:: A Directory of Electronic Mail Addressing & Networks
*Charts the networks that make up the Internet, including contact names & addresses.*
Donnalyn Frey & Rick Adams
ISBN 1-56592-031-7. O'Reilly & Associates. 1994

The 1994 Internet White Pages
*Lists over 100,000 active Internet users. Updated quarterly.*
ISBN varies. IDG Books.

The Big Dummy's Guide to the Internet
*Insightful, thorough introduction to the Internet. FREE!*
Available at keyword: EFF
Electronic Frontier Foundation

The BMUG Guide to Bulletin Boards & Beyond
*Encyclopedic Macintosh-oriented guide to everything telecom, from a one-person BBS to the Internet.*
Bernard Aboba
ISBN 1-879791-03-X. BMUG, Inc.

Cuckoo's Egg
*Reads like a novel of espionage, but it's all true! A must-read for perspective.*
Cliff Stoll
ISBN 0-671-72688-9. Pocket Books. 1990

Cyberpunk
*Outlaws and hackers on the computer frontier.*
Katie Hafner & John Markoff
ISBN 0-671-77879-X. Touchstone Books. 1992

Exploring the World of Online Services
*Prodigy, CompuServe descriptions.*
Rosalind Resnick
ISBN 0-89588-798-3. Sybex, Inc. 1993

Free Electronic Networks
*Communicate anywhere in the world for the price of a local
telephone call.*
William J. Shefski
ISBN 1-55958-415-7. Prima Publishing. 1993

Hackers: Heros of the Computer Revolution
*Three premises ring true in this book: 1) access to computers should be
unlimited and total, 2) all information should be free, and 3) authority and
decentralization should be promoted. This is the voice of anarchy and thus
one of the literary precepts upon which the Internet has been maintained.*
Steven Levy
ISBN 0-385-31210-5. Dell/Doubleday. 1985

Internet: Mailing Lists
*The Internet List of Lists, containing a comprehensive listing of all the
mailing lists currently running on the Net. Updates are available by
subscribing to the New-Lists mailing list, described in Chapter 4.*
Vivian Neou and Rich Zellich
ISBN 0-13-289661-3. Prentice-Hall. 1993

Internet Roadside Attractions
*Sites, sounds & scenes along the information highway. Nearly a thou-
sand great links, all of which are available in hypertext format on the
included CD-ROM.*
Various authors.
ISBN 1-56604-193-7. Ventana Press. 1995.

The Internet Starter Kit for the Macintosh (or PC), 2nd Edition
*You don't need the kit, but you'll like the clear & thorough introduction
to the Net.*
Adam C. Engst
ISBN 1-56830-111-1. Hayden Books. 1994

The Internet Yellow Pages
*THE most clever way to explore the Internet.*
Harley Hahn and Rick Stout
ISBN: 0-07-882023-5. Osborne McGraw-Hill. 1994

The Official America Online for Macintosh Tour Guide, Second Edition
  *You need this book if you plan to use America Online for more than Internet access. In fact, you need ten copies of it. Buy them now before the rush.*
  Tom Lichty
  ISBN 1-56604-012-4. Ventana Press. 1994

The Online User's Encyclopedia: Bulletin Boards & Beyond
  *An encyclopedic treatise ranging from buying a modem to saving money on phone bills.*
  Bernard Aboba
  ISBN 0-201-62214-9. Addison-Wesley Publishing. 1993

Modem USA
  *Online commercial and private services, listed by state.*
  Lynne Motley.
  ISBN 0-9631233-6-X. Allium Press. 1994

Net Guide
  *More than 4,000 forums on CompuServe, Genie, Ilink and the Internet.*
  Michael Wolfe and Peter Rutten
  ISBN 0-679-75106-8. Random. 1994

Neuromancer
  *Classic novel. Origin of the term "cyberspace."*
  William Gibson
  ISBN 0-57503-420-X. London: Gollancz.

OPAC Directory
  *"Online Public Access Catalogs" — 300 library catalogs nationwide, including dialing instructions*
  Regina Rega (editor)
  ISBN 0-88736-883-2. Meckler Media. 1993
  ISBN 0-088736-962-6. 1994

Snow Crash
  *Insightful novel of what the Internet may become ten years from now.*
  Neal Stephenson
  ISBN 0-553-56261-4. New York: Bantam Books. 1993

Using Computer Bulletin Boards, Second Edition
*How to log on & navigate a typical BBS; how to set up your own BBS.*
John Hedtke
ISBN 1-5828-196-7. MIS Press. 1992

The Virtual Community: Finding Connecton in a Computerized World
*Homesteading in the Electronic Frontier.*
Howard Rheingold
ISBN 0-201-60870-7. Addison-Wesley. 1993

Walking the World Wide Web
*Your personal guide to the best of the Web, with free Online Companion and CD-ROM.*
Shannon R. Turlington
ISBN 1-56604-208-9. Ventana Press. 1995.

The Whole Earth Online Almanac
*A worldwide view of online services.*
Don Rittner
ISBN 1-56686-090-3. Brady Compu Books. 1993

The Whole Internet User's Guide & Catalog
*The premiere Internet book, thorough, friendly, and insightful.*
Ed Krol
ISBN 1-56592-025-2. O'Reilly & Associates. 1992
ISBN 1-56592-063-5. 1994

# INDEX

## Colophon

This book was produced on Power Macintosh computers using PageMaker 5.0. Postscript files were printed to disk and output directly to film using a Linotronic 330 imagesetter.

The body text is set in Palatino. Subheads, running heads and folios are set in varying weights of DTC Kabel. The sidebars are set in Adobe Futura Condensed. Illustrations were produced using Aldus Freehand 3.1 and Adobe Illustrator 5.0.

# Design & Conquer

### Looking Good in Color

*$29.95*
*272 pages, illustrated*

Like effective design, using color properly is an essential part of a desktop publishing investment. This richly illustrated four-color book addresses basic issues from color theory—through computer technologies, printing processes and budget issues—to final design. Even the graphically challenged can make immediate use of the practical advice in *Looking Good in Color*.

### Looking Good in Print, Third Edition

*$24.95*
*462 pages, illustrated*

For use with any software or hardware, this desktop design bible has become the standard among novice and experienced desktop publishers alike. With more than 300,000 copies in print, *Looking Good in Print, Third Edition*, is even better—with new sections on photography and scanning. Learn the fundamentals of professional-quality design along with tips on resources and reference materials.

### Newsletters From the Desktop, Second Edition

*$24.95*
*392 pages, illustrated*

Now the millions of desktop publishers who produce newsletters can learn how to improve the designs of their publications. Filled with helpful tips and illustrations, as well as hands-on tips for building a great-looking publication. Includes an all-new color gallery of professionally designed newsletters, offering desktop publishers at all levels a wealth of ideas and inspiration.

Books marked with this logo include a free Internet *Online Companion*™, featuring archives of free utilities plus a software archive and links to other Internet resources.

# Maximize Your Mac

### Walking the World Wide Web

*$29.95*
*360 pages, illustrated*

Enough of lengthy listings! This tour features more than 300 memorable Websites, with in-depth descriptions of what's special about each. Includes international sites, exotic exhibits, entertainment, business and more. The companion CD-ROM contains Ventana Mosaic™ and a hyperlinked version of the book providing live links when you log onto the Internet.

### HTML Publishing on the Internet for Macintosh

*$49.95*
*500 pages, illustrated*

Create your own Web page! *HTML Publishing on the Internet* covers everything from using a service provider to constructing information centers and virtual storefronts. Offers step-by-step instructions for creating a site that meets the needs of developers and viewers alike. Packed with tools for publishing documents on the Internet, the included CD-ROM contains HotMetal PRO™, Internet Assistant™, Netscape Navigator™ plus additional graphics viewers, templates, conversion software and more!

### Internet Roadside Attractions

*$29.95*
*376 pages, illustrated*

Why take the word of one when you can get a quorum? Seven experienced Internauts–teachers and bestselling authors–share their favorite Web sites, Gophers, FTP sites, chats, games, newsgroups and mailing lists. Organized alphabetically by category for easy browsing with in-depth descriptions. The companion CD-ROM contains the entire text of the book, hyperlinked for off-line browsing and online Web-hopping.

# A Great Gift Idea!

Give your friends or relatives everything they need to join the digital revolution and juice up their online literacy. With *The Official America Online Membership Kit & Tour Guide, Second Edition*, they can explore the nation's fastest-growing commercial online service **at no risk**.

## The Tour Guide shows readers how to

- **Get news** from dozens of online wire services, newspapers and magazines.
- **Exchange e-mail** with friends on the other side of the world.
- **Explore the Internet** through America Online's new Internet services.
- **Download** tens of thousands of software files for a Macintosh or PC.
- **Get expert computing advice** from top hardware and software companies.
- **Access stock quotes**, buy and sell stocks online and track investments with an online portfolio management system.
- **Discuss politics** and current affairs in AOL's chat rooms.
- **And much more!**

**Get the most from your time online!** This readable, richly illustrated "traveling companion" includes the America Online starter disk and **20 FREE hours of online time** for new members!

Find your place in the emerging digital global village. While you're at it, find a place for a friend, too—a great gift for novice and experienced online users alike!

**Kits available for Windows and Macintosh.**

To order, use the form on the order page, or contact your local book or computer store.

# To order any Ventana Press title, complete this order form and mail or fax it to us, with payment, for quick shipment.

| TITLE | ISBN | Quantity | | Price | | Total |
|---|---|---|---|---|---|---|
| Advertising From The Desktop | 1-56604-064-7 | _____ | x | $24.95 | = | $ _____ |
| America Online's Internet for Mac, 2nd Edition | 1-56604-284-4 | _____ | x | $24.95 | = | $ _____ |
| HTML Publishing on the Internet for Mac | 1-56604-228-3 | _____ | x | $49.95 | = | $ _____ |
| Internet Roadside Attractions | 1-56604-193-7 | _____ | x | $29.95 | = | $ _____ |
| Looking Good in Color | 1-56604-219-4 | _____ | x | $29.95 | = | $ _____ |
| Looking Good in Print, 3rd Edition | 1-56604-047-7 | _____ | x | $24.95 | = | $ _____ |
| Looking Good With QuarkXPress | 1-56604-148-1 | _____ | x | $34.95 | = | $ _____ |
| Mac, Word & Excel Desktop Companion, 2nd Edition | 1-56604-130-9 | _____ | x | $24.95 | = | $ _____ |
| Newsletters From the Desktop, 2nd Edition | 1-56604-133-3 | _____ | x | $24.95 | = | $ _____ |
| The Official America Online for Macintosh Membership Kit & Tour Guide, 2nd Edition | 1-56604-127-9 | _____ | x | $27.95 | = | $ _____ |
| The Official America Online for Windows Membership Kit & Tour Guide, 2nd Edition | 1-56604-128-7 | _____ | x | $27.95 | = | $ _____ |
| Photoshop f/x | 1-56604-179-1 | _____ | x | $39.95 | = | $ _____ |
| The System 7.5 Book, 3rd Edition | 1-56604-129-5 | _____ | x | $24.95 | = | $ _____ |
| Voodoo Mac, 2nd Edition | 1-56604-177-5 | _____ | x | $24.95 | = | $ _____ |
| Walking the World Wide Web | 1-56604-208-9 | _____ | x | $29.95 | = | $ _____ |
| | | | | **Subtotal** | = | $ _____ |
| | | | | **Shipping** | = | $ _____ |
| | | | | **TOTAL** | = | $ _____ |

## SHIPPING:

For all standard orders, please ADD $4.50/first book, $1.35/each additional.
For "two-day air," ADD $8.25/first book, $2.25/each additional.
For orders to Canada, ADD $6.50/book.
For orders sent C.O.D., ADD $4.50 to your shipping rate.
North Carolina residents must ADD 6% sales tax.
International orders require additional shipping charges.

Name _____  Daytime telephone _____

Company _____

Address (No PO Box) _____

City _____  State _____  Zip _____

Payment enclosed ____VISA ____MC ____ Acc't # _____ Exp. date _____

Exact name on card _____  Signature _____

**Mail to: Ventana • PO Box 13964 • Research Triangle Park, NC 27709-3964 ☎ 800/743-5369 • Fax 919/544-9472**

**Check your local bookstore or software retailer for these and other bestselling titles, or call toll free:** **800/743-5369**